ONE
BY ONE,
THE STARS

SERIES EDITOR

Nicole Walker

SERIES ADVISORY BOARD

Dan Gunn
Pam Houston
Phillip Lopate
Dinty W. Moore
Lia Purpura
Patricia Smith

ONE BY ONE, THE STARS

ESSAYS

NED STUCKEY-FRENCH

THE UNIVERSITY OF
GEORGIA PRESS
ATHENS

Published in 2022 by the University of Georgia Press
Athens, Georgia 30602
www.ugapress.org
© 2019 by Ned Stuckey-French
Foreword © 2022 by the University of Georgia Press
All rights reserved
Designed by Kaelin Chappell Broaddus
Set in 10/13.5 Dolly Pro Regular by Kaelin Chappell Broaddus

Printed and bound by Lakeside Book Company, Harrisonburg, VA
The paper in this book meets the guidelines for permanence
and durability of the Committee on Production Guidelines
for Book Longevity of the Council on Library Resources.

Most University of Georgia Press titles are
available from popular e-book vendors.

Printed in the United States of America
20 21 22 23 24 P 5 4 3 2 1

Library of Congress Control Number: 2021952978
ISBN: 9780820361802 (pbk.: alk. paper)
ISBN: 9780820361796 (ebook)

CONTENTS

Foreword, BY JOHN T. PRICE ix

PART 1
Nightmares 3 ★ South Side 6
Backyards 20 ★ Termites 28
Who Should Be President in 1968? 47
Meeting Bobby Kennedy 71
Rowing 92 ★ Mass General 104
Walking the Tracks 121

PART 2
The Edsel Farm 127
"Don't Be Cruel" *An Argument for Elvis* 142
Thank You, Jon Gnagy 155
The Book of Knowledge
Essays and Encyclopedias 161

PART 3
Our Queer Little Hybrid Thing
Toward a Definition of the Essay 175
An Essayist's Guide to Research and Family Life 186
"Dear John" *Facts and the Lyric Essay* 205
My Name Is Ned *Facebook and the Personal Essay* 212

Acknowledgments, BY ELIZABETH STUCKEY-FRENCH 221

FOREWORD

"Hey there, you rascal."

This was how Ned Stuckey-French greeted me during our final phone call, shortly before his death from cancer at age sixty-nine. It was June 2019 and he was in a Tallahassee hospital fighting a related infection, but his warmth and wit were undiminished. These had been hallmarks of his personality from the first time I met him, in the early 1990s, when we were attending graduate school at the University of Iowa. We were both students, but not equals. I was in my early twenties, from small-town Iowa, having just finished an indecisive undergraduate career split between the sciences and humanities. I had applied to the English MA program as a kind of safe harbor where I might explore a growing yet still tentative interest in nonfiction writing while pondering what to do with the rest of my life. Ned was in his late thirties and married, with a degree from Harvard and another on the way from Brown. He was already locked in on the subject that would become the central focus of his life as a scholar and writer: the personal essay.

Iowa was an ideal place for both Ned and his wife Elizabeth to pursue their literary interests. Elizabeth had been accepted to the Writer's Workshop in fiction. Meanwhile, Ned would study literary nonfiction with Professor Carl Klaus, who was (and is) a nationally respected, pioneering scholar in the history and craft of the essay. Carl and his colleagues were in the process of building the nonfiction program into a national destination for those interested in studying and writing literary nonfiction, including one of the first stand-alone MFA degrees in the genre.

I didn't fully appreciate any of this at the time. I had taken a couple of nonfiction classes, written a few essays, but was far from committed. And I was, as Ned affectionately called me, a bit of a rascal—

more interested in socializing than studying. I didn't take myself or whatever talent I might have very seriously. I first met Ned in an informal workshop of an essay I'd written about my conflicted relationship with the Midwest, during which he'd offered some helpful suggestions. Afterward, he told me that he, too, had been raised in the Midwest, in Indiana, and that he would share with me a list of essayists from our home region that I might find helpful. He then invited me to join an essay-reading group he was forming. This was the beginning of a friendship that would last nearly thirty years.

This moment also revealed something essential about Ned's character. He loved making new friends and creating new communities. He loved teaching. During the next few years, in that reading group and others, and in various classes together, Ned would introduce my contemporaries and me to authors and ideas that would give shape to our own futures as essayists. He also modeled an honest yet supportive, good-humored approach to writerly critique that became a touchstone during our time in the program and well beyond. We became better writers and teachers because of him.

Just as I knew very little about the essay when we first met, I knew even less about Ned. Ned French was born in 1950 in West Lafayette, Indiana, where he graduated from high school as class president. His father, Charles, was a professor of agricultural economics at Purdue University. Ned attended Harvard, where he played football and graduated magna cum laude. Following college, Ned worked as a janitor at Massachusetts General Hospital as part of an effort to organize workers into a union, and then returned home to Indiana to teach and coach at a local high school. In January 1986, he met Elizabeth Stuckey at a mutual friend's birthday party. Elizabeth had recently moved back to West Lafayette, where her father was a professor of English at Purdue, though she and Ned had never met. They got married only a few months later.

In 1990, they moved to Iowa to pursue their graduate studies, renting a beautiful old house in the small town of West Branch, which became a gathering place for writers and other friends. Before leaving the University of Iowa with their respective degrees in 1997, they also became parents. Flannery arrived in 1995, and Phoebe joined them in 1997. I remember my wife Stephanie and me joining young Flannery for "Pooh Bear tea" at her birthday party, and being in awe at the grace Ned and Elizabeth displayed as parents while also finishing graduate school. It was a feat we would further appreciate, years later, when we became parents ourselves.

In 1999, Elizabeth and Ned were hired at Florida State University. As a professor at FSU, and during visiting appointments at St. Lawrence University, Columbia University, and here at the University of Nebraska at Omaha, Ned created a remarkable legacy as a colleague and teacher, mentoring and inspiring countless students—as he had once done for me.

In 2011, the University of Missouri Press published Ned's critical study *The American Essay in the American Century*, which is still among the most important and influential works on the subject. Equally significant was his collaboration with friend and former professor Carl Klaus on *Essayists on the Essay: From Montaigne to Our Time*, published by the University of Iowa Press in 2012—the first book dedicated to the evolution of the essay as described by the essayists themselves. This book began as an informal study group among graduate students—another educational, community-building effort Ned had encouraged me to join. Demonstrating his literary dexterity, Ned teamed up with Elizabeth and Janet Burroway to coauthor later editions of *Writing Fiction: A Guide to Narrative Craft*. Add to this many invited book chapters and essays and reviews, conference presentations and invited lectures, and you have a portrait of a remarkable public scholar.

Ned's literary work always carried a sense of responsibility beyond the page. This included serving as book review editor at *Fourth Genre*, joining editorial boards (such as the Crux Series in literary nonfiction at the University of Georgia Press), and offering advice and assistance to countless faculty who were developing and/or defending nonfiction programs.

That sense of responsibility was no more evident than his effort, in 2012, to save the University of Missouri Press. In May of that year, University of Missouri president Timothy M. Wolfe announced the defunding of the University of Missouri Press and the firing of most of its staff. Ned's relationship to that press was personal. They had published *The American Essay in the American Century*, and Missouri was the home state of his father, who had attended the University of Missouri on the GI Bill. As he stated many times, however, he primarily viewed the closing of the press as an assault on public higher education and on freedom of speech. Channeling his experiences as a labor organizer, he teamed up with university press sales representative Bruce Joshua Miller and *Publishers Weekly* journalist Claire Kirch, among many others, to raise public awareness and exert local and national pressure on university administration. He started a vigorous Facebook campaign and was interviewed in national venues, including a feature on NPR. He convinced fifty-eight scholars representing 138 titles to ask for their publishing rights back from the press. Characteristic of Ned, he reached across political divisions to earn support from Republican state lawmakers. Six months later, President Wolfe reversed course, restoring the university subsidy to the press, as well as rehiring the staff and the editor-in-chief, Clair Willcox. Ned would advocate on behalf of presses facing similar challenges at the University of Kentucky and University of Akron.

In 2020, Ned was posthumously named the inaugural Stand UP honoree by the Association of University Presses, intended to honor those "who through their words and actions have done extraordinary work to support, defend and celebrate the university press community." During a tribute video for the AUP 2020 meeting, Greg Britton, editorial director of the Johns Hopkins University Press, remarked, "Ned's activism transformed the way our community mobilizes. . . . In standing up for us, Ned taught us how to stand up for ourselves." Those words speak for many of us who have benefited from Ned's advice, help, and encouragement over the years.

In the spring of 2017, Ned underwent surgery to remove a cancerous tumor, and the procedure appeared to be successful. The next year he was well enough to attend the AWP Conference in Tampa—a community of scholars, writers, and teachers that had always been important to him—where he reunited with friends and presented on yet another frontier in nonfiction writing, "Teaching the

Video Essay." In spring of 2019, he was scheduled to give the keynote address at a conference in Malta dedicated to the essay, further evidence of his growing international reputation. Unfortunately, the cancer returned and he could not attend.

The disease progressed much faster than many of us, including Ned, anticipated. During our last phone conversation, while he was in the hospital, there was much reminiscing and laughter, as always. Typical of Ned, he spent a lot of time asking about me and Steph and our three boys. "What a gift a family can be," he said, and expressed how proud he was of Flannery and Phoebe. His voice was full of affection and gratitude. We talked a little more about his treatment, about what steps came next, but then the nurse arrived and he had to get off the phone.

"Love you, brother," I said.

"Love you, too."

Those were the last words between us.

And then they weren't.

Following Ned's death, there were two memorial events. The first was in Tallahassee and the second in Iowa City, hosted by Prairie Lights Bookstore, and attended by friends and former professors from his grad school years, some of whom traveled from as far away as New York and North Carolina. Carl Klaus was one of the speakers. My nineteen-year-old son Ben, a first-year student at Iowa, also attended, witnessing some of the many ways college friendships could become meaningful well beyond the school years. It was a joyful gathering, just as Ned would have wanted it to be.

A few months later, this manuscript emerged. Ned had talked for years about a collection of essays he had been working on, and some of us had had the opportunity to read or listen to individual pieces, but it remained unfinished at the time of his death. At the memorial gathering in Iowa City, Carl and Elizabeth discussed what remained of the manuscript and later reached out to me about the opportunity of reading and editing it, and exploring the possibility of publication. I was, of course, honored that they trusted me with Ned's book—he had many friends and admirers who would have gladly done this work on his behalf. But I confess I felt some major hesitancy. Ned was no longer here to guide the process or to finalize any edits. How could I, or anyone, honor his wishes?

But then the manuscript arrived, and the first thing I noticed was Ned's familiar handwriting covering the pages. He had left extensive editing notes throughout, everything from sentence-level changes to follow-up research questions to plans for reshaping and rearranging the chapters. I knew then that whatever additional work needed to be done, Ned would, in a significant way, be there to guide it.

Most importantly, I was struck by the beauty and force of the writing itself. I hesitate to summarize in a short foreword what readers will delight in discovering on their own, but I think it is important to state that this is much more than a random collection of Ned's essays. Together, the essays create a compelling story of one person's awakening to his core convictions. It begins with a childhood nightmare that leads four-year-old Ned "to worry about everything, especially grown-ups. Who could trust them? What did they know? What didn't they know? Why did they do what they did?" Trust. Knowledge. Ignorance. Motivation. Action. The relentless questioning of "why things were the way they were." These are the foundational concerns that would later become the center of Ned's life and work.

Throughout the essays to follow, personal reflection often gives way, sometimes subtly, to social commentary. The first four essays center on Ned's childhood in a Midwestern, middle-class, late midcentury family and place. These personal experiences, however, are carefully located within larger social and historical contexts that begin to complicate his otherwise privileged, white perspective. In "South Side," for example, set during 1962, when Ned was twelve—"the summer after the Freedom Riders, the summer before Birmingham, Medgar Evers, and the March on Washington"—Ned reflects on his liberal parents' unintentionally patronizing behavior toward the Black mechanics who generously offer to fix their car, after a midnight breakdown in Chicago. "It was the night," he concludes, "I felt the color line."

The essays that immediately follow describe Ned's discovery of other boundaries he would later work to break down. In "Backyards," middle-class stratification is revealed in a boy's observations of neighbors' more manicured lawns, as well as their condescension toward his parents. One of those neighbors is his father's boss, Earl Butz—a name that lives in infamy with many rural Midwesterners of my generation. Butz would become the secretary of agriculture under Nixon and the architect of the "get big or get out" policies that led to the 1980s farm crisis, devastating my Iowa hometown and many others. In "Termites," Ned braids the intensely personal story of his parents' dissolving marriage together with a school insect project. On a quest for specimens, he and his friends embark on a bicycle trip across the countryside, passing by the Eli Lilly factory, producer of antibiotics, but also poisonous waste and herbicides and, later, Prozac—a fact that resonates with his mother's ongoing struggle with mental illness. Young Ned was traversing, it seems, a place of personal, social, and ecological imbalance, but one that taught him that a "bigger part of learning is simply finding out as much as you can."

That spirit certainly informs "Who Should Be President in 1968?," which marks the beginning of Ned's political activism. During high school, motivated by a desire "to reach beyond my own life"— including the claustrophobia of his parents' crumbling marriage and his evolving feelings about the Vietnam War—he mailed a presidential poll to 130 highly influential people, conservative and liberal, asking what issues mattered most to them. Those polled included nationally known writers, scientists, politicians, economists, political scientists, and journalists. Their responses to this eighteen-year-old Indiana kid offer a powerful, and still deeply relevant, montage of the times, while also moving Ned farther along in his progressive beliefs.

In "Meeting Bobby Kennedy," also set during his senior year, Ned steps outside of his own class to canvass for RFK on a side of town he had rarely visited, viewing poverty up-close for the first time. The assassinations of Bobby Kennedy and MLK shortly before his graduation from high school lead to an understandable despondency but not apathy. During a tension-filled car ride with his parents, returning from his first semester at Harvard, Ned gazes out the window at the Indiana countryside: "The landscape looked mysterious and inviting. I wanted to throw myself out across the fields and join the troops of sumac assembling themselves at the edges of the forest. I wanted to be a part of their slow and peaceful march. King and Kennedy were dead, but something had to be done. We, the sumacs and I, would lead a succession of oaks and hickories out into the open, and Indiana would be forest again." These lines capture perfectly Ned's ethical imagination, recognizing the interrelatedness of people and places, the possibilities of individual and communal action.

Those possibilities are explored further in "Mass General," Ned's engaging account of his time as a hospital janitor, and his efforts as part of a "Marxist-Leninist" group to organize his fellow workers into a union. The experience leads Ned to new insights about the challenges and ongoing promise of progressive political ideas when "grounded in the experiences of people's lives"—especially those from backgrounds vastly different from his own.

There emerges, as well, in the essays to follow, a reconsideration of the "middlebrow" culture of Ned's parents, which he and others had once denigrated. In essays on Elvis, the popular television artist Jon Gnagy, and his parents' encyclopedias, he engages the class complexity of the term "middlebrow" that has too often "been equated with smugness and avidity, an unseemly grasping after status, the contamination of real culture." The essay form has itself been dismissed as middlebrow, he argues: "That translator of specialized knowledge, that kissing cousin of the journalistic article, that product of memory and research rather than imagination and art, that service genre used to explain the more literary genres such as fiction and poetry, that fourth genre that, as E. B. White reminded us, 'Stands a short distance down the line.'"

Consistent with his convictions, however, these theories and cultural critiques are grounded in the particulars of individual lives and personal relationships. This includes his discovering new compassion for his father on a Canada fishing trip, touring Memphis with Elizabeth, learning to paint with his ten-year-old daughter, reflecting on the life and death of a high school friend, and earning, thanks to his father, his first paid writing assignment composing an encyclopedia entry on U.S. agriculture. So, too, he discovers new appreciation for the smaller beauties of the Indiana countryside and starry skies while on a walk with Elizabeth—the essay from which we drew the title of this book.

In this middle cluster of essays, we see Ned coming home, with new understanding, to the people and places that have made him who he is, while embracing the ideas that will carry him forward in his calling as a writer and teacher.

It is important to disclose that Ned's original manuscript ended with "The Book of Knowledge: Essays and Encyclopedias." Neither Elizabeth nor I knew if Ned had planned to add essays, though he had talked informally about writing books on middlebrow culture and on the craft of essay writing. Considering that this might be the last opportunity to publish Ned's essays under one cover, Elizabeth and I discussed the possibility of including some additional pieces that were important to him and to those who knew and respected his work. Much of that work was dedicated to writing and teaching about the essay form, so it should be no surprise that the four selected pieces focus heavily on that subject. "Our Queer Little Hybrid Thing: Toward a Definition of the Essay," originally published in *Assay: A Journal of Nonfiction Studies* (and listed as a "Notable Essay" in that year's *Best American Essays*), has been used in countless classrooms to introduce students to this sometimes ill-defined, elusive form. But these final pieces also continue the autobiographical thread into Ned's later years as a teacher, writer, and father, especially "An Essayist's Guide to Research and Family Life."

Additionally, these final pieces help chart the ways the social and political activism of Ned's earlier life find new but related expression in his efforts as a literary advocate, particularly on behalf of the personal essay—a form he believed was profoundly democratic, welcoming a diverse range of voices and acts of witness, anchored in the particulars of experience. "When I went away to college in 1968," he writes in "The Book of Knowledge," "at the same time as I was getting a heavy dose of high culture, my classmates and I were marching in the streets and occupying buildings, fighting not just to end the war but also to democratize culture. We were arguing for women's studies and African American studies programs, for a canon that included women and minority writers as well as dead Englishmen." Championing the personal essay when he became a professor himself was an extension of that earlier activism, but now took the form of teaching, giving conference presentations, composing accessible scholarship, facilitating faculty and student workshops at other institutions, and famously fighting to protect the university presses that publish and promote essayists.

The essay form, for Ned, is an ethical force, one rooted in truth. He gives passionate yet humorous expression to this belief in his satirical breakup letter "Dear John: Facts and the Lyric Essay." The focus of this piece is on John D'Agata's then recently published book *The Lifespan of a Fact* (coauthored with Jim Fingal), and Ned originally presented it at the 2012 AWP Conference. As anyone who attended will recall, Ned's reading provoked a *very* loud debate among audience members. "And well it should," Ned told me afterward. Whatever side you fell on, he felt strongly that the relationship between fact and artistry was an essential, defining discussion among readers and practitioners of the form, particularly when it came to writing about individual human lives. I know he would appreciate the opportunity this piece offers current teachers and students to explore such questions.

The essay form also embodied Ned's ongoing commitment to community building. This is directly addressed in the final essay, "My Name Is Ned: Facebook and the Personal Essay," in which he explores, with self-deprecating humor, his well-known "addiction" to this social media platform. He also describes his efforts, on Facebook, to respectfully converse with those holding radically different political views than his own, even within his own family. Many expressed admiration for Ned's boundary-crossing discussions on Facebook and have deeply missed them during this time of national division. Elizabeth and I felt this essay (also originally an AWP talk) was the ideal ending to the book, because it so beautifully captures

Ned's desire to connect with others, as expressed in his final lines: "I close in the hope that we essayists might be able to use Facebook not only as material but also as a place to create a community. In that vein, I hope that by the time I get back to my hotel tonight, I'll have some new friend requests from a few of you."

By publishing this final book by Ned Stuckey-French—his only collection of essays—it is our hope that it will indeed create new admirers of his work. New friends. This includes teachers and their students, who will find invaluable writing instruction but also, through Ned's coming-of-age story, be drawn into conversation and reflection about the questions and issues that mattered most to him—and should matter to us all.

For those of us who did have the privilege of knowing Ned in life, however, his continuing influence will never be in question.

On the day he died, following the message from Elizabeth, I was walking among the redwoods on the campus of the University of California–Davis. It was 2019, but the election was already in full swing. At a nearby farmers market, campaign tables were set up among the crates of organic fruits and vegetables—a juxtaposition I thought Ned would have appreciated. I was in Davis attending the ASLE Conference, a biennial gathering of environmental scholars, writers, and scientists. Almost every session I attended focused on the ways that art, scholarship, and teaching can, and should, advance the cause of environmental and social justice. We were all, in our own ways, responding to the questions Ned asked himself as a young man: When and where do I get involved? How do I make my own work meaningful? In the immediate wake of his passing, I saw Ned everywhere, not least of all in my once unlikely presence there, engaged in those vital conversations and community. As I considered the turbulent times ahead, I wondered what I would do without his guiding voice and vision.

I thought of this again a month later, visiting my wife's family in Idaho, when I signed up to take my first whitewater rafting trip, at the age of fifty-three. As I reluctantly stepped into the boat with my three sons, hearing the distant rumble of the water, I was reminded of Edward Abbey, to whose work Ned had first introduced me during that essay-reading group in graduate school, specifically Abbey's 1981 essay "Down the River with Henry Thoreau," which recounts his reading of *Walden* while navigating the rapids of Utah's Green River. Ned loved nature and nature writing, especially very *long* nature writing, and he coerced me into reading a number of other pieces that would later, seemingly against my will, shape me into the Midwestern environmental writer I never in my wildest imaginings thought I would become. But Ned did. For my thirtieth birthday, on the edge of my doctoral graduation, he gifted me the hardcover edition of the *Norton Book of Nature Writing*, in which he wrote this dedication: "To John Price, Nature Writer." That was, I believe, the first time I ever saw myself referred to by that honorific.

Approaching the first rapids on the Payette River in Idaho, scared out of my mind, I found myself thinking of my friend and the final lines from Abbey's essay that he had forced on me all those years ago. For me, they continue to capture Ned's guiding spirit, which remains, in memory and on these pages, a faithful companion through whatever turbulent waters lie before us:

> We load the boats, secure the hatches, lash down all the baggage, strap on life jackets, face the river and the sun, the growing roar of the rapids.... We feel the familiar rush of adrenaline as it courses through our blood. We've been here before, however, and know that we'll get through. Most likely. The odds are good. Our brave boatman and boatwoman... ply the oars and steer our fragile craft into the glass tongue of the first rapid. The brawling waters roar below, rainbows of broken sunlight dance in the spray. We descend.
>
> Henry thou should be with us now.
>
> I look for his name in the water, his face in the airy foam. He must be here. Wherever there are deer and hawks, wherever there is liberty and danger, wherever there is wilderness, wherever there is a living river, Henry Thoreau, will find his eternal home.

So, too, Ned Stuckey-French.

John T. Price
University of Nebraska at Omaha
May 2021

ONE
BY ONE,
THE STARS

PART 1

Nightmares

In 1954, when I was four, our family lived in a little bungalow on Vine Street in West Lafayette, Indiana. It had just a scrap of backyard—no room for a swing set or even a sandbox—but I wouldn't have played out there anyway because the Crazy Man lived behind us.

I knew he was crazy, because Nancy Harshbarger told me so and she was in third grade. Nancy said that when his garden wouldn't grow right he started yelling at it, yanked his tomato plants out by the roots, and hurled them and their stakes against the side of his garage, screaming at them to "die, motherfuckers!"

Our house was tiny. An old coal-burning furnace, its rusty ductwork snaking out from it, dominated the cobwebby half-basement. I hated nights in that house, for it was then that I heard the sound of the coal as it burned and settled—its sudden rattles like the sounds of hell rushing up through the register and into my room. My bed sat against a wall, and the window in that wall looked down into the Crazy Man's yard. I tried to sleep with my back against the window, hoping I wouldn't roll over and wake up to him grinning in at me from the dark with his fingernails pinching into the sill and his eyes wide like those of a Kilroy gone bad. My mother said later it was my worst year for nightmares because it took so long to convince me they weren't real. She'd hear me scream and rush in. Through the tears and snot, I'd blubber out what I had just seen, what I was seeing still—witches in purple hats, growling dogs with pink drooling mouths, the head (just the head!) of the Crazy Man floating down from the ceiling and stopping next to my bed, where it wobbled and laughed.

I began to worry about everything, especially grown ups. Who could trust them? What did they know? What didn't they know? Why did they do what they did? Why did they throw tomato plants and swear?

Each worry led to another. One afternoon I found myself sitting in our little living room next to the fireplace. I began thinking and worrying. I looked at the bricks in the hearth and at the built-in bookcase next to the hearth. I looked at what was there before me, and I thought about why things were the way they were—the rough surface of the bricks, the spidery lines in the grain of the wood. Soon, my thoughts had carried me somewhere I had not been before. I wanted to remember everything about where I was at that moment and what it looked like. I thought no one had ever thought what I was thinking.

Maybe that sounds self-important now, but I was a kid who had been set on his heels. I didn't feel important. I felt helpless. I was trying to freeze the moment so as to have something to hold on to. I wondered: Why are there trees or mountains? Why are there people? Why is there anything?

I got up slowly, fearing that the floor might slide away into nothingness, taking me with it, and I went into the kitchen to find my dad. He was at the table balancing his checkbook, and as I came in he looked up at me from his bills. A cup of black coffee sat next to him on the white enamel tabletop.

These new thoughts had stolen up on me quickly and they might leave quickly so I out and asked him, "Dad, why is there anything? Why are there people? Why isn't there just nothing?"

He stared at me, pursed his lips, and put down his pencil. He must have felt he had a live wire on his hands. "That's a big one." He looked away to gather his thoughts and then looked back. "A lot of people go to church to try to answer those kinds of questions. Some people get their answers, some don't. But they're good questions. You should keep asking them." Then he paused, waiting to see if he had said enough. My eyes and my silence must have told him he hadn't. Not really. "You and I are here right now. There are other people in the world too—your mom, your brother, lots of people. That's a good thing, right?"

I nodded, mostly for his sake. I could tell he was done.

All of this happened a long time ago and my dad is dead now. I think he gave me about as good an answer as you can give a four-year-old. As my mother had when I'd screamed about my dreams, he reassured me and waited and told me to wait too, knowing that answers to the biggest questions—questions about horror, uncertainty, and origins—come or don't come with time, and that all we can do is wait and ask for answers and live our lives.

We lived on Vine Street for only another year, while my parents built a bigger house out near the edge of town. Once, during that year, sitting on my tricycle at the corner of Vine and Sylvia, I saw the Crazy Man come out on his porch to get his mail. I froze, hoping he wouldn't see me. He took the letters from the box, looked through them, and then turned around and walked back in, just like anybody might. The fact that he acted normal when he wasn't both thrilled and terrified me. I rode away as fast as I could, trying not to think about the inside of his house and whether or not it was anything like my house, and I wondered what he might be doing and whether he was doing things my own father did like drinking coffee and paying bills, and I kept on trying not to think about the Crazy Man all the way home.

South Side

It is the summer of 1962. Our family's white Plymouth station wagon limps through the night. A red warning light has just lit up on the dash. The problem, whatever it is, is a big one because of where we are. We're on the South Side of Chicago. Ten minutes ago, orange cones and detour signs forced us off Lake Shore Drive and down into the darkness.

We're heading home from Minnesota to West Lafayette, Indiana, where my father teaches at Purdue. Up north, my dad, my brother, and I fished on Lake Winnibigoshish. Winnie, as we call it. My mom and sister stayed in Northfield, south of the Twin Cities, and visited Mom's relatives.

We got a late start and now it's after midnight. My brother and sister are asleep in the second seat. I'm all alone in the third seat, what we call the back-back. There are four limits of walleye and northern pike, filleted and freezing on dry ice in a Scotch cooler on the floor next to me. I was reading *Strike Three!*, one of the Chip Hilton sports series, by flashlight, but now I'm listening to the nervousness up front.

"What do you think it is?" my mother asks.

"A broken fan belt, I hope," says Dad. "Could be the alternator."

"Can't you just drive with it till we get home?"

"We're living off our battery. It's not recharging."

"Just till we get back onto the throughway?"

"No." This no is too emphatic. Enough, he's saying, leave me alone, you do not know what you're talking about, you're out of your realm, leave this to me. I've been here before and can hear all of this in the snap of his no and in the length of her injured silence.

The detour signs are leading us into an industrial sector. Chain-link fences, warehouses, ailanthus trees breaking though the cracked blacktop of parking lots, night watchmen dozing in trailers. Dad long ago shut off the radio to conserve electricity. The stark light from street lamps makes it hard to tell if the headlights are even on so he turns on the windshield wipers to see how much juice he's got left, if any. The wipers crawl to a halt halfway through their arc. They're stuck now, ominous at forty-five degrees. He flips off the switch to keep the wipers from trying to move. The soft hum of their failed attempt goes dead.

The neighborhood is turning more commercial. It's a hot night, but our windows are up, and our doors are locked. Five young Black men laugh and jostle each other under a street lamp. They don't see us. My father runs a yellow light and rolls through the stop signs. Grates guard the pawnshops and liquor stores. Only the taverns are open. We pass three gas stations. They're all closed.

I see only the backs of my parents' heads, but I can hear them talking.

"We'll be okay," says my mom. "Let's just calm down."

"Look, I know cars, I know neighborhoods, and I know we better find something soon."

"You 'know neighborhoods'?"

"Oh, please," says Dad. "Don't start that."

My mother points up ahead. "The light's on at that Gulf station."

"I see it. Try not to wake up the kids."

As we pull in, I can hear my brother stirring. The station looks raunchy and defeated. Its orange cinder blocks and blue trim are peeling and gray with grime. Moths and June bugs circle drunkenly in the cones of light above the pumps. Old notices are taped to the plate glass window, and a couple of curling, hand-printed cardboard signs sit propped on its sill: "No Credit!" and "Night Clerk Does Not Have Key to Vault." We roll to a stop, parallel to the front of the building. My father gets out, but leaves the engine running. My mother locks his door behind him. This little bit of commotion wakes my sister, who whimpers and asks if we're home. My brother keeps sleeping. His head is thrown back and there's drool on his chin. I want to get out, but know better.

I'm barely twelve and don't know much. Don't know much about racism, for instance, or ghettoes, but I do know that it's dangerous here. My parents are liberals and use vacations as "learning experiences," but this lesson is unplanned. In Detroit, we toured a Ford plant. In New Orleans, we walked down Bourbon Street and my parents laughed when I peeked through the swinging doors at the dancers. Dad joked about "the world's oldest profession." They always point out the sharecroppers' shacks when we're on our way to Florida, where Grandpa Albers winters with his new wife and his emphysema. But increasingly my parents fight, and the lessons get tangled up with their attempts to undo each other. My mother is from the North and sees herself as a bonafide liberal; my father is from Missouri, a border state, and so—in her eyes—is suspect.

"It's okay," Mom says to my sister. "We're just stopping for a minute. Go back to sleep." Her white lie works. Sara is asleep again so fast I wonder if she was ever really awake. My mother sees that I am awake. Not sure her eye contact is enough, she puts her index finger to her lips to keep me shushed.

The customer bell dings as my father opens the door to the station. A stout and balding Black man comes in from the garage, wiping his hands on a red rag. My mother and I can't hear them, but we watch. It's as if they're in a terrarium, or the control booth at a recording studio.

The garage guy listens to Dad, and nods deliberately a couple of times. Dad is talking quickly and using his hands more than usual, gesturing out toward the car and back up the street toward the detour signs. When he points toward the car, the man looks out at us. He has on blue coveralls with Gulf orange piping and a white oval name patch over his heart. I can't read it from here. He nods to my mother and me, smiles a perfunctory smile, and turns back to my father. He swings a thumb one way and a finger back the other, indicating, I realize, that he'll pull the car in the bay out so my father can pull in. I can read Dad's lips. He says "Thank you" twice, nodding nervously and looking the man straight in the eyes.

As he steps through the station door my father sheds his air of supplication. He's back in control. His stride is firm and he snaps open the door just as Mom unlocks it.

"They'll look at it right away. He seems to know what he's doing." He's nonchalant, even a little bit loud. His remark strikes me as odd. Why wouldn't he know what he's doing? This is a garage. He's a mechanic.

Sara and Hugh are stirring. Dad tells us to pile out and wait in the office. There's some stretching and blinking, a little whining, but soon we're all inside, where Mom placates Hugh and Sara with a PayDay from the vending machine. She perches on the windowsill; they plop onto the two chairs. The seats on the chairs are faded red vinyl; the chrome tubes of the frames are pocked and rusting. On the end table, there's an overflowing ashtray—a green aluminum dish that's scratched and nesting in a beanbag. Next to it are some dog-eared copies of *Jet* magazine. The manager's desk is littered with receipts, message pads, four empty Coke cans, and a car parts catalogue in a black three-ring binder.

I'm standing at the doorway to the garage area. Like the bear that went over the mountain, I want to see what I can see. I have not been to this mountaintop before. There are no Black kids in my school, no Black families in my town. None.

Inside the garage two Black guys wait for Dad to pull in and for the manager to return from parking the other car. One man is to my left, leaning against a stained and rancid slop sink. His legs are crossed at the ankles and his arms are folded. It's a studied ease. He's wearing dirty khakis, black engineer's boots, and a white T-shirt. The whiteness of his T-shirt makes his black face and black arms look even blacker, almost the color and sheen of patent leather, or an eggplant. He's tall, sinewy, and expressionless. Occasionally he works some gum as he stares toward the doorway through which Dad slowly drives our glowing, whiter-than-white Plymouth. On top of the car is the luggage rack my dad made. It's jam-packed. A green canvas tarp is stretched tight across it. I'm now watching all this through the eyes of the Black man and it suddenly looks silly to me. Why do we have all this stuff? Why do we have it on top of our car?

On the workbench a radio is playing. The announcer is selling "pomade." Whatever that is. The other man is pudgy and short. He's standing by the workbench at the back of the garage, sucking on a bottle of Orange Crush and sporting brown-and-white spectator shoes, tan slacks with an impressive crease, and a shirt with wide lapels and a geometric print the brown of which echoes that of his shoes. He's color-coordinated. He's got up nice, too nice for a gas station at one in the morning. He doesn't look as if he works here. I wonder if it's his car we've cut in on or if he's just hanging out. He swallows a gulp of pop and calls to the other guy.

"Ellis, direct the mister in. Where your manners at, man?"

The tall man throws him a dirty look, but steps across the lift and into the top of the H it makes on the floor. He raises his hands, palms toward himself, and flicks his fingers fast and often as he steps slowly backward. Dad follows this keep-coming sign up onto the lift. When all four wheels are positioned, the guy suddenly flips his hands back around and freezes them. Dad brakes. The tall guy's right hand moves quickly to the grille, searching for the hood release. As Dad steps out of our car, the manager returns from the outside. Behind him, through the bay door, I can see the streetlight turn green at the corner. A car screeches away, trailing the blare of its radio behind it—Sam Cooke singing "Bring It on Home to Me."

Most every night at home when my parents fight in their bedroom, I press the black Bakelite headphones of my short-wave radio hard against my ears and wrap my pillow around my head, trying to read while also listening to WLAC, the home of soul in Nashville, Tennessee. "This is John R. talking to you for Ernie's Record Mart. We got the beat, we got the soul. You keep that dial where it is, heah? Right where it is, deep in the heart of Dixie." James Brown, Chuck Berry, Little Richard, Aretha Franklin, and on Sunday night the spiritual hour and a sermon from Detroit's New Bethel Baptist Church by Aretha's father, the Reverend C. L. Franklin. It takes me to a world beyond my parents' trouble, a world outside my white bread town.

> You know I'll always be your slave
> Until I'm buried, buried in my grave
> Oh, oh, bring it to me,
> Bring your sweet lovin'
> Bring it on home to me, yeah, yeah . . .

Sam Cooke has two years to live. Gospel is becoming rhythm and blues. Eight-tracks and boom boxes are pretty much a decade away.

"We'll fix you up," the manager tells my dad. This is the first bit of their conversation I've actually been able to hear. My dad is fidgeting with the change in his pocket and still nodding too agreeably. I can tell that he wants out of here. Pronto.

"I had to put in a new alternator just last winter," my father tells the man. He's being ambiguous, for this could mean that he put it in himself or that he had it put in at a garage. He wants the first possibility to hang in the air, one that communicates competence, authority, know-how, and says *don't think you've got me, even if you do.* Then he adds, "Probably just needs a fan belt and a battery charge. Can you check the date on that battery while you're at it? We'd like to get on our way." He's pushing it too far, telling the guy what to do in his own shop.

The manager surprises. He's been all patience, not deference but patience. Now he turns to my dad. "You know you're in trouble." The tone is direct and no-nonsense, a statement of fact, but it's softened at the end with the hint of a smile that also conveys reassurance.

I can feel Dad flinch, but he recovers, looks the man in the eyes, and says, "Yes, yes, I do."

"Don't worry," the man answers. "We'll take care of you." He pauses, gets another nod from my dad, and adds, "You may be right. Could just be a fan belt. Either way we'll get you out of here soon."

My father thanks him and takes the post near the slop sink the tall guy has vacated. A sign above the workbench says "Authorized Persons Only in the Garage Area—No Tools Loaned." Either my dad hasn't seen it or has decided it doesn't apply to him. But, in any case, he's away from the engine now, outside their realm, and watching but not meddling.

The tall guy pops the hood and lays his work light on the engine. The light's bright bulb sits in a cage of rubber-coated wire. He turns and takes a soft pack of Kools from a tool chest to his left. He taps one out, pops it twice on the face of his wristwatch and lights it deliberately with a match before easing back under the hood. He removes the battery, hooks it up to the charger, and then returns to our car to begin his diagnosis.

I step out of the way as the chubby guy, dapper in his brown-and-white, comes through the door from the garage. Hugh and Sara are drawing pictures on deposit slips my mother tore out of the back of her checkbook. The man says hello to all of us, puts his Orange Crush bottle in the return case, and gets an Almond Joy.

"They'll get you fixed up in there," he says to my mom.

"I hope so. It's late and we've got to get these kids home."

He turns to Hugh and Sara. "You're doing your artwork now though, aren't you?" They look up at him and stare. They're still half asleep and to them the man is some sort of dream. A brown man in a dream.

Then my mother surprises me a bit. She introduces us one by one. "This is Hugh... Sara... and that's Ned. I'm Dolores."

"I'm James... James Floyd."

Is he formalizing with his last name, because he's unsure that we should all be on a first name basis so quickly? Or is it just that trick from *How to Win Friends and Influence People?* Say your first name, and then repeat it with your last name so people can get the whole thing and remember it. But my mom turns it into a joke.

"Dolores French," my mother responds, but then she pushes back through the little awkwardness with a joke. "It's nice to meet you James Floyd. So you've got two first names? Does that ever cause you problems?"

He laughs. "Now and then."

I try to case this out. Her joke assumes he's quick and has a sense of humor. It assumes the best in fact, and she seems to be right. He's smiling. But I'm not completely sure. We're in the wrong world and the wrong time, and I'm not sure what's what. Sometimes my mother just likes to talk to people; sometimes she likes to prove that, unlike my father, she is at home with anyone, anywhere, anytime. Maybe she is.

James Floyd tears the wrapper from his candy bar and shakes out the first of its halves into the palm of his left hand. He holds it toward my mom and, with a raised eyebrow and a nod her way, asks silently whether she wants it. She does. She takes it and promptly, unhesitatingly, takes a bite, as if drinking from the same cup.

"I knew a Dolores once," he says. "Is it D-E-L or D-O-L? They always mixed hers up."

"D-O-L," she answers. "But my nickname is Diz." She finishes off her candy and licks a spot of chocolate from her thumb. Things are a little too friendly.

I know about these blurred boundaries. At home, when my father is not at home, I'm left with my mother. More and more, my father stays late at the office and goes out of town on business. To her, he's simply absconding. As their marriage unravels—and it unravels slowly: it will be another fourteen years before they finally divorce—she turns increasingly to me. I'm her eldest, her eldest son, her confidant, her little man, her crutch, a surrogate when Dad's away.

Sometimes when he's away, things feel almost normal, even fun. She jokes; I act silly. She makes up funny songs; I dance. I balance a yardstick on my chin and she counts out the seconds I keep it up. Nine. Ten. Eleven. We watch the news together, read *Time* magazine, arrive at shared opinions. Kennedy's tax cut makes sense. The Test Ban Treaty must be ratified. The Freedom Riders are right. Maybe things will work out.

Then she talks to my father long distance and everything goes bad again.

My door creaks open. The light from the hall seeps in. "Ned? Are you asleep?" She knows I'm not. I'm sitting up reading. "I need to talk."

"What is it?"

"Can you just come in the other room for a minute?" I look up and can see her head floating at the foot of my top bunk. Her eyes are red and puffy. She turns and heads out the door, knowing I'll follow. I mark my book and follow her down the hall and into the family room. Dad will be in Washington an extra day, she tells me. It's snowing there.

"Why," she hisses, "didn't he get a flight out this afternoon?" She's sitting at the table, twisting a paper napkin. I know she's looking at me, but I don't look back. I'm past her and into the kitchen, opening the refrigerator door and putting it between us.

"Maybe he had to meet with people for dinner," I say matter-of-factly. "Maybe he didn't hear the weather report." I'm walking a fine line here. I'm trying to be reasonable and merely explanatory without seeming to side with him. I find some leftover vanilla pudding, take it out and close the door. I set the bowl on the counter and peel off the Saran Wrap. As I turn to get a spoon from the silverware drawer, I sneak a glance and gauge her response. She seems to have accepted the possibilities I've proposed; seems to have bought my nonchalance.

"Yeah, maybe," she says. The napkin is unknotted now and on the table. She's smoothing it flat. She stands up and walks back toward the hallway to the bedrooms. "Why don't you bring your pudding with you? Carson's almost on."

"In a minute. I'm going to get some Hi-C too."

When I get there, she's lying in bed, two pillows propping her head. Her reading light is on but she's staring at the TV. *The Day Lincoln Was Shot* lies next to her, open and facedown. I sit on the floor, my back against the foot of their king-size bed. It's the usual arrangement and leaves me about four feet from the screen. Johnny has started his monologue. I eat pudding through the rest of the monologue and the first commercial. Johnny and Ed are back now and in their seats. Johnny is smoking. They banter a bit, making fun of Doc's plaid jacket. Doc feigns both pride and injury. Another commercial break, and still my mother is silent, though I'm sure we're not yet done with my dad. I eat my pudding deliberately; I sip my Hi-C slowly.

"We're back," says Johnny. "Our first guest tonight is Godfrey Cambridge. I never know what this man is going to say, but he always makes me laugh and he always makes me think. Not all comics do that."

"No, they don't. I've noticed that," says Ed, who then smirks at Johnny. Some of the audience laughs. Johnny does a slow burn, letting the insinuation sink in. Rising laughter.

"No, Ed, not all comics do, but Godfrey Cambridge does, and without further interruption..." Another look at Ed. A no-hard-feelings wink. "... without further ado, Mr. Godfrey Cambridge."

Carson is right. Cambridge's routine is provocative. He twists all sorts of stereotypes, making fun of Black people as well as white. But especially white people. He moves constantly between a kind of elevated, almost British brand of Standard English and street jive. He's funny. He's polished. His routine is over. The audience loves it. Ed loves it. Johnny loves it. Johnny even wipes his eye once to let us know he laughed so hard he cried. Over the continuing applause and through his grin, Johnny says with an excessively appreciative, how-does-he-do-it shake of his head, "We'll be right back with more from Godfrey Cambridge."

Dissolve to the commercial. My mother finally talks.

"You know it took me two years to get your father to call them 'colored people.'" She's found her opening. "And I don't know how long it was before he could say 'Negro' without having to stop and think about it."

I am meant to understand that he's not only cruel to her but also to Black people. He's a racist. Or was before she fixed him. I know however not to rise to her bait. I say nothing.

Johnny's kept Cambridge on the couch and he's praising him profusely. Cambridge accepts the compliments with grace. The two of them turn serious for a minute and discuss how comedy can bridge the gap, and how laughter transcends race. Then, knowing exactly when to lighten things again, Johnny slides into some set-ups so Cambridge can get more laughs, especially from Johnny, who always leads the way with his twinkling eyes, his guffaws, and his surprised, coughing puffs of cigarette smoke. There's an implicit agreement among us all that this is improvised. Johnny is the surprised and gracious host, not the polished straight man.

The next act is a girl singer. I stay so as not to seem to be running, but after the next commercial, I get up and take my bowl and glass into the kitchen sink. On my way back, I say good night as I pass by her bedroom on the way to my own. She doesn't answer, but from the hallway I can see she's still awake and watching Johnny.

James Floyd has decided to stay a while in the waiting room. My mom keeps chatting him up. They're on their second Almond Joy.

"So you really think Daley's a good mayor?" she asks skeptically.

"Well, I don't say that exactly, but the system takes care of those who take care of the system."

"What about the president? You like him? I do."

"Yeah, I like him." Then he laughs. "I guess we all owe our jobs to the mayor."

"Yeah, well, a rich daddy doesn't hurt either."

I'm fascinated. The only other time I can remember seeing my mother talk this long to a Black person was at International Student Night at the Purdue Student Union, but that was an African exchange student. The interaction was formal, if also friendly. How many Nigerian students are there at Purdue? Do you plan to return to your country? All the while, we kids circulated among the booths and card tables, getting our names written in Arabic, Swahili, and Farsi.

I search my memory for other possibly instructive encounters, but my repertoire is thin. How does one talk to Black people? Where have I seen it happen? Maybe my father and a bellhop in New York or Washington, or my mother asking a maid for extra towels in a hotel corridor. I do remember tagging along with my grandfather, my father's father, to the blacksmith's shop one summer in Missouri. Several farmers, including a Black one, talked together while they waited for a wagon tongue or a mower blade to be repaired. They shared the same subjects—weather, crops, hog prices, illness. The Black man talked as much as anybody, but later, after we'd left, my grandfather identified him to my uncle as that "nigger" who farms over by so-and-so's place. The word shocked me. I'd heard my grandpa refer to Brazil nuts as "nigger toes," but that was abstract and removed somehow, an adjective tucked in a silly, unconsidered, nearly buried metaphor. This was different. He was identifying a real man with whom he'd joked and gossiped, a man he seemed to like.

I never heard the word in West Lafayette, my hometown, at least not from an adult. Among kids, yes. They might say it. It was a regular, in fact, in "Eeny meeny miny mo." But even there I knew it was risky and a bad habit that shouldn't slip out in front of adults. So I switched, as did others. We began to catch Russians by their toes.

I look into the garage again. The tall Black guy with the cigarette and the manager in the blue coveralls have still got their heads under the hood. I've seen the manager's name up close now, in the white oval on his chest, and it is Curtis. They're fixing the problem now, which is just a fan belt after all.

Now Sam Cooke is on this radio. It's the summer of this song. It will reach number 2 on the R & B chart, number 13 on the pop chart. Sam Cooke has crossed over and figured out how to converse with whites.

If you ever change your mind,
About leaving, leaving me behind,
Oh, oh, bring it to me . . .

The tall, sullen man pulls from the engine the remnant of the broken belt. It flops in his hand like an injured snake. His Kool hangs from his lip. He looks triumphant. In five minutes they install a new one. The drama is over.

My father strides in from the garage.

"Looks like we're ready to go." He's smiling and satisfied, proud to have gotten his family through this. The manager follows him in, once again wiping his hands on his red rag. He drops the rag on the counter, sits down at his desk and begins to write up a receipt. The tall guy has pulled our car out of the bay and is swinging it around in front of the station.

My mother says to her candy friend, "It was nice to meet you, Mr. Floyd. Good luck with your mayor and his system." My father registers this with a soft sigh I hope only I have noticed. Sara holds up her drawing. It's a cat. She played with the barn cats in Minnesota and wants one of her own. Hugh's will be a design of a Soap Box Derby car. It always is.

"Three dollars, Mr. French," says Curtis the manager. He hands the receipt to my father. I linger to watch while everybody else heads chattering to the car. I want to see this scene to its end.

"You sure? You've really helped me out here."

"It was just the fan belt."

"I know, but I . . ."

"Happy to help." He has interrupted my father, not rudely but to make clear that the bill is fair to all involved, that people should help each other, that there's no need to blow this out of proportion, that there's no need to be paternalistic.

"Thank you," says my dad and he gives the man a ten.

As the man counts out the change, he says, "Remember, two more lights and then you'll swing left and back up onto Lake Shore. You'll be in Indiana in fifteen minutes."

"Thanks again. Come on, Ned."

So nothing happened. It was just a fan belt. People helped each other out. But anything could have happened. It was the summer after the Freedom Riders, the summer before Birmingham, Medgar Evers, and the March on Washington. It was the night I felt the color line.

In the car, I leave my light off. I don't feel like reading. I lie on my back and watch the streetlights flash by. I'd seen my parents out of their element. I'd seen three ways Black people, these three Black men anyway, relate to white people—one smooth, one standoffish, one businesslike. I'd seen two ways white people, my parents anyway, relate to Black people. My mother a bit too eager to prove she's a friend; my father a bit too eager to be in charge.

Sara and Hugh have already quieted down. The lights and excitement of the gas station are behind us. We swing up the ramp and onto the expressway. The radio is playing so softly I can't make it out. My parents are quiet. There will be no summing up right now, no assessment of who did and didn't do what. There will be no fight.

In fifteen minutes we're in Indiana; in twenty, I'm asleep.

Backyards

One Saturday in August 1962, perched high in a maple tree in our backyard, I handed my father a nail. We were building a tree house. I was twelve. My brother Hugh, who was about to turn nine, stood below us on the ground, sending boards up with a pulley and standing clear in case we dropped something.

Across a little lane, I could see the remnants of Tom and Bill Butz's tree house. The Butzes' backyard sloped downhill away from ours so their tree house was below us. Beyond their parents' house, I could see all of West Lafayette, Indiana, spreading out toward the red tile roofs of Purdue University. Tom and Bill were older than me and had already left for college, but most of their tree house was still there. It was a pretty good one, especially considering they had built it by themselves—two small stories, simple platforms really, the first maybe six feet off the ground, the second a few feet above that. It had no fencing or roof. You couldn't sleep in it. Ours would be better.

Most of our plans were still on paper that first afternoon, however, and I didn't know if we'd even finish framing the floor that weekend. Twice I'd asked my dad how long it would take, but he'd told me to be patient, that it was more important to get it right, so I'd stopped asking.

Looking back on it now, I wonder if my dad wasn't being a little bit competitive, too. Tom and Bill's father was Earl Butz, the dean of agriculture at Purdue, and as such, my dad's boss. He was the same Earl Butz who would become Nixon's secretary of agriculture. Though he was a friend of agribusiness who argued that "food was a weapon" and farmers should "get big or get out," he helped Nixon win the farm vote. After Nixon was forced to resign, Earl stayed on as Gerald Ford's secretary of agriculture. Though it wouldn't be long before Earl, like Nixon, was asked to resign. On a plane home from the 1976 Republican National Convention, Butz was sitting in first class with Pat Boone, Sonny Bono, and, unfortunately for him, John Dean. Boone, always the earnest teenager, asked Earl why the party of Lincoln couldn't win Negro voters. An honest answer would have acknowledged that the Republicans had written off Black voters after LBJ pushed through the Civil Rights Act of 1964 and were now pursuing a southern strategy based on racist code words such as "law and order," "forced busing," and "states' rights." Instead, Butz joked, "All the coloreds want is tight pussy, loose shoes, and a warm place to shit." Dean, whose testimony had done Nixon in three years earlier, was on assignment for *Rolling Stone*. He reported the joke, it appeared in *Rolling Stone*, and a few weeks later, Earl Butz was out of the White House and on his way back to Purdue.

All that was yet to come, but my dad's relationship with Earl Butz was already, in the early sixties, long-standing, personal, and complicated. Earl had been his major professor in graduate school and then hired him as an assistant professor. We also attended the same church as the Butzes and it was usually there that I saw Earl and his wife, Mary Emma. Our exchanges with them in the foyer or church parking lot intrigued me. My mother was a liberal and liked to tease Earl and try to get a rise out of him. "Oh, Earl, you don't mean that. You're just mad Kennedy's in the White House and you aren't." Dad, on the other hand, was professional and polite, though sometimes, I thought, too deferential. Later, I'd hear from others that he sometimes disagreed with Earl at work, though I suspect Dad picked his battles carefully.

"That's solid," Dad said of the floor joist we'd just finished, "but I think we better cut another long one for over there, and maybe a short cross piece to connect these two."

We're never going to finish, I thought. I wanted to be done laying floorboards so our tree house would start looking like a tree house. If we didn't finish today, that would throw us into tomorrow, which was Sunday, and then Dad would probably invoke his no-work-on-the-Sabbath rule, and before you knew it, we'd still be framing next week. I was ready to have my friends over so we could read comic books in the tree house, wage water balloon fights, and sleep out all night.

But Dad was the boss, and after he'd checked his measurements, we climbed down the ladder, joined Hugh, and headed back across the yard toward the basement, the lumber, and the table saw.

The high whine and unforgiving blade of my father's power saw scared me, but with deadpan instructions, he'd insisted that I learn how to use it. "Keep the board straight or it'll jump up and bite you. Hold your hands wide. You may want those fingers later in life."

Fortunately, the tree house boards were too big for me to cut. All I had to do was hold the long end of each one level while my dad guided the shorter, marked end through the blade. "Remember," he said, "slow and easy. You just hold your end of the board. I'll set the pace."

Hugh stood on the other side of the room, his fingers in his ears. My dad reached under the saw and flipped the toggle switch. The screech of the spinning blade reverberated off the concrete walls, turning shockingly shrill when board met blade. It was like being inside a jet engine.

My dad built the table saw himself. Its frame was made of wood and the saw itself was powered by a motor he had salvaged from a worn-out washing machine. He'd made it when he was remodeling our old house on Sylvia Street, putting in two bedrooms and a bathroom on the third floor so student renters could help pay the mortgage.

I knew where he had learned how to improvise and salvage like this. Every summer, I went to my grandparents' farm in Missouri for a couple of weeks, tagging along while they did their chores. My dad always called his parents' place "a beef and pork operation," but the word "operation" seemed grandiose to me even then. I loved staying there and doing the things he had done when he was a kid—gigging frogs, fishing the farm ponds for bluegills and bullheads, shooting sparrows with the same little single-shot twenty-two he had used, and helping my grandmother gather eggs from the chicken coop—but sometimes the whole place felt as if it were held together by baling wire, hard work, and more than a little luck.

Once, at breakfast on the farm, my grandmother asked me how I wanted my eggs. Earnest and self-important, I replied, "Over well with the yolks broken. Can you do 'em like that?"

She laughed and said, "I think so. I've made them that way for your dad for thirty years."

A summer or two before we built the tree house, my dad and I made a cage for my two pigeons. We put the cage in our backyard just outside a garage window so that in winter we could run a heavy orange extension cord out to it and keep a forty-watt bulb burning so the pigeons stayed warm. The floor of the cage was made of the same wire mesh as the sides and top so I could hose it out when it needed to be cleaned.

Our backyard also had a high jump pit, a rope swing, and a row of tomato plants. Dad liked to keep tomatoes. I think they reminded him of his mother's garden. August evenings he'd go out back with a saltshaker to eat them off the vine and smell the crushed leaves on his hands. He'd pick a tomato, bite into it like an apple, and, after swallowing, always say the same thing: "This is as fresh as they come."

It was past the cooing pigeons and the pungent tomato plants that we toted what I hoped would be the last two floor joists of the day.

From my perch in the tree, I could also see the Sandersons' backyard next door. James and Louise Sanderson's youngest daughter, Julie, was a year younger than me, and her brother Scott and sister

Abby were, respectively, four and six years older. Despite the difference in our ages, Scott and I were good friends. He was small for his age, but, like me, loved sports. We played endless games of basketball in my driveway and staged our own two-man track meets on the sidewalk out front. But Scott and I were the only real link between our families. Abby babysat us occasionally and taught us how to play solitaire, but our parents didn't really have much to do with each other. Louise was cool and distant; Mr. Sanderson was a nice enough guy, but not around a lot. I think he respected my father professionally, for he was also a professor at Purdue and his specialty, applied statistics, probably helped him appreciate my father's growing reputation as an economist, even if Dad was just an *agricultural* economist. Louise, on the other hand, stayed trim playing golf and kept her distance from my mom, whom she likely dismissed as just another Book-of-the-Month-Club intellectual. The Sandersons drove a new Oldsmobile convertible and belonged to the country club.

The Sandersons' backyard was divided into two parts by a retaining wall built out of railroad ties. The upper level was a nice lawn, big enough for croquet games. A second-floor deck that extended almost the full length of the house hung out over a patio that adjoined this upper part of their yard. French doors opened onto the deck from their family room. On it were a glider, several deck chairs, a chaise longue, and a round table with an umbrella—their version of a tree house.

The area beyond and below the retaining wall, though wilder than their croquet court, was not as wild as any part of our backyard, with its underbrush, Tarzan swing, and cage of filthy birds. A small stream lined with chunks of granite trickled through this lower section, and next to the stream the Sandersons had put in a putting green. It was only a little larger than a living room floor, thin in spots and kind of weedy, but a putting green nonetheless.

Up in the tree house, my dad wedged himself between two trunks so he wouldn't fall. When he hit the first nail, the sound rang out across the neighborhood—loud, metallic, and shocking. He swung a second time, but the sound was wrong. He had mis-hit. The nail was a twenty-penny, big and thick, a spike really, but it bent. Dad sighed, flipped the hammer, and placed the claw to pull out the nail. He tossed the useless nail down to Hugh. I knew better than to say anything. I handed him a fresh nail.

He rolled his shoulders and I could hear his spine crack like knuckles in a couple of spots. He sighed again and started in on the next nail. His concentration was fierce, but it was not enough to overcome the fact that he was tired and working with a short swing, and after a few hits, he bent this nail as well. As he pulled it, I looked at him but got no eye contact. His sideburn was wet with sweat and plastered flat. There was a spot of eczema on the back of his neck, just at his hairline. He was in his own world, more focused than ever on doing this right. I handed him a new nail. Bang. Bang. Bang. The hits were true and the nail was home. I was reaching into my apron for another one when we were shocked by a voice from below that was not Hugh's.

"Whatcha you doing up there, Charley?" The voice was male, adult; familiar, but not.

It was James Sanderson, as composed and placid as a TV dad. He was in topsiders, khakis, and a burgundy knit shirt. His hair was neatly parted and his glasses had tortoiseshell frames. His arms were folded across his chest and he was craning a little bit to get a good look at us. The pose suggested he'd been there a while. His question was friendly enough, but it was pretty obvious what we were up to.

My dad pulled himself right side up and turned, like he was doing a sit-up. He blinked and reached a finger behind his glasses to wipe the sweat out of his eyes. He'd been caught off guard. Then he focused down to the ground, at Mr. Sanderson, and spoke, "Oh, I'm just trying to get this damn thing up."

I had heard my mother's uncles swear. They were big, beer-drinking German dairy farmers. I had heard them swear in my father's presence, and I'd even seen him appreciate, perhaps even envy, their swearing, but I have never heard my father swear. Never.

"Damn thing"? I thought. What is he saying? This is our tree house. This will be the best tree house in town. "Damn thing." How could he say that?

I stared at him, but he wasn't looking at me; he was looking down at Mr. Sanderson and smiling. It was an awkward, sheepish smile, a smile that was meant to look nonchalant, but was not. Up here, up close, I could see a twitch near his eye. The effort and concentration my father and I had shared a moment before were gone.

"Tree house, eh?" asked Mr. Sanderson.

"Yeah, the boys say they're ready for one. This seemed like the place to put it." Dad fished for his handkerchief.

"Quite a job," said Mr. Sanderson. Then he unfolded his arms and hitched his belt a little bit.

"Yeah, more work than I thought it would be," said my dad, "but we're about done for today."

"Well, I was watering some flowers and heard you. Just thought I'd see what you're up to. Good luck up there. See you later, boys." Then he turned and headed across our yard toward his own. My dad and I watched him as he passed the Tarzan swing without seeming to give it any notice. Then he moved out of the shadow of the oak tree into the late afternoon sun. All he was doing was walking home, and yet to me, his back seemed full of rebuke.

It would be years before I began to understand the awkwardness in my dad's smile and unlock the reasons why he might have been willing to say *damn* in front of his boys. The reasons had to do with marking himself as an adult after having been caught hanging from a tree like a kid, but it was more than that. Mr. Sanderson's presence cast a spotlight on our backyard, the way throwing a dinner party makes you notice the smudges on the light switches or the chips in Grandma's china. We might have disagreed with the Republicans whose backyards adjoined ours, but they could still intimidate us. There was always in my dad, even later when he worked in the Carter White House or represented the United States at international conferences, a hint of self-doubt that I don't think he let many people see. It was as if these "Country Club" people, these people who drove a new Oldsmobile convertible when he drove a six-year-old Plymouth station wagon could see him for what he was—a dirty-faced kid who fished farm ponds for bullheads and sold gooseberries at a stand by the side of the road so he could buy his first rifle, a little single-shot twenty-two.

My dad wedged himself back into the fork in the tree and situated himself the way he was before Mr. Sanderson surprised us. I handed him the last nail. He banged it home in five quick strokes, and we headed down the ladder to wash up for dinner.

As we walked across the yard together I registered everything in a new light. I was only twelve and I didn't know all that these backyards can symbolize, but I registered the differences.

In the bare spot under the Tarzan swing, the exposed roots of the oak tree had been polished by thousands of sneakered feet. The leaves of the tomato plants hung wilting and brown in the late summer heat. The tomatoes themselves were swollen and split— Big Boys, Early Girls, Beefsteaks. The pigeon cage, with its galvanized wire, gray and leaden, and its wooden frame of salvaged, mismatched wood, stank in the shadows. Under the cage there was a splattering of soggy bird shit, and in the cage two pigeons blinked and watched us as we walked by.

Termites

The summer before ninth grade, the summer of 1964, we collected insects. During most of the summer we assumed termites would be easy to find so we didn't look very hard for them. Lepidoptera—butterflies and moths—were not only bigger, flashier, and more interesting, they were more fun to catch. Chasing a swallowtail across a meadow or touring street lights late at night for big moths was more romantic than kicking apart rotten stumps or dismantling woodpiles, which was what you had to do to find termites. But August arrived and found us without termites. I was the one who proposed the shortcut. One of the exterminators around town must have some. My friend Bill Harrison was not sure this was on the up and up, but we all needed termites and I prevailed. I checked the Yellow Pages and started calling exterminators. The first five thought I was crazy to imagine they kept any termites, but finally, on the sixth call, I had some luck. The man said, almost apologetically, that he only moonlighted as an exterminator, but that he did have some termites. He put them in an old terrarium and watched them just like he'd watched his ant farm when he was a kid.

"My queen is something when she's pregnant," he said. "She puffs up to the size of your little finger. I can give you all you want."

He lived about five miles south of town. "Just beyond the Eli

Lilly plant, where they make the pharmaceuticals," he said. The ride would be long and hot, but that was OK. In a way, we would be working for the termites after all.

The next afternoon, Mike Dobbs, Leonard Johnson, Bill Harrison, and I set off on our bikes to get the termites. Dobbs had a ten-speed with thin, hard tires and as we worked our way up the Ninth Street hill I heard the click-click-click as he down-shifted to his lowest gear. He pulled next to me, stood on his pedals, churned them hard, and blew on by. Almost as if he was riding on level ground he swept past Bill, and, finally, Leonard. Once in the lead he slalomed back and forth, flashed a grin, and threw a taunt back over his shoulder at Leonard. "Come on, lard butt. It's only a hill."

Leonard was working his old Schwinn as hard as he could, but it had big balloon tires and even from where I was I could hear them sticking to the squishy asphalt. They made a muffled tearing sound. While Dobbs scooted about like a water strider, Leonard huffed and puffed and cussed to himself.

Dobbs and Leonard were next-door neighbors and best friends but totally unalike. Leonard was the biggest, slowest kid in class. He had freckles everywhere and his hair was all cowlick. The next spring, he would drive to school, the first kid in our class to get his license. Dobbs, on the other hand, was short and quick, a halfback who used the holes Leonard opened for him at right tackle. Dobbs's father was the head of Army ROTC at Purdue University, where my father taught agricultural economics. Dobbs had jet-black hair, laughed at everything, and chattered constantly. For Leonard words were the enemy. He could talk about a few topics—his family, cars, his girlfriend Vicki, sports—but even then it was a struggle. When his sentences started to tangle his eyelids would flutter and drop shut. Then he'd raise his chin and trembling lips, and stutter out what he could. I rarely knew what he was going to say and I found it hard to watch him try. Once, when a few of us were playing poker, Leonard drew two cards to a full house. He raised a quarter to open the next round, the limit in our penny-ante games, and then, uncharacteristically, tried to hurry the betting.

"Do...do...do you...do you...ah...do you...?"

"No," answered Dobbs to the question that hadn't been asked. "I don't see your quarter. I fold."

Everyone else folded too, and Leonard won eight cents with his full house. This time, Dobbs's "help" cost him, but more often, there was a kindness and nonchalance in the way Dobbs finished his sentences that Leonard seemed to appreciate.

Dobbs and Leonard were friends of mine, but I was closest to Bill. He and I had known each other since kindergarten. We'd done chemistry sets and built shortwave radios together. At my house we made bombs that didn't really explode and rockets that didn't really fire. The bombs sizzled and burned blue and green flames, and the rockets tipped over and skittered across the driveway. Bill was compulsive and orderly but also willing to be reckless. In that sense he was like his father, a surgeon who chain-smoked Camels.

I enjoyed spending time at the Harrisons'. My parents' marriage was falling apart and Bill's house offered some sanctuary. The Harrisons were well off and had a big yard with a pool, but the attraction for me had more to do with the easy sociability I found there. The radio was always on. Friends of all three of their kids were usually around. Dr. Harrison was home a lot, though unobtrusively so, showing up from time to time during our afternoon-long Risk games to see who was conquering what continent and bring us a tray of Cokes. When Bill had sleepovers and we played poker, Dr. Harrison sometimes sat in, making sure to lose back anything he'd won before he went to bed. He and his two sons always had projects going. At Christmas, they strung lights along their eaves, fastened a sleigh and reindeer on the peak of their roof, stuck Santa halfway into the chimney, put four-foot candles and a crèche on the lawn, and always got their picture in the paper. Bill and his father built a series of Soap Box Derby cars, each one more sleek and shiny than the last, employing the latest in graphite lubrication and fiberglass bodywork. One year over Christmas vacation, the family spent five straight days completing a big, round, all-white jigsaw puzzle. Though Bill shared this penchant for hobbies with his father, he looked more like his mother—blonde, tall, skinny, and serious. She kept busy with her own projects, though you could hardly call them hobbies—wall-papering, weeding, cleaning the pool.

My own mother's bipolar disorder had already hospitalized her once. These were the days before lithium. She was bouncing from one shrink to another, and each one prescribed something different. None of them knew what the others were doing and the prescriptions piled up. My mother lived in a haze of Thorazine, Seconal, and Valium that left her helpless, watching television all day in her bedroom with her sunglasses on and the curtains drawn. Meals were often up to me. After getting lunch for my little brother and sister, I'd fix my mom something—maybe a grilled cheese sandwich, of which she'd eat half, or some Campbell's soup. Later, before we finally rousted ourselves to meet Dad somewhere for dinner, a delivery often arrived from Arth's Drugs. I signed for it, always leaving the receipt on my dad's desk so he could deduct it at tax time.

In seventh grade I came home from school one day and saw our minister sitting with my parents in the living room. None of them got up. "Your parents and I have been talking, Ned, and they have something to tell you," said the minister.

My father spoke first: "Your mother and I have decided to get a divorce." I didn't know what to say. I looked at my mother. She wasn't even crying. "Everything will be okay," she said. It all seemed planned out, and worst of all, beyond my control.

In fact it had been planned. My brother and sister weren't there (I found out later that some of my parents' friends had picked them up at school and taken them to their house). My parents had been fighting more and more, and my mom had been sad since she'd had a miscarriage, but still, I hadn't expected this. Usually, I was the little man, but this time I lost it and screamed, "No! No! No! You won't! No!" As my father started to get up, I jumped away from him past the piano bench and crawled behind the sofa, where I balled up underneath a print of an Utrillo street scene. I stayed there and yelled and hit them when they tried to get to me. Finally they called my mother's psychiatrist. When he arrived, all four adults went into the family room for a minute to consult. Then the psychiatrist came back into the living room. He sat on the couch and leaned over the back of it to talk to me privately. I'd never met him before. I was surprised to see he wore a hearing aid. He said he knew it was tough, and maybe I could come to his office sometime and he could help me figure out what to say to my parents. By that time I was getting tired and even a bit embarrassed by the commotion I'd caused.

"Okay," I said, and came out and sat on the couch.

When my parents and the minister returned, my father said that he and my mother had talked and they were going to stick together after all and keep working at it. I was shocked. I had hidden behind the couch because divorce terrified me. I had not imagined that going behind the couch would give me the power to keep my parents together.

In reality, it didn't. My father began to spend more and more time at his job. He went back to his office after dinner and didn't come home until eleven or so. Once he was home, I tuned in WLS out of Chicago or WLAC, the "home of soul" in Nashville, Tennessee, and hugged a pillow against the black plastic headphones of my shortwave radio so that I didn't have to listen to them fighting in the next room.

On the day we went after the termites, I put my parents' problems out of my mind. Bill thought we ought to take our nets with us, figuring we might see some good butterfly fields on the way. Dobbs and I talked him out of it. The ride was going to be long and hot—a mile or two of it would be gravel. The termites, we argued, would be bugs enough for one afternoon.

As we passed the county fairgrounds and headed out of town, the road flattened out, traffic thinned, and soon, in every direction, there was nothing but corn and soybeans. It was hot, and we were already tiring a bit and getting quiet. Dobbs must not have liked the silence, because he started us singing. "Duke of Earl," "Wah-Watusi," "Da Doo Ron Ron," "Louie Louie"—songs Leonard knew the words to. The slow pace of the bicycles opened the countryside up to us in a way car rides never did. On the electric lines red-winged blackbirds hunkered their shoulders and screeched, warning us that we were now in their territory. Goldfinches scattered from elderberry bushes and flew along a fence row and out across a cornfield. I thought how the surging hurry-and-glide of their flight pattern made them look like they were on a roller coaster. The bottom halves of the cornstalks were brown. Monarch butterflies worked the last milkweed flowers of the summer. On our right was an alfalfa field. I could smell the third batch of hay, which was raked but not baled yet. In another week, double sessions for football would start. I couldn't wait. I was ready for school to begin again and fill my time.

That summer adolescence hit me. Hit all of us, I suppose. Bill's older brother, John, gave him some inkling of what was ahead. As an oldest child, I enjoyed no such help, but relied instead on Bill for information—locker room reports from John about which cheerleaders did it, or the image of a hand inside a swimming suit, described to me by Bill, who had spied on one of John's pool parties. Adolescence arrived at different rates for each of us. Some of us were already riding puberty's locomotive while others were still waiting in the station, checking our watches. One moment you were wearing corduroys with knee patches, and life was all squirt guns and yo-yos. Every day was a happy slide from breakfast to the time when the streetlights clicked on and started to hum, and you begged your mother for another five minutes outside. But now, this summer, the girls had showed up at the pool in their new bodies and their two-piece bathing suits, and everything had changed. At night, I would sneak out of bed and do pushups in the dark.

The insect collections gave to the summer a second, much-needed focus, besides girls. The collections were a big deal because they were our first assignment for high school, but more than that, they had become an academic tradition in our academic town. They were part of the post-Sputnik emphasis on science in the schools. The previous spring, the high school biology teachers had visited our eighth-grade classes to explain the requirements. We would be expected to do a special project, which could be completed any time before the end of the first semester.

Handouts described our options. Besides insects, one could collect leaves or enter the science fair. Most of the girls went these latter routes because it was harder for them to get out at night to collect nocturnals like moths and beetles, but my friends and I knew already we would do insects. Collecting gave you an excuse to roam the county, even at night, and besides, most of the older guys we knew had done insect collections. Often that summer we spoke respectfully of the collection Kit Kildahl had turned in the year before—172 total specimens, including both a unicorn beetle and a mole cricket. Bill had shown me the five perfect cases his brother had submitted four years earlier. Though he was a senior now, John still kept his collection in his bedroom and we had to ask to see it. It was legendary and included three whole cases of lepidoptera, and one of those was nothing but big moths—a perfect royal walnut, a polyphemus, a cecropia, an imperial, several kinds of underwings. Every year in West Lafayette, sophomores-to-be sold their old nets, purple fluorescent bug lights, and mounting boards to incoming freshmen. We bought collection cases at the ag co-op, field guides at the university bookstore, and began collecting with the arrival of the mourning cloaks in late March.

Each afternoon during the summer we walked remnants of the tall grass prairie, rhythmically sweeping our nets for thirty yards before stopping to check them for wasps, leafhoppers, and other species slow to rise from their flowers and their work. Each night we checked a regular set of street lights and neon signs for beetles and moths. Every specimen had to be mounted perfectly and labeled correctly: order, family, and common name on the first label, and on the second, eight millimeters further down the pin, the date and site of capture. Our instructions were explicit.

> Pin butterflies and moths through the thorax slightly to the right of center. Center the insect's body between the two sides of the mounting board (the two surfaces raised so as to lift each wing seven to eight degrees above level) and by hooking the bent tip of a dissecting needle under the wing (far enough out on the wing so that you can gain leverage but not so far that it might tear; also, be careful not

to puncture the wing or smudge the powder on the wings of Lepidoptera), fan the upper wing up toward the point at which its bottom edge is ninety degrees to body. Secure the wings by pinning strips of paper over them as indicated in Diagram 5. Straighten and spread the legs. They should appear life-like and not droop. Align the antennae (taking care not to damage the feathering if it is a moth). You may find a magnifying glass helpful.

One night I was pinning a big hawk moth at my desk in our basement. It was a beautiful specimen—gray with some pink and lavender highlights, a six-inch wingspan, and a body the size of a field mouse. It had taken me almost an hour to net it. I had to shinny up a streetlight, under which the moth was swooping like a bat, and wait for it to come within range of my net. Now, having mounted the left wing perfectly, I carefully lifted the right upper wing when, to my horror, the moth's abdomen started to contract and slowly twitch.

The respiratory systems of insects are made up of a series of openings, called spiracles, which line the sides of their bodies. The anterior spiracles are generally used for air intake, and the posterior ones for carbon dioxide exhalation. In killing insects, the collector shuts down this respiratory system with carbon tetrachloride or cyanide. Cyanide is more effective, but also more lethal to humans and so harder to obtain. Carbon tet is available in both cleaning and lighter fluids.

I grabbed some lighter fluid and dripped it onto the abdomen, then sat back, took a breath, and waited to make sure the moth was definitely dead. I had been moved to act quickly because my specimen might have torn a hole in its wing or broken a leg, but at the same time I now knew this moth well. I had bent over it for most of an hour already, examining it, learning its colors, feeling the strength of its wings, and I was revolted at having to kill it a second time. In the field, one killed specimens immediately, often while they were still in the net, but even if you removed them from the net and held them in your hand as you squirted the lighter fluid, the kill was part of the catch, done almost without thought. To have to kill the hawk moth during mounting revealed to me the tension between science and empathy that had been there, dormant but real, all summer.

Two very different teachers taught biology—Mr. Witters and Mr. Bush. Mr. Witters was an academic, a genuine intellectual who as often as not referred to a species by its scientific rather than its common name. After school, he stayed late working with students on the many science fair projects he sponsored. Even at night, when I had a student council meeting or was getting back late from an away game, I would see him in the biology labs working on his own experiments, his PhD research. His lab was busy and messy, the air abuzz with Drosophila, or fruit flies, the floor littered with cedar chips and droppings from the rat cages.

Mr. Witters had just gone through a divorce, which had followed the deaths of his two children. A son and daughter had died about a year apart from genetic problems caused by radiation poisoning Mr. Witters had unknowingly suffered while working in the Life Sciences Building at Purdue. Now his work was everything.

Mr. Bush, a stocky man with a crew cut, also served as the line coach on the football staff. He too had been touched by illness. His oldest son, John, who was my age, had been born a blue baby. Open-heart surgery, a new procedure in the fifties, had saved him, and though he was now healthy and bright, John was slight and pale, with thick glasses, two hearing aids, and a speech impediment.

The two biology teachers respected each other and worked well together, but they had very different approaches to the insect collections. Mr. Witters offered an opportunity for extra credit; Mr. Bush didn't believe in it. In Mr. Witters's class, you could earn ten points for each order of insect above twenty you were able to include in your collection. Until school started and you received your schedule, you didn't know which teacher you would have—Bush or Witters—but we all hustled for orders in hopes that we would get into Mr. Witters's class. Book lice are an order, earwigs another. Stone flies and scorpion flies are each an order. There is even a microscopic order called Strepsiptera that spends its life between the plates in the abdomens of wasps. One had to catch and kill a lot of wasps to find one Strepsiptera. Termites were an order in and of themselves—Isoptera.

Some orders were especially hard to find in Indiana. Brent Beebe spent the summer at his grandparents' house in Seattle and was able to bring back a dozen earwigs, common in moist, coastal environments but rare in Indiana. He traded earwigs for his whole collection. I gave him a mourning cloak and a giant swallowtail for one earwig, but considered it a good deal because I had doubles of both those butterflies.

Within many orders there are odd or rare species that we especially valued. Hymenoptera, for instance, are simply bees, wasps, and ants, but the order includes unusual species such as velvet ants, cuckoo wasps, and the cicada killer, a hornet-like creature that captures cicadas in flight, paralyzes them, and drags them into underground nests where its larvae can feed on them. Another form of Hymenoptera is the ichneumon fly, which looks like many other wasps except that winding out from the tip of its abdomen is a stinger, or ovipositor, that is three or four times as long as the rest of the insect. The females curl this long, thin tail back up over themselves, bring it down at a right angle to their bodies, and work it into the bark of dead or decaying trees. The wire-like ovipositor chisels deeper and deeper into the tree until it reaches the tunnels of another insect's larvae. As the wood-boring hosts tunnel through the wood they create vibrations the female ichneumon fly detects with her antennae. She deposits her eggs into those tunnels so that when her brood hatches they can live in and on the other insect's larvae. The several species of ichneumon flies are host specific, parasitic of the larvae of particular beetles, sawflies, wasps, or, more rarely, spiders and pseudoscorpions.

One night, when I came home from playing basketball at Bill's, my little sister, who was then eight, met me at the door. "Dad's got a really big bug for you," she said. I was surprised that she was up and not in her pajamas yet, and that my dad was home from the office. I wanted to see what kind of bug they had, but I wasn't going to get my hopes up. I assumed it was some big but common moth—a luna or a tomato hornworm sphinx—and that they had torn it up trying to catch it. My dad had the insect in a shoe box. He was smiling.

"It's some sort of big wasp," he said. "Sara saw it on the window. I couldn't find your net, so I just put this box over it."

I got my net and killing jar from the basement, and holding some nylon netting over the shoe box, I slid the cover back. It was a perfect very large female ichneumon fly. The body was about an inch and a half long, and unfurled, its ovipositor would stretch to almost six inches. I looked up at my father.

"Weren't you afraid?" I said.

"I figured all it could do was sting me," he said. "Do you already have one?"

"I've never seen one that big."

I stayed up until eleven-thirty that night mounting my ichneumon fly and reading up on the species. When I was done I went upstairs to sit at the foot of my parents' bed and watch Johnny Carson's monologue with them. It was one daily ritual they still shared.

The next day I called Bill and asked him to check with his brother about how to mount the ichneumon's ovipositor.

John said I could just let the long tail curl out behind the specimen, using one or more pins to prop it up if it was flopping to the side. He said the white space that the tail created in your box where you would normally put two or three other insects could be very dramatic.

The insect collections were designed to teach us precision and accuracy, but they introduced us as well to deviation, blurring, and individuality. The color plates in the field guides, for instance, bespoke clarity and definition, but the captions and write-ups were more qualified. *Often confused with the... easily mistaken for the... thought to be a... often hybridizes with... in our region must be considered an accidental.* Our quest for orders was also a quest for order, but it was a quest that was finally futile, and looking back on it now I see that an acceptance of difficulty and incompleteness was some of what we were supposed to learn. I know now that a species is often difficult to recognize, hard to define. Some moths, such as the catalpa sphinx, are distinguishable only by the host plants they select and on which you find them laying their eggs. Beetles are so numerous it's been estimated that at least a third of their species remain unidentified. According to legend, when asked to speculate on the personality of God, the English biologist J. B. S. Haldane replied that the Creator seems to have "an inordinate fondness for beetles." As their rain forest habitat is destroyed, hundreds of species of beetles, the order Coleoptera, are passing away and will probably never be seen, named, or known, at least by humans.

Species mix, genes are shuffled. The naming of the animals, Adam's task, remains impossible. And yet, classification has its place. The existence of hybrids, for instance, is testimony to the fact that there are points at which nature draws a line. My grandfather used to tell me stories about farming with mules. They were stronger, smarter, less easily distracted, and harder-working than horses, he said, but they were also true hybrids and therefore sterile.

While collecting our insects, we learned Linnaean taxonomy—kingdom, phylum, class, order, family, genus, species, or "King Philip Comes Over For Good Soup"—and that nature is sly and slippery, and eventually defeats taxonomy. We also learned to look, to really look. I learned, for instance, that even within the same species there are individuals. Bill and I both caught female imperial moths—a yellow and brown member of the Saturniidae with a four- to six-inch wingspan and a body the size of your thumb—but mine was much smaller and darker than his.

As we rode toward the exterminator's, our habit of looking led us to scan the fields for swallowtails, even though we were without the nets to catch them. Then after a while we ran out of asphalt, and the country road turned to gravel, loose and treacherous. Just to pedal was difficult and required all our concentration.

At the Wea Creek bridge it was time for a break, and everyone but Dobbs headed down to wade, get a drink, and see if it might be worth coming back later to hunt for scorpion flies. Dobbs said he'd stay up top to keep an eye on the bikes, but really he was worried about poison ivy. He had spent half of June sitting in a bathtub with blisters the size of grapes between his knuckles. At the creek we saw only green darners and the little blue and black damsel flies that everyone had caught weeks ago. It was cool and dark under the sycamores and cottonwoods, but alive with gnats and mosquitoes. The path was lined with shoulder-high stinging nettles.

When we got back up to the bridge, we mounted our bikes and rode slowly up out of the ravine and back onto the prairie. After ten more minutes of pedaling, we came up on the first of the Shadeland Farm feed lots, where a herd of maybe seventy-five white-faced Herefords looked at us as they stood and chewed. Dobbs yelled at them to stop staring. Up ahead of me, Bill stopped his bike along the shoulder of the road. I pulled up next to him. He said, "We ought to check out that pasture for dung beetles."

"Perfect place for 'em," I said.

Big beetles fascinated us both, almost as much as big moths, and dung beetles were a type of scarab beetle neither of us had yet, though we both knew them well from our field guides. They are not as big as water scavengers or even some stag beetles, but they're a nice insect—wide and squat, essentially round, and unique in behavior. Their habitat is very specific—they live in and around cow shit. The adults encase their eggs in a ball of fresh manure. Then, like Sisyphus, though with more success, they roll it and roll it till it is firmly packed and perfectly round. Finally, they dig a hole and bury each ball in the ground. The balls are as big as the beetles themselves, about the size of a shooter marble. When the larvae hatch, they feed on the dung ball for protein, conveniently leaving some of it in the ground to fertilize the soil. To the uninformed they might seem like a joke, but to anyone who has seen them at work, they aren't. The Egyptians made the dung beetle a symbol of fertility and rebirth. They're just rolling shit, but the way they do it with their little forelegs is amazing—a wonderful skill, involving as much patience and delicacy as the tying of a surgeon's knot or the gathering and weaving of strands of spider web for a hummingbird nest.

Dobbs spoke up for Leonard and himself, saying that they did not want to climb into the cow pasture. I could tell that the steers had him spooked. Bill and I climbed the fence and the cattle scattered, loping just far enough away from us to feel safe. As we rooted around among the cow pies, I thought about how what we were doing was slightly nuts, but in less than ten minutes each of us had a perfect dung beetle—legs and antennae intact, their shells a deep obsidian with bronze and green highlights, like an oil slick. Having established whose was whose, we put the beetles in my killing jar, leaving Bill's empty for the termites.

Bill and I got back on our bikes and we all took up our ride again. Sunflowers stood tall and still in the ditch along the road, their flowered heads drooping under the weight of their seeds. Sparrows scuffled in the dust.

"You guys probably saw about eighteen gazillion dung beetles in there. But did you get any for us?" said Dobbs.

"You could have climbed the fence," said Bill.

"You two are going to turn into a couple of gigantic dung beetles," said Dobbs. He started imitating, not a dung beetle exactly, but some kind of insect, sticking out his neck, staring blankly at nothing, holding one of his hands up like a claw and swiveling his head in small, mechanical motions. Bill and I were laughing at his craziness when all three of us heard Leonard yelling. He had ridden on ahead of us and stopped about fifty yards down the road, where it made a turn to the right. He was calling and pointing. "Hey, you guys, look! Look!" As we approached him it became clear what all the ruckus was about. Just past him, maybe a hundred yards down the hill from where he stood, was the Eli Lilly plant. The exterminator had mentioned the plant in his directions, but in an inconsequential way, saying only that we were to take the second left after we passed it. None of us had been down this road before, and the enormity of the factory brought us to a dead halt.

No one said a thing. We just looked. The plant loomed menacingly on the far side of a huge lawn, looking like the Emerald City gone bad. Painted gray, it shimmered in the heat like a mirage. It was bigger, much bigger, than the Purdue football stadium. A chain-link fence surrounded the compound, and wired to the fence in front of us was a sign declaring "No Admittance. Authorized Personnel Only." Scores of smokestacks studded the plant, and interspersed among them were dozens of gigantic cylindrical tanks. Some of the tanks stood upright like silos, others lay on their sides. The clanging, metal-on-metal sounds of machinery were punctuated occasionally by loud, whooshing releases of steam. The plant included several buildings, connected by enclosed corridors at ground level and by open catwalks above. Past the buildings there was a parking lot of several acres. It was full of cars.

In West Lafayette, where we lived, you could smell the Eli Lilly plant when the wind was from the southeast. Whenever that happened my mother would trot out her tired joke about how at least they were making penicillin. I had seen the plant before, but always from the other side of the Wabash, the West Lafayette side, and then only occasionally when my dad and I drove out to Rumpza's produce stand for fresh sweet corn. From our side of the river the plant's smokestacks, rising above the trees, looked benign, even romantic, like those of an ocean liner just back from Buenos Aires or Monaco.

My mother was right about the penicillin, but only half right. Eli Lilly did make antibiotics, but they also made soybean herbicides and, later, the antidepressant Prozac. During the 1950s and 1960s, before the establishment of the EPA, the Lilly plant buried its waste in underground tanks. Eventually, the tanks rusted and leaked, and the waste leached into the ground water. At first, Lilly distributed carbon filters to its neighbors for use on their taps, but the water continued to smell of chemicals, and eventually the company had to buy a subdivision of twenty-two homes because its wells were poisoned. Lilly bulldozed all the houses except one, a brick farmhouse that dated from the 1850s.

The four of us stood at the fence in silence, when all of a sudden, as if from another world, Dobbs snapped, "Hut to, gentlemen! You have a mission to complete." As we started to ride again, Dobbs organized a game of "catch the leader" to break the tension. Single file and leapfrogging, we headed cross-country, following a range road that scored the prairie in a line as straight as a string pulled across a table, as straight as the X-axis of an infinite coordinate.

The exterminator lived in a little prefabricated house that sat up on a rise, a small heap of terminal moraine left from the last glacier. He was a young man, maybe twenty-five. He wore a De Kalb seed cap, madras shirt, and jeans. His cowboy boots were muddy and scuffed, their heels worn. His house, pole barn, and yard were surrounded by cornfields. He had planted a windbreak of white pines along the north and west sides, but the trees were only waist high and did not provide much protection yet. The whole effort, both the buildings and the windbreak, seemed to me, even then, to be both hopeful and earnest.

He gave us a drink of well water, which was so cold it hurt your head to drink very much, but we were thirsty. He had a beagle that kept yapping and jumping up on Leonard, who talked baby talk to the dog and scratched its ears. The exterminator apologized that he couldn't give us a king or queen termite, explaining that there was only one pair to a colony and they were hard to find. But he could give us as many workers and soldiers as we wanted. Even Bill, who wasn't afraid of wasps or even cicada killers, looked relieved when the exterminator put the termites into the killing jar for us. The soldiers, who grow wings only during their migratory, or colonizing, phase, were currently wingless. They had strong, threatening mandibles, or pincers. The workers were a little scary, and also possessed a fierce and prehistoric ugliness. They spend their entire lives underground and are white, sexless, puffy, and translucent. Like fish and crawdads that live in caves, they had no eyes. The cyanide in the killing jars snuffed them immediately.

We rode back toward town in pairs about twenty yards apart—Leonard and Dobbs in front, Bill and I following.

I asked him, "What do you think is your best insect?"

"My Strepsiptera took the most work, but I like my royal walnut."

A royal walnut is a member of the Saturniidae family, the largest North American moths. Their wingspan can reach seven or eight inches. The main representatives of the Saturniidae in Indiana are the cecropia, luna, polyphemus, and royal walnut, the last of which is the biggest of the four. Bill had all four. I had the first three.

"What's your own favorite?" Bill asked.

"My ichneumon fly is nice, but my dad caught that. I guess I like my hawk moth best."

We talked on like that about our collections, distracting ourselves from the heat and dust, the termites, the Eli Lilly plant, and the fact that the summer was almost over. But our conversation wasn't distraction enough, at least for me. I thought about my father and whether he would be home that fall for all of my football games. If he was gone, away to give a speech or do some consulting, I knew it would be hard for my mom to come by herself, though she would do it. The afternoon I hid behind the couch had changed everything. I had backed my parents off and in doing so realized a power I didn't know I had and ultimately did not want. I hadn't crawled behind the couch to get that power. There had been no calculation in my scramble; fear and shock sent me behind the couch. True, I had started to feel the power quickly, for right away I could see fear in my parents' eyes and hear worry in their voices. But almost as soon as I felt the power, I began to feel embarrassment as well. I was embarrassed that I had been able to manipulate my parents and do it so easily, even though I hadn't planned to manipulate them. I had not behaved well, and my embarrassment about it was a reminder of the embarrassment I felt when my parents didn't behave well—when they fought in public. They fought in restaurants and at church, and in the other room while I watched television with my friends. I'd hoped that my new power would be enough to stop this kind of behavior and keep them together, but even then I knew that it wasn't, and that I would be embarrassed for a long time to come.

Besides the breeders (the king and queen), the workers, and the soldiers, there is a fourth caste among termites—the nymphs, who constitute a kind of reproductive reserve. They resemble the king and queen, with eyes and wing buds, but assume sexual and physical maturity only if the original king and queen are killed. In that event, the nymphs complete their metamorphosis, pair up, and begin to reproduce. The new queen becomes a full-scale egg producer, laying up to four thousand eggs a day and growing so enormous she can't move at all and is completely dependent on the food brought down through the tunnels to her by her blind white workers. But if the king and queen don't die first, the nymphs live out their lives as nymphs, lords and ladies forever in waiting.

In the 1970s, when my sister went away to college, my parents finally divorced. A few years later, Bill's father fell sick. I called Bill when I heard. Now a physician himself in Indianapolis, he told me how his father, who had lost seventy-five pounds, claimed to have histoplasmosis, a fungal disease that is endemic in the river valleys of the Midwest and can sometimes look like tuberculosis or old pneumonia scars on a chest X-ray. Bill had examined his father's X-rays himself and knew better. It was clearly lung cancer, though his father denied it. Our phone call was sad, but good. It showed me that we were old enough now for our parents not to embarrass us, and that Bill's parents, or his father at least, could be as stubborn and foolish as mine.

Bill and I were becoming adults, as some termite nymphs never do. It was a process that began the summer I looked at insects, and the entire world, differently. I could no longer rely on my parents, and even our biology teachers seemed to need the empathy of their students.

The fall of 1964, the fall after we got the termites, Bill was assigned Mr. Bush for biology. Mr. Bush, with his firm rules, aversion to extra credit, and immaculate, well-organized lab, was intimidating, but after school, on the football practice field, he revealed a sense of humor and a willingness to muck it up with us. His own frail son was the team manager, and when John received his letter sweater at the team banquet, his father cried.

I was assigned to Mr. Witters, who always arrived for class smiling and excited. I loved his class, but I could never look at him without thinking about his lost family and how hard he must have had to work to maintain his optimism and energy. In a fundamental and tragic way, his curiosity and his intellect had failed him. He was a brilliant man who worked hard and lost his family because of it. He couldn't salvage his home life, but he remains my model of a good teacher, full of lesson plans and knowledge and a complete devotion to his students. His insect assignment, with its strict instructions and Linnaean taxonomy, taught us the importance of method, but his extra-credit policy said that rules and method aren't everything. A bigger part of learning is simply finding out as much as you can.

I misidentified one of my two species of scorpion flies, and lost two points, but because I had twenty-two orders, I ended up with twenty extra-credit points and a total score of one hundred and eighteen. Bill had three perfect cases and the better collection, but because he had Mr. Bush, he scored only a perfect one hundred. His prize catch ended up being not his royal walnut but an Embiidina, a little-studied web-spinning insect rarely found in Indiana. He caught it one night late in August when he and I were checking bug lights out in the county. His particular specimen was a winged male. Embiidinae normally live in colonies (though without a caste system like termites), but the one Bill caught was alone and at least a hundred and fifty miles north of its normal range. The Embiidina was Bill's twenty-third order. Neither teacher had ever seen one.

Who Should Be President in 1968?

I don't remember when I started wanting to be president. In some way, I suspect, it was rooted in the fact that I was born on Washington's Birthday—February 22, 1950. Crest of the Baby Boom. My mother's father wanted my parents to name me George Washington French. They didn't, but when I was a kid Mom sent me to school on my birthday with a mix of red-, white-, and blue-iced cupcakes, each stabbed with a little American flag on a toothpick. That I shared a birthday not only with George Washington but also with Teddy Kennedy always seemed auspicious to her.

My mother was intensely political. She'd grown up in a family where politics was the field on which her parents fought out their own battles for power and control. Her dairy farmer father was a rock-ribbed Republican, named for the Grand Old Party's first presidential candidate, the explorer and Union general John C. Frémont, but her mother helped found the Minnesota Democratic-Farmer-Labor Party and rode Truman's campaign train in 1948. Fremont was sloppy and sentimental, Beatrice was frustrated and manipulative. Despite their differences they loved each other and ran a big, successful farm with a large herd of Holsteins and several hired women and men. Until his dying day, my grandfather talked proudly about shaking hands with Eisenhower at a campaign stop in Northfield, Minnesota.

I never knew my grandmother. One night on the way home from a church meeting, the car she was riding in was hit in the fog by a train at a rural crossing. I was a year old. My mother often reminded me that Hubert Humphrey sent flowers to the funeral. Years later, in 1966, in Washington with my dad for one of his professional meetings, they ran into Humphrey at the airport. Mom reminded the Happy Warrior about the flowers. Humphrey, who was then vice president, graciously apologized for not being able to attend the funeral and then traded stories about my grandmother. A photograph of this encounter became a kind of talisman in our house, marking our ability to run with the big dogs. In it my father and the vice president, who was famously loquacious, are listening to my mother make a point.

In any case, by the spring of 1968, the spring of my senior year in high school, I was as straight an arrow as you could find—football player, co-captain of the track team, and student body president. My plan was to get into an Ivy League school, escape my parents' troubled home, major in government, and become president.

Throughout that spring, I campaigned for Bobby Kennedy in the Indiana primary. He'd entered the presidential race on March 16, four days after Eugene McCarthy had scared President Johnson in the New Hampshire primary, losing by only 230 votes. McCarthy's critics called him an opportunist but I felt only that he could beat Nixon and so every night after track practice I knocked doors for him.

My other big project that spring was a presidential preference poll I sent to 130 experts and opinion makers. I patterned it after one done in 1960 by *Esquire* magazine that I had found in the stacks at the Purdue library; all it asked was "Who should be president in 1968?" and "What should the issues be?"

In high school I alternated between losing myself in novels and running for student council, and the people I polled reflected my own obsessions. Like me they were split between the literary and the political. They included writers such as Arthur Miller and James Baldwin, politicians such as Everett Dirksen and J. William Fulbright, liberals such as Arthur Schlesinger Jr. and Pierre Salinger, and conservatives such as William F. Buckley and candy millionaire and John Birch Society founder Robert Welch.

The poll was a way for me to reach beyond my own life, which, because of my parents' crumbling marriage, was feeling increasingly claustrophobic, and to establish some personal contact with people who were already a part of a world I wanted to enter. If I was going to be U.S. president someday, I needed to know what the nation's movers and shakers thought, so I wrote them and asked. I wanted to find out what was being said and thought in Cambridge, New York, and Washington.

Shortly before my eighteenth birthday in February 1968, I decided the war in Vietnam was wrong. A month earlier, in January, the student council, of which I was president, had decided to sponsor a convocation on the Vietnam War ("teach-in" was too strong a word for us, though something like that was what we had in mind).

My parents were Stevensonian Democrats, but our town, West Lafayette, Indiana, was fanatically Republican. It had elected a Democratic mayor when I was in seventh grade, but he was the first Democrat elected to any office in the history of the town. The Birch Society's influence was everywhere in West Lafayette back then. There were *Reader's Digest* reprints on the communist menace in doctors' waiting rooms. Fluoride, folk songs, and income tax were distrusted. An "Impeach Earl Warren" billboard welcomed you at one end of town; a "Get U.S. Out of the United Nations" sign said goodbye at the other.

When I was a kid, my mother told me that John Birchers signaled their membership by mounting faux cast-iron eagles on the walls above their front doors or garages. Her evidence was empirical. There was an eagle on the house of my orthodontist, and he was an open Bircher. He wrote letters to the editor, gave my mother pamphlets, tried to save her soul. The house of my friend Donnie Bain also had an eagle. His parents were archly conservative and his grandparents had retired to Valley Forge, Pennsylvania, apparently as a matter of principle.

When these Birchers, especially a retired colonel with kids in the schools, got wind of our plan to have a Vietnam event, they swung into action. There would be a convocation, but it would be properly framed. They brought in M. Stanton Evans, a conservative pundit, contributor to *National Review*, and managing editor of the *Indianapolis News*, as the speaker.

Normally, as student body president, I would have put on my herringbone sport coat and paisley tie and introduced the speaker, but this time, the colonel handled it. I was just another kid in the audience. Evans's talk was long and dry, but things warmed up during the Q-and-A. I asked a question myself, but it was innocuous. I still thought we could and should win the war. Wasn't it true, I asked, that North Vietnam, and especially Hanoi, is dependent on Haiphong for supplies? What if we were to mine the harbor? Wouldn't the war be over in a week? I was showing off. I knew about Haiphong. Here was a silver bullet McNamara had overlooked. For some reason, I thought that I had something on Evans, but he simply agreed with me, adding that my time frame was too optimistic, but yeah, sure, let's squash 'em.

Then Hester Harris walked down the aisle toward the audience mic. A senior like me, she was barely five feet tall. Her black hair was long and straight in the Joan Baez style of the coasts, and she was wearing an orange miniskirt, purple tights, and cowboy boots. She looked great, though my frat boy persona wouldn't let me admit it, even to myself. Hester was our hippie-in-residence, and a real hippie at that. Her father was Mark Harris, the author of the Henry Wiggen baseball novels, including *Bang the Drum Slowly*, and he had come to Purdue that year as a visiting writer from San Francisco State. Hester had grown up in San Francisco, had actually hung out in Haight-Ashbury. She had already caused a fuss in the school paper, acknowledging that yes, she had smoked dope, and yes, she was against the war, and yes (and this was the clincher) she believed in free love. When she headed down the aisle, everyone knew she was about to cause a fuss.

"Mr. Evans, isn't it true that the war in Vietnam is a civil war and no business of ours? And furthermore, isn't it true that officials of our own government have acknowledged that if open, nationwide elections were held in Vietnam today, Ho Chi Minh would almost assuredly be elected president of a united Vietnam?"

Evans pooh-poohed her with some version of the domino theory, but for me at least, Hester's clarity, assurance, and miniskirt had stolen the day.

After the convo we all milled around down front so we wouldn't have to head straight back to our fifth period classes, and Hester and I talked.

"We have no right to mine their harbors," she began. "What if they mined one of ours?"

"That was a good question, Hester. You really nailed him."

She smiled and locked me in with some serious eye contact. She looked pleased, but I couldn't tell if it was because of my compliment or because she knew she had me off guard. Then she answered her own question.

"We'd scream bloody murder and drop an atom bomb on them."

Everything she was saying seemed right, but I couldn't admit to it yet, so I flirted some more.

"Not as long as you've got the floor, Hester."

She smiled again. "Yeah, well, I've got something to show you. I'll bring it in tomorrow."

The colonel was at the mic now, ordering everyone to return to their classes.

Hester met me at my locker the next morning with a copy of *Ramparts* magazine. It was a year old—the January 1967 issue—and pretty dog-eared. It featured a twenty-five-page color spread titled "The Children of Vietnam" that showed little kids who'd been napalmed. They were blistered and scarred and some were missing digits or limbs. I read the article during study hall—the text was by Dr. Spock—but mostly I looked at the pictures. The eyes of the burned babies shook me loose and I decided Hester was right—the war was wrong and we should get out now.

Years later I would read that Martin Luther King Jr. had bought that same issue of *Ramparts* at an airport newsstand on his way to

Jamaica and had been similarly affected. I wondered how many people that article had nudged toward active opposition. Reading it and looking at those pictures must have been akin to reading *Uncle Tom's Cabin* in the 1850s.

Hester wanted me to support McCarthy, but I held back. I told her I didn't think he could win, but in retrospect I think it was largely a failure of nerve on my part. I didn't know anyone but Hester who was supporting McCarthy, and I wasn't ready to be called a hippie.

I thought of those burned children a month later, when I turned eighteen and went to register for the draft. As I drove out Earl Avenue looking for the address on the letter I'd received, I was confused. I had expected that the building would be substantial and intimidating, something on the order of the downtown post office, with its classical columns, shiny oak counters, high ceilings, and snack stand run by a blind man, but all I saw was a mix of shabby bungalows and small businesses—one-agent insurance offices, an auto parts store, some gas stations. The office, when I finally found it, was a leased storefront in a minimall. Inside, the lone clerk—an overweight white woman about my mother's age—stood behind the counter talking on the phone. When she finally got off, it took her all of three minutes to issue me my card and grant me my II-S student deferment. The card was paper, not even cardboard, let alone laminated. Its flimsiness seemed a physical manifestation of the anticlimax I felt.

Television back then, at least in our house, was black-and-white and pretty grainy. But even through the gray and lousy reception, what was going on in Vietnam was scary and clear. When I registered for the draft, the Tet Offensive had been exploding for most of a month. The North Vietnamese and Vietcong had launched coordinated attacks on twenty-seven cities in the south, including Saigon, where they seized the U.S. embassy for a while. Khe Sanh was under siege. Hue was lost, then won back. In two weeks, a thousand American soldiers, twenty thousand South Vietnamese, and thirty thousand North Vietnamese were killed. This was a mess to avoid.

On Thursday, March 28, three days before President Johnson called a halt to the bombing of North Vietnam north of the twentieth parallel and announced that he would neither "seek" nor "accept" the Democratic nomination for president, I mailed out my poll. Return mail brought the first responses, and almost invariably they listed Vietnam as the primary issue. Eventually, more than two-thirds of my respondents said Vietnam should be the main issue, and others, who answered with a narrative rather than a list, almost always included it.

McCarthy was in the race as an antiwar candidate and so, as one would expect, his supporters always emphasized Vietnam. Anthropologist Margaret Mead said we must figure out "how to escalate the political negotiations to end the war in Vietnam and de-escalate the military involvement." Historian Henry Steele Commager said it was the only issue. Novelist Fletcher Knebel listed it second after race, but every other McCarthy supporter put it first.

Norman Thomas had run for president six times on the Socialist Party ticket, but in 1968, at the age of eighty-four, was not running and, in fact, had only nine months to live. His quavering handwritten response, however, came from someone who was thinking ahead: "My present preference [for president] is Senator McCarthy." As for the issues, Thomas put Vietnam first, but added that "equally important [was] a congery of issues related to race—housing, education, etc."

Like Thomas, Bobby Kennedy's supporters were quick to add domestic issues to their lists. Kennedy was running a broader-based campaign than McCarthy. He was trying to win Wallace Democrats back to the party and keep the support of mainstream Democrats who were concerned with traditional bread-and-butter issues. Kennedy supporter and economist Paul Samuelson offered a typical response. There were, he said, two issues—"Peace in Viet Nam" and "Reconciliation within the Dynamic Great Society."

Republicans knew that Vietnam was key, but they usually framed the question differently, especially the Nixon supporters. Peace alone was not enough for them; they still wanted to win (just as I had earlier that winter, with my talk of mining harbors). But they knew that was probably no longer a majority position, and so their responses were ambiguous formulations that allowed for victory without demanding it. Wabash College political scientist and Nixon supporter Benjamin Rogge, for instance, said the main issue in the campaign should be "ending the war in Viet Nam." How and when it might end was left open. Indiana congressman and former House minority leader Charles Halleck was even more vague. He claimed it was too early for him to endorse a candidate (he would eventually support Nixon) but did say that "this nation's involvement in the Vietnam conflict" was the number one issue. Not peace, not withdrawal, not negotiation, just "involvement."

In 1968 there were still Rockefeller Republicans. Among my respondents, these included Cornell political scientists Walter Berns and Andrew Hacker, and *Esquire* editor Harold T. P. Hayes. These men were more likely to be antiwar and less likely to hide behind euphemisms. "Get out of South East Asia," wrote physicist Volney Wilson, "as quickly as possible."

Following the assassination of Martin Luther King Jr. on April 4, rioting erupted in most major cities. I heard of King's death that night, accidentally, while at a party with my drunk high school friends. Two of us returned to my house to watch the news, but there were few details. It all felt so unreal. The next week, however, I stepped out of the haze and back into my leadership role, and convinced the student council to organize a fund-raising drive for a community center on the south side of Chicago that was helping people displaced by the riots. We raised a few hundred dollars.

That same week, I received a response to my poll from my congressman, Charles Halleck, who bemoaned "the plight of the American farmer." Halleck dropped his rhetoric of victimization, however, when he argued that something must be done about "violence in the streets," "spending," and "the threat of higher taxes."

Benjamin Rogge, the conservative political scientist at Wabash College, agreed with Halleck. He said we needed to curb "the tendency of government to expand its control over the lives, incomes and properties of its citizens" and focus instead on "maintaining law and order in our society," never mind that such a step might lead to more government, more police, and more control over the lives, incomes, and properties of certain citizens.

Neither Rogge nor Halleck mentioned race when they talked about violence in the streets, but they didn't need to. Undoubtedly, these conservatives also meant to clamp down on the predominantly white student movement, but that was secondary. Except for Berkeley in 1964, the major campus confrontations were yet to come—Columbia was a few weeks away, Harvard wouldn't happen till the next spring, and the Jackson State and Kent State shootings were two years away. Urban riots, however, had been happening every summer since 1964, when Harlem exploded. There was Watts in 1965; Atlanta, Chicago, Cleveland, Dayton, San Francisco, and St. Louis in 1966; Boston, Cincinnati, Newark, and Detroit in 1967. In the previous three years over a hundred people had been killed in urban riots and almost thirty thousand arrested.

The kinds of responses I received about race were skewed by the fact that only 10 of the 130 people I polled were African Americans and that none of those ten responded.[1] I polled no Native, Latin or Asian Americans. Though my racial blind spots left me with a pool of all-white responses, those responses did expose much about the attitudes of white Americans toward Black Americans in 1968.

Liberals feared the violence as much as conservatives did. They worried about how to achieve "racial peace" (Walter Berns), "racial amity" (Andrew Hacker), "reconciliation of the races in the United States" (Arthur Schlesinger Jr.), "improved racial relations" (Richard Hofstadter), or "reconciliation" (Paul Samuelson). But rather than sending in the cops, they talked about how to send in the money. Margaret Mead, for instance, urged the candidates to discuss how America might "expedite the reorganization of the inner city and provide for a massive attack on education and opportunities for the disadvantaged."

Spending on housing and education seemed to me necessary but

---

1. The African Americans I polled were James Baldwin, Senator Edward Brooke, Margaret Danner, Charles Evers, Richard Hatcher, John Johnson, Martin Luther King Jr., Adam Clayton Powell, Bayard Rustin, and Whitney Young.

not sufficient. I sensed, albeit dimly, that without confronting the white supremacist attitudes that underlay both the conservatives' overt racism and the liberals' paternalism, money was not enough. Of my respondents only Richard Hofstadter even hinted at this. Racial peace, he said, required "racial justice."

That April, which had begun so cruelly with King's murder and the resulting riots, grew kinder, at least for me. While I waited for more replies and Primary Day, my attention turned toward regular high school concerns, including the opening of track season, the countdown toward prom and Senior Week, and the arrival of admissions letters from colleges.

I expected to get into Cornell because I'd been recruited by their football coach, but I'd also applied to Harvard, mostly because my dad said he was paying the application fee anyway and you only apply to colleges once and, well, why not? My parents and I were amazed when I got in, and we floated about in disbelief and joy for the next few days. The letter stayed on the kitchen counter by the phone, and one or another of us picked it up every now and then and read it again. As we well knew, several U.S. presidents had attended Harvard, including John F. Kennedy and his brother Bobby.

Later that same week, the City College of New York historian Arthur Schlesinger Jr. came to town to campaign for Bobby Kennedy. I went with my parents to hear him talk to a group of forty or fifty people of older people, mostly from Purdue. We met in a cushy meeting room in my dad's office building. It was my first exposure to an adults-only strategy session, and I felt out of place, at once both very young and suddenly grown up.

Schlesinger wore a seersucker suit, horned-rimmed glasses, and a bow tie. He wouldn't have carried much weight with farmers and workers, but he seemed just the ticket with these college town activists. He was wry and stunningly bright, but also self-satisfied and prone to name-dropping. He explained how important it was to nominate Bobby Kennedy, how he offered not only a continuation of the Roosevelt-Stevenson-Kennedy tradition but also the possibility of victory in the fall.

The audience seemed tired and subdued, more interested in letting Schlesinger know they'd read one of his books than in actually plotting strategy. In the end, a rumpled, heavyset cynic with a bulbous nose and a red, veiny face went off about the impossibility of arguing liberal causes in Indiana before finally veering into some intraparty, county-level squabble.

Schlesinger looked at his watch, and the county chair came forward to adjourn the meeting. People filed out, and my mom, as always, found friends to chat with. My dad insisted that he and I "say hello" to Schlesinger.

We waited for some other sycophants to do the same thing, then my dad stepped forward. Schlesinger looked resigned. The meeting had been disappointing and his graciousness was waning. My dad introduced us.

"Why yes, it's nice to meet you," the great man replied, shaking my dad's hand and then turning to reach for mine.

"Ned's starting Harvard in the fall and recently sent you a poll he's doing about the election."

"Really?" said Schlesinger. "I've been out of the office campaigning since mid-March. What's your poll about?"

"I asked who you support and what you think the issues should be."

"Well, I hope I answered both those questions tonight." He looked at my dad and the cluster of groupies standing with us and smiled, cueing them to chuckle along with him. I nodded and tried to smile, but I wished my father hadn't said anything about Harvard or the poll. I wished I wasn't even there. It all felt phony and irrelevant.

"I'll look for your letter when I get back to New York. Good luck in Cambridge. It's a great town."

To his credit, Schlesinger did write back. His response arrived a couple of weeks later at the end of April. It was short and clear. He declared for Kennedy and listed the key issues as peace in Vietnam, racial relations, and an "attack on poverty, urban and rural." I read that last adjective as perhaps a nod to my dad the ag economist, but it might have been there because of my Indiana postmark or Kennedy's own famous tour of Black sharecropper cabins in the Mississippi Delta. He made no mention of having met me.

When I sent out my poll, I made a mistake. I had assumed my subjects would sign their responses so I didn't code my return forms or SASEs. Six forms came back unsigned. Sometimes the postmark explained who it was, but usually not.

In the middle of April, an unsigned response arrived from Boston. I wanted the writer, who was a Kennedy supporter and offered a liberal-sounding set of issues, to be the economist John Kenneth Galbraith, but I had no way of knowing. I'd written to a lot of people in Boston.

Galbraith had taught with Schlesinger at Harvard since the Kennedys were undergraduates. Until Schlesinger left for the City College of New York the two of them had been backdoor neighbors and later both became JFK appointees—Schlesinger a White House aide, Galbraith ambassador to India.

During the winter of 1967–68, Galbraith, unlike Schlesinger, decided he couldn't wait to see if Bobby would announce and had begun campaigning for McCarthy. But by mid-February, Galbraith was meeting with Kennedy behind the scenes. In his memoir, social activist Tom Hayden recounts that one evening, he and Bobby Kennedy had a long discussion about Vietnam. Kennedy asked him to stay for dinner with Schlesinger and Galbraith at his apartment in New York.

By early April, when he received my poll and Kennedy had declared, Galbraith may have moved closer to Kennedy, but he was still openly supporting McCarthy, so it made sense that at that moment he might list Kennedy as his choice but not sign his reply.

I also suspected that this response was from Galbraith because it listed "Peace in Viet Nam" as the number one issue, but then, after a dash, tacked on "and a Sounder Foreign Policy in Asia." This addition also seemed as if it might have come from Galbraith, whose experience as ambassador to India might have led him to put the war in a regional context.

And yet such a perspective could also have come from another

Harvard professor and JFK appointee I had written—Far Eastern specialist and former ambassador to Japan Edwin O. Reischauer.

I had two reasons for wanting the response to have came from Galbraith. First, I possessed a tenuous personal connection with him. Galbraith, like my father, had received his training in agricultural economics, and once, when Galbraith had come to Purdue to deliver a lecture, my father had been his escort. The comical pairing of my five-foot-eight-inch father with the six-foot-eight-inch Galbraith was made all the more so, my dad said, by the fact that Galbraith was on crutches, having just broken his leg while skiing in Switzerland.

I also wanted it to be Galbraith because his analysis of U.S. priorities carried such weight at the time. *The Affluent Society* had been a tremendous influence on my dad and his generation of economists. It had also been a best seller. My mother and I read it, and later I bought my own copy. Several of the social thinkers *Esquire* had polled in 1960 referred to the book's argument that private affluence in America had come at the expense of public investment and the country's infrastructure. Crane Brinton, literary critics Mark Van Doren and Albert J. Guerard, sociologist Daniel Bell, and economist Louis Keyserling as well as Galbraith himself had all called in the 1960 article for a righting of what Bell labeled "the crazy, growing imbalance between high, consumer spending for private goods and the lagging expenditures for public services."

Galbraith, like Schlesinger and other members of the Americans for Democratic Action, was an avowed anticommunist, though some conservatives saw him as being duped by the Reds. Or worse. He might be arguing for a mixed economy, with the welfare state tempering and humanizing the markets, but they saw him as trying to sneak socialism in the back door. In the *Esquire* article, for instance, even Leo Keyserling, who had chaired Truman's Council of Economic Advisers, argued that we must steer a middle way "between the Scylla of totalitarian planning and the Charybdis of the *laissez-faire* philosophy." But even such apparent moderation contained the code word "totalitarian." Ayn Rand was more direct. She declared, "There is *only one basic issue* in the world today: Free Enterprise vs. Statism."

In 1968 some of my respondents were still arguing with Galbraith, though often in a veiled way. *Esquire* editor Harold Hayes, a Rockefeller supporter, worried about "restoring balance to the economy" but didn't say what was causing the imbalance. Crane Brinton, hiding once more behind ironic quotation marks and a historian's apparent objectivity, said that the presidential campaigns should confront "the degree to which the 'welfare state,' 'creeping socialism' or 'social justice' is to be realized through *federal* govt." Others were more explicit. Conservative congressman Charles Halleck said he was concerned about "the state of our economy, spending, [and] the threat of higher taxes."

None of these men made the economy the number one issue. Only former general and ambassador James Gavin did that. His main concern was with "improvement in the *domestic condition*: i.e., adequate schooling and training for employment; adequate housing; opportunity for adult education; medical care in advanced years; [and] inspiration to do more than acquire material things."

More commonly, my respondents worried that Johnson couldn't afford to wage war on poverty and Vietnam at the same time. Richard Hofstadter's thinking about this issue evolved as he listed his issues:

1. Peace in Vietnam
2. Racial justice and improved racial relations
3. Urban development and improvement
4. The maintenance of prosperity through the transition from a war to a peace economy

(The last three issues are intimately related.)

Indeed, all four are.

In a carefully crafted paragraph, Pierre Salinger, JFK's press secretary, described the same problem: "I believe the central issue of the 1968 campaign is the achievement of true equality in America and the need to make a massive attack on the problems of our cities and the ghettoes. The need to bring an end to the war in Vietnam is closely correlated with the problem of our cities, because if we are to make the kind of massive attack on our own problems that is necessary to achieve any kind of success, we must be rid of the burden of the war in Vietnam." Hofstadter and Salinger were both Kennedy supporters, and I adopted their argument (at least in part) when I canvassed for Kennedy that April. The war was not just wrong, it cost too much—in both dollars and lives.

I made other mistakes besides not coding my return sheets, mistakes that some of my respondents felt obliged to correct.

A clerk in the Office of the Budget let me know that Charles Schultze had resigned as director of the Bureau as of the end of January. He also scolded me for not using zip codes in all my correspondence. Zip codes had been introduced in 1963, but I'd used an old stamp of my father's to address my return envelopes and it didn't include our zip.

Hofstadter corrected my questionnaire, noting that I must mean, "Who should be *elected* president in 1968?" because the new president would not be inaugurated until January 1969. It was an error I'd inherited from *Esquire*, but it was something you learned in junior high civics (or in my case from reading *Time* magazine over my mother's shoulder as a kid), and I kicked myself for having missed it.

Fletcher Knebel and Crane Brinton took up my use of the word "should." As Knebel, the author of the political thriller *Fail-safe*, put it:

> People make the issues. The word "should" is misplaced. I believe the issues people will want candidates to discuss clearly will be in this order:
> 1. Race
> 2. Viet Nam war
> 3. The economy

I told myself that the word "clearly" in Knebel's response might also be seen as misplaced—"discuss clearly" or "clearly in this order"? I also questioned his list. The people certainly wanted issues discussed clearly, but it wasn't so clear that race trumped Vietnam among America's predominantly white electorate.

Professor Brinton said nothing about the fact that I misspelled his name as "Briton" on the forms I'd sent out, but he too criticized my use of "should" to indicate probability. He displayed a historian's concern for precision and objectivity. Concerning the issues, for instance, he claimed that he "could pretty confidently write 'will be' instead of *should*." I felt that he, like Knebel, was separating himself from "the people" who would be deciding the issues. Weren't novelists and historians also citizens?

As revealing as their propensities for correcting me were the ways some of my respondents declined to answer.

One of the first responses I received was from Paul W. Cook Jr., the president of Wabash College. He replied that foreign policy was the number one issue but that it was intimately connected to a second issue: "The domestic problem complex—negroes, cities, poverty." Then he listed a third issue: "How to get Ned French to apply to Wabash." This was flattering, of course, but it also seemed to be a violation of the unwritten rules of the poll. His humor was at odds with my earnestness, and to me it felt cloying, silly, and a little desperate. I naively and proudly thought it was okay to be recruited as a football player but not as a pollster. I hadn't thought that a small liberal arts school, especially if it was all male and tucked away in an Indiana River valley as Wabash was, might need to work hard to recruit students and that even its president would be involved in that recruiting.

I should have commended President Cook, for I wrote to three other college presidents, Kingman Brewster of Yale, Nathan Pusey of Harvard, and James A. Perkins of Cornell, and one former president, Clark Kerr of Berkeley, and none of them wrote back.

I did get a letter from Katharine V. Ashmead, President Perkins's "executive assistant," who thanked me for writing and added that "regretfully, the questions you raise are just too weighty for Dr. Perkins to consider right now. I know he wishes he had the time to be able to sit down and ponder these questions with you, but, unhappily, it would take more time than he has available.'

The questions weren't weighty, I thought, just loaded. And I wasn't asking him to "sit down and ponder" them with me, just to dictate a quick response. I was being patronized and knew it, especially when Ms. Ashmead added that President Perkins applauded me not only for writing but for my "spirit in taking on this poll." You've got a lot of pluck, young fella. I could almost feel him patting me on the head.

On May 28, several weeks after I'd found out that I got into Harvard, I received another Cornell response that redeemed the university for me. It came from the office of Cornell historian Clinton Rossiter, whose book on the presidency I admired. His assistant Jane P. Weld wrote to explain that a mix-up had meant that my letter and several others had been misplaced, leading to "what must have seemed a very rude neglect of your request." Professor Rossiter, she added, had been out of the country since early January and couldn't have responded anyway. Ms. Weld said that she would keep the material I sent and show it to him when he got back from his sabbatical, and she wished me well in my "massive effort."

To me her explanation was easier to buy than the one I'd received from President Perkins's assistant. My own father was a professor, and I knew how hard he worked to protect his writing time. When a professor was on leave, he was on leave.

I received letters from some other gatekeepers as well. Arthur Miller's agent explained that the playwright had switched to their firm only recently, it had taken a while for my letter to be forwarded, and by the time it had arrived, Mr. Miller had left the country and would not be back for "some time." Again, I was disappointed but understood why the agent hadn't chased Miller down in a foreign country with my questionnaire.

Sharon Miller, secretary to Robert Vaughn, the liberal actor who played Napoleon Solo, the "Man from U.N.C.L.E.," notified me that Mr. Vaughn wouldn't have time to answer until he finished his PhD exams in May. Her letter came on heavy, embossed stationery and was something I could actually brag about with friends at school. They didn't know who Norman Thomas or Margaret Mead was, but a letter from Napoleon Solo's secretary impressed them.

I also got a letter from William F. Buckley's secretary, who signed it "Frances Bronson (Miss)." I couldn't figure out whether the parenthetical addition was a come-on, some sort of anti-feminist political statement, or both. Miss Frances explained in what seemed to be a form letter that "Mr. Buckley is drastically in arrears on commitments he has made—in addition to the heavy schedule he normally carries (a weekly television show, three syndicated newspaper columns a week, the editing of *National Review*, etc.)." I wanted to know what these other commitments were—talking for hire on the lecture circuit? Campaigning for Nixon? It was fine with me that he was too busy to write, but she seemed to me merely to be bragging on her boss.

Walter Cronkite sent me a form letter too, but he identified it as such and apologized for sending it. And besides, his letter was funny and well-written, really a kind of anti-form letter. He signed it himself, serving in name at least as his own gatekeeper. "Dear Mr. French," he wrote,

> This is a form letter, and I deplore the necessity of answering your communication with it.
>
> However, my unexpected three-week trip to Vietnam in February, the week-long series of special reports on my return, and the rapidly escalating political campaigns have simply put me so far behind the flow of incoming correspondence (almost 1,000 letters a week) that there is no hope of catching up without clearing the backlog.
>
> Still I have almost no time left in a normal day—and there seem to be few of these—to keep up with the most urgent matters.
>
> If, however, you wish to re-submit your letter, I shall try to give it consideration as soon as possible.
>
> Again, a thousand apologies, and I can only beg your understanding of the difficult circumstances.
>
> Sincerely yours,
> Walter Cronkite

Cronkite had itemized his busyness just as Miss Bronson had itemized Buckley's, but for me at least, Cronkite's was the better set of excuses.

Cronkite arrived in Vietnam just as the North Vietnamese and Vietcong launched the Tet Offensive. His reports were grim and shocking, and forced him to face the fact that America wasn't winning the war after all. In an hour-long special report on February 27 he urged the United States government to negotiate a settlement and get out—"to negotiate not as victors, but as honorable people who lived up to their pledge to defend democracy and did the best they could."

Cronkite's report was strong stuff. White House press secretary George Christian said of it later that "shock waves rolled through government." The president himself admitted that if he'd lost Cronkite, he'd lost the support of the American people, and a month later he announced he wouldn't run for re-election.

Answering personally that you couldn't answer didn't always win me over. University of Chicago economist and political conservative Theodore W. Schultz scribbled on the back of my self-addressed stamped envelope that he didn't have time to answer my questions. My dad laughed when he saw it and said, "Ted's always been kind of full of himself."

Senate Foreign Relations Committee chairman J. William Fulbright of Arkansas also said he was too busy to respond. I wondered if I'd have gotten more than a form letter if I'd been writing from Arkansas rather than Indiana.

Fulbright was a Democrat and a dove, so it disappointed me when he didn't respond and Republican Senate leader Everett Dirksen of Illinois did. Dirksen demurred regarding a presidential choice and merely forwarded some reprints of his speeches as a way to answer my question about the issues, but it was more than I got from Fulbright.

Other government figures wrote to say they could answer neither of my questions. Supreme Court justice Hugo Black said they were "too political in nature." Federal Reserve Board chairman William McChesney Martin admired my efforts but then added a short lecture about the Federal Reserve Board. The board, he wrote, was "established by the Congress in 1913 as a nonpartisan agency of the Government and has maintained its nonpolitical character throughout its existence. For that reason, I'm sure you will agree that it would not be appropriate for me to take part in your poll." Even then, in

1968, I questioned whether "nonpartisan" and "nonpolitical" were synonymous. I was pretty sure that in a sense every decision by the board to raise or lower interest rates carried political implications, but I did understand why he might not want to take a position on who his new boss should be.

It was harder to understand why John Birch Society president Robert Welch wouldn't say who he thought should lead the nation. His personal assistant wrote to say that Welch didn't want to offer a "personal opinion as to whom he thinks should be President of the United States, lest it be construed that the Society is taking a political stand." I could understand how the Federal Reserve Board could be construed as nonpartisan, maybe even nonpolitical, but not the John Birch Society. I realized later that his reticence probably had to do with his organization's nonprofit status, but then I wondered why he didn't say that.

What he did say was "that the President of the United States should be a man of honor and integrity; who believes in and will uphold our Constitution; who is motivated by a love of God, family and country; who is more a statesman and less a politician and should, when he makes a decision be able to say of it according to his conscience, it was morally right." Two things were interesting to me about this statement. First, the statement seemed, when coupled with his unwillingness to speak to any specific candidate's ability to measure up to these criteria, to carry the implication that some of them—perhaps even all of them—were unqualified; that some, or perhaps all of them, made their decisions without considering them to be morally right. Secondly, Mr. Welch, who had said he could not offer "even a personal opinion as to whom he thinks should be President of the United States," did include a copy of a pamphlet he'd written titled "IF I WERE PRESIDENT."

On Primary Day, Tuesday, May 7, I couldn't vote; the voting age was still twenty-one. Still, the next morning, I was proud to think that my canvassing had helped Bobby Kennedy earn a decisive victory in Indiana, including my home district.

Most of the responses I got to my poll had arrived the month before, in April. I waited through May, hoping for more, but only four came in. The last one arrived around Memorial Day from Robert Vaughn's secretary, telling me that the day the "Man from U.N.C.L.E." successfully completed his PhD exams at UCLA, "he was signed to do a film in Czechoslovakia" and was now en route to Europe. She apologized that he hadn't been able to complete my questionnaire, but said he'd be there for four months and so she was returning my materials. I wasn't too disappointed because I thought other results might still trickle in, and in any case it was Senior Week and I wouldn't be writing my poll up for a while yet.

When Bobby Kennedy was assassinated barely a week later, I lost interest in my poll. I wore a McCarthy button but knew he wouldn't win. Nixon was evil incarnate, and Humphrey seemed without principle. The flowers at my grandmother's funeral didn't redeem him. There were lots of funerals now, and still he wouldn't come out against the war.

Now and then that summer, I sorted through the responses to my poll, looking for clues as to what to do next. The response I returned to most often had arrived in the first batch of return mail, months before Kennedy's death. It was from Hester Harris's father, novelist Mark Harris, who, like me, was a reluctant McCarthy supporter. His response was a narrative, not a list:

Who should be president in 1968?

None of the accepted political candidates is really right. But when I vote I tend to vote for someone who might possibly win. Among candidates publicly mentioned I favor them in the following order: McCarthy, Kennedy, Rockefeller. I do not think, at the moment, that I can bring myself to vote for LB Johnson or for Nixon.

What should the issues be?

The thing we need is an entirely new vision of things, whether on the international scene, or at home. In general, the problem is alike abroad or at home—more equal distribution wealth, the reduction of hunger, the increase of education, and the general removal of the causes of war by those means; i.e., by the improved distribution of wealth, food, education, and the civilized pleasures.

I'd be pleased to talk more about this. Just drop around some time. I'm around the corner, which is more than I can say for most [of] the gentlemen (only one lady?) on your list. I'm even closer than [William H.] Gass.

Yours truly,
Mark Harris

It was an auspicious and provocative reply to receive in my first batch of mail—at once tactical ("someone who might possibly win"), removed ("candidates publicly mentioned") and cautious ("tend...do not think...bring myself"), but also impassioned, egalitarian, and sweeping. Civilized pleasures, I thought, civilized pleasures. Not only must "wealth, food, [and] education" be equally distributed but also the civilized pleasures.

That word "civilized" had also appeared in the response I received from the novelist John Dos Passos. I had written him and John Steinbeck because they were former left-wing novelists who were now anticommunist conservatives. I felt myself moving left, and I wondered why they had moved right. Steinbeck, who would die in December just a day after Norman Thomas, didn't respond, but Dos Passos banged out a short, messy response on his manual typewriter. Nixon, he said, "now looks like the best bet," and there was only one issue: "The survival of the United States as a civilized community after eight years of destructive management at home and abroad." Here the word "civilized" seemed to be a marker separating the United States from savagery, destruction, and chaos. Harris's use of the word might share some of the same racist Eurocentricism, but to me, especially then, it seemed to be mainly about generosity and inclusiveness rather than exclusion.

Harris was also right to criticize my sexism—though the 130 people I'd sent my poll to had included four women, not one—and maybe it was the idea that the father of a girl I had the hots for would notice such an error that kept me from ever taking him up on his invitation to stop by, though it probably had more to do with Hester being a hippie and me being a jock.

That summer of 1968, as I pondered what remained of my political dreams, and the nation's, the one man I didn't poll about who should be president was my father.

In a way, though, I didn't need to. Like my mother, he was a staunch Democrat, but their backgrounds were very different. Unlike her Minnesota family, who owned a big farm and shook hands with presidents, his parents raised seven kids on a dirt farm outside a little town north of Kansas City. They ate out of the garden, butchered their own meat, held machinery together with baling wire, and plowed with mules. They lost two farms to the banks during the Depression but proudly stuck it out in the Dust Bowl. My dad's father had only an eighth-grade education but served a couple of terms on the school board.

Even as child, I knew that Dad was interested in politics—he and Mom always hosted election night parties at our house—but I had not known the intensity of his personal aspirations until he revealed them during a late-night car trip. It was sometime in the late 1950s, when I was only eight or nine. We were on a family trip, perhaps to Minnesota, where my mother's family lived, but more likely to or from my dad's home in Missouri. It was nighttime, my little brother and sister were dead asleep on a mattress in the back-back of our station wagon, where the third seat had been folded down, and my parents were talking to me as if I were grown up, in the way you do sometimes with your oldest.

"If you could be anything you want to be when you grow up, what would you be?" my mother asked.

"A forest ranger," I replied, "or a farmer." I couldn't articulate it yet, but it was the quiet, the autonomy, and the long views that I wanted. I'd spent the summers on my grandparents' farm in Missouri; our family had been west to Berkeley for my father's sabbatical from Purdue in 1957, and so I had seen the Rockies.

My father couldn't let this go by. He was an agricultural economist and knew the trends. "Those jobs are hard to get," he said. "They're spotting fires by airplane now and every year there are fewer and fewer family farms."

His irrelevant realism angered my mother, but she kept cool and tacked in a direction that surprised me. "What about you?" she asked him. "What did you want to be at Ned's age?"

He kept his eyes on the road and responded, as I had, without hesitation. "What I still want to be, I guess—president."

My mother barked out a little laugh and said, "It's a little late for that, don't you think?"

A long, hard silence followed, which my father finally broke. "It's never too late." Then, deliberately, he switched on the radio and began searching through the Top 40 and country stations for a night game.

Meeting Bobby Kennedy

Spring comes late in Indiana. March drags into April, and for weeks and weeks everything is awful. The sky is gray and cloudy. The fields are endless and muddy, and you know that somewhere out there a flash flood has surprised a young possum and drowned it. Then a few pussy willow buds sneak out and finally a day arrives when you wear a jacket to school but can carry it home. That's the day the sky lifts and, finally, life seems worth living again.

It was a sunny day like that, the first of May, 1968, when I met Bobby Kennedy. A couple hundred of us had gathered at the Purdue University Airport in my hometown of West Lafayette to greet Kennedy. Housewives, Purdue students, the party faithful—we all pressed against a rib-high chain-link fence to see what we could see. Now and then we broke into a half-hearted chant, but mostly we just waited. At the other end of the fence from where I stood, a paltry little rock band played something, though I can't remember what.

I had just turned eighteen and was the student body president at my high school. I was a student council nerd, managing editor of the literary magazine, co-captain of the track team, everybody's designated driver. That fall, when I went away to Harvard, I was going to play football and major in government, and then, in time, become president of the United States. Law school, the U.S. Senate, president. I was full of big ideas, full of myself.

Bobby Kennedy had big plans too. He was running for president, and the Indiana Primary was essential. It was his first primary, and he had to win it. Eugene McCarthy, the senator from Minnesota, had been campaigning all winter against President Johnson and the war. In the middle of March, McCarthy shocked everyone when he came within 230 votes of beating Johnson in New Hampshire. Suddenly the president was vulnerable, and four days after New Hampshire, amid accusations of opportunism, Kennedy jumped into the race.

Johnson's support continued to free-fall, and two weeks later, he withdrew his candidacy. His pullout might seem to leave things simple in Indiana—McCarthy and Kennedy head-to-head—but there was a ringer. Indiana governor Roger Branigin was running as a local son and stand-in for Vice President Humphrey, who would probably enter the race himself. Neither Branigin nor Humphrey had come out against the war. Like McCarthy, Kennedy had been speaking against the war, but he had argued as well and more often and more convincingly than McCarthy that we couldn't fight a war on poverty *and* a war in Vietnam, and that the issue of race was central to all of this.

Since his brother's death, Kennedy had grown fatalistic and serious—reading Emerson, Greek literature, and Camus, climbing mountains in the Canadian Rockies, running for the Senate in New York. In 1966, he'd traveled to South Africa, visited Soweto, and criticized apartheid; by 1968, he was even picketing with the United Farm Workers in California.

When his plane finally appeared in the clear blue sky and began to drift down toward us like a balsa wood toy, we let up a wild, un-Hoosier-like cheer. As it landed and taxied in, the sun's reflections danced off its windows like a planned effect. We regained our composure and took up our chant. *Bob-by! Bob-by!* The whine of the engines drowned out most of our noise and the wind blew the rest across the prairie, but we didn't care. I held up a blue-and-white Kennedy sign and yelled as loud as anyone.

The Purdue Airport was a little thing—two runways, a three-story control tower, and a waiting room the size of a motel lobby—but we were proud of it. "A lot of airport for a town this size," my mother used to say. Purdue had focused early on aviation—Amelia Earhart taught there in the 1930s—and now, in the spring of 1968, the university was calling itself "the home of the astronauts." Gus Grissom, Roger Chaffee, and Neil Armstrong had all gone to Purdue and flown at its airport. Grissom and Chaffee had burned to death in their Apollo 1 command module during a training session the year before; Armstrong was getting ready to fly to the moon.

My parents did not come with me that afternoon to meet Kennedy at the airport. My father, a professor of agricultural economics, must have been at his Purdue office; I don't remember where my mother was. It was her kind of scene—she'd taken me to see John Kennedy in 1960 and Johnson in 1964 when they'd campaigned in Indiana—but she wasn't there this time.

Kennedy's plane came to a stop about thirty yards out on the tarmac. The pilot shut off the engines and as they wound down, we revved up, filling the air with our yell. *Bob-by! Bob-by!*

From the Purdue Airport, Kennedy would take ground transportation across town to a little crop-duster of an airfield where he was going to speak to a group of farmers. Then he'd motorcade downtown to his Lafayette headquarters to thank the volunteers, finally ending up at the Purdue Hall of Music for the main event—a speech before an audience of six thousand, which would include my parents. I would miss the middle stops because I had an afternoon class I couldn't cut and then track practice, but I'd be at Purdue for the big speech.

Kennedy's plane was a big one, bigger than the puddle jumpers that flew out of West Lafayette, connecting us to Cleveland and St. Louis. As we continued to cheer, a guy in a jumpsuit, his headphones now dangling around his neck, eased the portable stairs up against the plane's fuselage. After a while the door opened and a stream of aides and reporters began to trickle down the stairs. I tucked my placard under my arm to get a better look.

A few weeks earlier, Kennedy had flown into Indianapolis to speak outdoors in a Black neighborhood. The night was cold and windy, more March than April. Johnson had pulled out of the race five days earlier. This would be Kennedy's first speech in Indiana before an African American audience. En route, he was told that Martin Luther King Jr. had been shot and killed. Kennedy's wife, Ethel, and his aides, including John Lewis, the civil rights activist from Georgia who had served with King throughout the South and had been nearly beaten to death on the Edmund Pettus Bridge in Selma, asked him to cancel the speech. He refused. The Indianapolis police chief washed his hands of it all by yanking Kennedy's escort. In 1968 the Secret Service guarded only the president, not the candidates.

When Kennedy arrived, he found that the audience had not yet heard about the assassination. In the middle of a vacant lot, he climbed onto the back of a flatbed truck and broke the news. The crowd gasped as if gut-punched. Some started to sob. He reminded them that his own brother had been killed, and by a white man. He challenged them to rise above violence and lawlessness, and instead embrace "love and wisdom, and compassion toward one another, and a feeling of justice toward those who still suffer within our country, whether they be white or they be black." Then he quoted Aeschylus from memory: "In our sleep, pain which cannot forget falls drop by drop upon the heart until, in our own despair, against our will, comes wisdom through the awful grace of God." It was a line that was at once tough and consoling, a literary line. I remember thinking when I heard it the next day on TV that this was not the way politicians talked. Kennedy needed the Black vote, and King's killing demanded a response, but his speech was more than that. He believed that the crowd could find solace in the same ancient and elevated words in which he had found it.

As word of King's assassination spread nationally, rioting started almost immediately in most major cities. But not in Indianapolis.

The night that King died and Kennedy gave his speech, my friend Louis Klatch and I were checking out a party at Tom Herreid's house. Herreid was a year younger than we were and we knew him from student council, though we didn't usually hang out with him. His single mother was out of town and he'd told us to stop by if we wanted. As we approached his house, a little story-and-a-half bungalow near the Purdue campus, we could see that the front door was open even though the night was chilly. Inside, a stereo was blasting "I'm So Glad" from the *Fresh Cream* album. You could almost feel Clapton's guitar lines through your feet. Three juniors were staggering around the front yard, drunk and laughing. Herreid was one of them and, by all appearances, the drunkest. He was dancing a silly, stumbling jig and singing, "The king is dead! The king is dead! Long live the king!" When he saw us, he stood up straight, saluted and laid out his palm to give us five. "Loooo-ie, my man!" he said. "Mr. Ned! What's happening?" I slapped his hand unenthusiastically. He seemed to recognize the gulf the beer had put between us because he shrugged sheepishly. Then he sank back into his drunkenness and began his chant again. "The king is dead! The king is dead!"

I turned to one of his friends, a big blond kid I knew from football and who now seemed sober. "What's he talking about?"

"God, you haven't heard?" said the blond kid. "Martin Luther King got shot."

"He's dead?"

"Yeah. They shot him at a motel." Herreid rolled his eyes back in his head, screamed like a howler monkey, grabbed his neck and fell onto the grass in mock death.

There were no Black kids in our school, no Black people in our town, except for some athletes at Purdue and an occasional international student from the Congo or Nigeria. King's murder felt distant and unreal. Herreid was drunk, perhaps for the first time, and couldn't, I knew, be held absolutely accountable. And yet it was disgusting.

Louis and I left the party and, back at my house, watched the news. It didn't tell us much—only that King was dead in Memphis, the motel was the Lorraine, and there had been no arrests.

The next week at school, Louis and I, along with the student council, organized a fundraising drive that sent a few hundred dollars to a neighborhood center on the South Side of Chicago, an area that had been hit hard by the riots that followed the assassination. Tom Herreid helped take up the collection.

Herreid's party had been on a Thursday night, and the only reason I had been able to be at it was that my parents were out of town. They were in Indianapolis—my mother to shop and my father to meet with some people from Kennedy's advance team.

My father understood agriculture and Indiana farmers, and he knew Birch Bayh, the Indiana senator who was strong for Kennedy. Birch Bayh and Teddy Kennedy had been in a plane crash together four years earlier. Teddy broke his back when the plane went down, and Bayh helped drag him from the wreckage.

Bayh asked my dad to be part of the Indianapolis strategy session. My father told me later that when the meeting finally turned toward the farm question, a fast-talking advance man with a Boston accent asked what Kennedy could do to pick up some rural votes. Dad smiled at the guy and said, "Well, I think the best thing he could do is have his picture taken with a pig."

Mr. Boston stopped short, stared down my dad, and snorted, "And who is going to tell the senator *that*?"

The discussion returned to price supports and the future of family farming.

Kennedy was counting on both African American and white voters in Indiana's few industrial cities, but he also hoped to split the antiwar vote with McCarthy and even win over some of the more conservative rural Democrats who were only beginning to question the war.

I had turned against the war myself, just a few months earlier. My support for the war had already been waning, and then my hippie classmate Hester Harris started working on me. When she showed me the pictures of young napalm victims in that famous issue of *Ramparts* magazine, it finally shook me loose. I began to work on my parents and, sometime in February, I won them over. They were going through a rare good patch in their marriage, brought together, as they sometimes were, by their politics. Maybe the fact that their nest was beginning to empty scared them toward each other. I was their oldest and about to leave for college. At any rate, they listened to me and to what I was saying.

What I was saying carried new weight because I had just registered for the draft.

Walter Cronkite helped too. He was recently back from covering the Tet Offensive in Vietnam and announced in an hour-long primetime special that the war could not be won.

Every evening that spring, I took my new convictions and my parents' blessings out after track practice to canvass for Kennedy.

Governor Branigin was from Lafayette, and most of the doorbells I rang were in his home precinct, which was an odd mix of rich and poor. Branigin's house (his own home, not the governor's mansion, which was in Indianapolis) sat on a bluff near those of the Purdue president, the local Catholic bishop, and much of Lafayette's old money. From these big houses the precinct fell away toward the river, literally crossing the tracks, until it arrived at Wabash Avenue and a working-class neighborhood called the Tow Path. It got that name because it was built on the levee that had run beside the Wabash and Erie Canal. The canal had been filled in long ago, but in its heyday before the arrival of the railroads, mules had walked the levee, dragging boats across mud flats when the water was low. Fugitive slaves had followed it north. Now the Tow Path was a rough collection of bars, thrift shops, corner groceries, and tired little houses with gray porches and sagging gutters.

At the top of the hill, maids would sometimes dismiss me out of hand. When Mister or Missus did answer the door, I could see their eyes drift past my young face and down to my Kennedy button. They might indulge me for a minute, maybe even take a pamphlet, but they'd invariably beg off when I began to ask my questions. "Are you registered? Do you plan to vote in the Democratic Primary? May I ask who you think you might vote for? Do you know what Senator Kennedy plans to do for Indiana and America?"

Down the hill, it was a different story. There, under a yellow porch light or in the dark landing of a walk-up, I'd try the bell and when it didn't work, I'd knock. Two or three kids, thrilled at the novelty of a visitor, would stampede to the door and fight to see who was there. Sometimes the oldest would say hello; sometimes they would all just stare. The light of a big console TV, which was occasionally color (uncommon in those days), outlined the dim shape of their father slouched on the couch. My eyes, still adjusting to the dark, couldn't see if he was ignoring me or really asleep. From the kitchen the mother yelled, "Mary Louise, who is it?" A dog barked in the backyard and Maxwell Smart talked to Agent 99 on the TV.

"It's a man," said Mary Louise.

A man! I felt flattered, instantly older and very cool. And then Mom came out, wiping her hands on a dishtowel, and I began my spiel.

"I'm registered," she answered, "but he's not." She nodded toward the couch. "He thinks they're all crooks." Her husband rose to this bait and grunted something I couldn't make out.

"Can it, Harold," she snapped. "This young man's here to talk to us about Bobby Kennedy."

At the sound of the name he rousted himself from the couch and asked, "You want a beer or something?" I couldn't tell if he was really interested or just determined not to be left out.

"Thanks, but I better not. I've got a lot of houses to get to yet. The primary's only two weeks away." I didn't want to admit I didn't drink.

"They're such a sad family," she said. "I felt so bad for Jackie. And that Ethel, gosh, all those kids!"

I looked down at their kids, who had been gazing at me the whole time as if I were a Martian. Theirs was a life I hadn't seen up close like this. My parents tried to teach us about poverty—they purposely drove us through East St. Louis on the way to Dad's parents' farm in Missouri; he brought back color slides of Rio's slums; we collected for UNICEF—but that was all armchair sociology. Our windows stayed rolled up, our doors locked. This was different. This was my hometown, and I was in this family's living room.

I reminded them that the primary was May 7 and thanked them for their time. He shook my hand goodbye; she promised to get him registered.

Kennedy's plane continued to sit on the runway. We kept waiting and chanting. All along the fence people rubbernecked, trying to see through the doorway and into the darkness. Every time a man in a suit edged into the light, our hopes lifted. Then the man would turn toward us or step out and we could see that he wore glasses or was carrying a clipboard and was not Bobby.

Finally, he appeared. We could see the hair and the smile. It was Bobby Kennedy. He stopped at the top of the stairs and waved. For a weird instant, the chanting stopped and then, just as weirdly, the silence was filled by an intense and scary squeal.

Four years earlier, I'd seen the Beatles in Indianapolis on their second American tour. It had felt like this, though there, at the state fairgrounds, the squeal had never stopped. It might ebb a bit as the crowd tried to tell whether the Beatles were playing "She Loves You" or "Twist and Shout," but it never stopped. Now, at the airport, our squeal faded away and we began again to chant. Bobby! Bobby! For an instant, however, the mania felt the same.

As Kennedy reached the bottom of the steps there seemed to be some slight confusion about which way to go. Ethel was with him. She was wearing a sleeveless shift and no hat. She was less elegant than Jackie, but by now just as familiar, a celebrity in her own right. She glanced toward the far end of the terminal, where the band was playing and a set of microphones waited, and I figured they'd go straight there for some kind of welcoming ceremony before leaving to visit the farmers. But then Bobby took Ethel's elbow and steered her toward the fence, and they began to shake people's hands. They were no more than thirty feet away, just to my right. I was still trying to think what to say when I heard Ethel say "Hello" to the woman next to me. Ethel's simple greeting set the woman bouncing up and down. She was a young woman, maybe a graduate student or an assistant professor's wife. Her blonde hair was teased high on her head.

Ethel took her hand and said, "Thank you for coming."

Not bouncing quite so much now, the woman said, "Good luck, Mrs. Kennedy! Good luck!"

Ethel smiled politely and said, "Thank you." I remember wondering at the time what it felt like to be called "Mrs. Kennedy" and whether "good luck" might carry an ominous ring.

Ethel let go of the bouncing woman and reached over to shake my hand. "Hello," she said, "It's good to be in Indiana." I still didn't know what to say. She held my hand and smiled. I nodded and nodded, as mechanical as Howdy Doody, as mute as Disney's Clarabelle Cow. By the time I finally got it together to say "Thank you for coming," she had released my hand and taken her smile to the next person in line.

I turned back to my right, intent on not screwing up a second time. A gap had opened between the two Kennedys. He was a few people away from me. The band was playing and people were screaming, but more and more this felt like a reception line instead of a mob scene. Bobby was shaking one person's hand at a time, not two. He was moving quickly, but deliberately. The bouncing woman was still bouncing.

"It's good to see you," he told her. "Thank you for coming."

"Good luck, Senator! Good luck!"

"Well, thank you," he said with friendly exaggeration and a flirtatious grin.

Then he turned to me. We shook hands. "Thank you," he said. "Thanks for being here." He was shorter than I expected and very tanned. He had freckles on the bridge of his nose. His eyes were shockingly blue.

I was ready to say what I had to say, but when I did, it felt blurted and obnoxious. "I've canvassed over three hundred houses for you, Senator." He dropped my hand but held my gaze. And he didn't move on.

"How does it look?" he asked. His response was immediate and matter-of-fact, as if we were the only two people here. We were, I realized, about to have a conversation. I had thought—to the extent I had thought at all—that he would simply thank me and move on. But it seemed he really wanted to know what I had to say. He wanted to hear some news from the ground.

"It's close," I said. "You're ahead, but it's close. A three-way split with a lot of undecideds." He was still looking straight into my eyes.

"How many undecideds?"

"Ten, maybe twelve percent—at least in Lafayette where I'm canvassing."

"That's a lot. Thanks for talking to them. I really appreciate it."

And then it was over. We were done. The bubble of intimacy he had created was gone. The noise of the crowd washed over me—the band, the screaming people, the bouncing woman next to me saying, apparently to herself, "Oh my God. Oh ... my God."

Immediately I began to second-guess myself. Should I have said more? Should I have told him I was going to Harvard in the fall? That I too wanted to be president someday? Would that have been dorky and pretentious? Would that have been sucking up? Who was I?

Kennedy had moved down the line. I kept watching him, listening to him, thinking about what he'd said and how short he was. I gazed at him and slowly began to register the rest of him—his blue suit, his striped tie, the two nervous security guys moving along behind him. His size and his freckles made him look boyish, but his clothes and his manner were tailored and assured. It was a potent combination of vulnerability and power.

He was gone now. I could no longer make out his voice.

A young man in a sport coat and open collar approached me from Kennedy's side of the fence. He asked, "What were you talking about?" He didn't say who he was. I thought at first he was a reporter, but he didn't have a notebook, so he might have been an aide. He seemed cocky and full of presumption. Part of me didn't want to answer him at all, but I did.

"I told him I'd been canvassing for him, and he asked me how it was going."

"What'd you tell him?"

"I said it's close. I said there's a lot of undecideds."

"Oh." He turned and walked back toward a gaggle of people who, like him, were trying to look important and sure of themselves. They seemed very happy to be over there on their side of the fence.

The band stopped playing and a local politician stepped up to the microphones to introduce Kennedy. The amplifier popped so loud it made you jump and there was the whine of feedback. Someone made the adjustment and Kennedy was introduced. Everyone cheered as he stepped to the microphone. He thanked the politician for the introduction, thanked us all for coming, and said how happy he was to be here in Indy-an-AH, comically exaggerating the final *a*. Some of the Indiana papers had seized on the fact that he'd previously substituted a Boston "er" when saying the word, pronouncing it "Indianer." These stories were meant to demonstrate that he wasn't one of us, wasn't a Hoosier like Governor Branigin. Kennedy made a point of correcting himself, explaining that the earlier miscue had been made by "his younger brother." This second joke had the advantage not only of brushing away the attack with good humor but of reminding voters that Teddy was the younger brother now and that he, Bobby, was older, seasoned, the heir apparent.

Then he added another wrinkle. Deadpan, he reversed himself by telling us how especially happy he was to be here in "Lafayetter." After the laughter, he introduced Ethel, telling her in a stage whisper, "Don't forget to smile," though both of them were already grinning big, horsy grins. Next he took a jab at Branigin, who, commentators had said, was angling for the vice presidential spot should Humphrey get the nomination. Kennedy suggested that if the governor were running for vice president he should do just that. "But," he said, "I want you to know I'm running for president." This prompted much applause. He closed with some quick generalities about bringing the nation together and moving it forward.

He was good. He knew how to campaign and seemed to enjoy it. His speech was practiced but relaxed. Certain of his gestures—a way he had of folding his hands across his stomach while talking, a hesitant half-nod when acknowledging applause, the nervous brushing away of his hair from his forehead—evoked what seemed to be a genuine shyness. He was human, appealing, and new.

I found out in the paper the next day that when he left us and spoke to the farmers, the crowd had included a sixteen-year-old girl on a horse. She lived close by and had ridden over. It was an easy way to get there, and once she arrived, she was high up and had the best seat in the house. The photo on the front page showed Kennedy standing on the platform and gazing down at the girl on her horse. In the picture, he looks short, standing as he is between two tall local politicians, but he also looks relaxed and in charge. He's smiling approvingly at the girl. The two Hoosiers on each side of him look nervous, as if the sight of a girl on a horse might somehow prove embarrassing to Kennedy, or, more importantly perhaps, to Indiana. The photo's caption said that when he addressed the crowd "the senator called for bargaining powers for farmers and legislation for low-interest loans to enable young men to remain in the farming business." That line was pretty much the one my father had recommended when he'd met with the advance team in Indianapolis. And in the end, it seemed to me, the photo opportunity wasn't so different from the one my dad had suggested either, though a pretty girl on a horse is more charming than a pig in a poke.

Six days after I met Bobby Kennedy, he won the Indiana primary. I couldn't vote for him myself. In 1968, you could be drafted at eighteen, but you couldn't vote.

In the three-way race, Kennedy received a solid plurality, getting 42 percent of the vote statewide to Branigin's 31 percent and McCarthy's 27 percent. He won two-thirds of the state's counties and nine of its eleven congressional districts, including Tippecanoe County and the second district, where I lived. He beat Branigin in Branigin's home precinct, Fairfield 2, where I had done most of the canvassing.

With the primary over and Kennedy's campaign having moved on to Oregon and California, I returned to the spring of my senior year in high school—the prom, track meets, student council, and finally, Senior Week. Besides baccalaureate and commencement, Senior Week included a canoe trip and a chaperoned street party.

Everyone went to the sanctioned events, but the real parties happened later each night at Kathy Kemmer's family's cottage out on the Tippecanoe River. Kathy had swiped a key to the cottage from her father—a bold move, I thought, given that he was a stern, straitlaced Republican judge. These parties were infused with that sad mix of nostalgia and fear that marks everybody's last week of high school, especially in a small, stable Midwestern town like ours, where most of us had known each other since kindergarten. People cried and talked, and some lost their virginity. There was a lot of beer, even a little marijuana, though this was Indiana in 1968 and dope wouldn't be commonplace for another year or two. I stayed at these parties as late as anyone did, but I was the good son, Mr. Student Body President and thinking ahead to Harvard, so I never drank or smoked. Like most of my friends, I was and wasn't ready to get out of town. I wanted to get away from my parents and their fights, but I also worried that when I got to Harvard I'd be revealed as the bumpkin I knew I was.

Commencement was held on the evening of Wednesday, June 5. In the gymnasium, we passed the word down the rows of folding chairs that there'd be a party later on at the Kemmers' cottage.

The party felt old hat. Things had fallen into a routine by then—

the drinking and dancing to 45s downstairs, the pairing off in the bedrooms upstairs, the sad and happy last hurrah.

When I got home at about three in the morning, I crashed on an old double bed in our basement rec room. I liked to sleep down there because it was cool, and in the morning it stayed darker and quieter later than it did upstairs in the bedroom I shared with my brother.

Sometime midmorning my parents came down together to wake me. I knew immediately something was wrong. They never woke me up, and especially not together. My mother spoke first.

"We've got something to tell you." She paused and looked toward my dad. I felt a familiar rush of fear. Were they finally getting a divorce? Deep down, I knew it was inevitable, but I hadn't thought it would happen now. My dad looked at me and gave me the news.

"Senator Kennedy was shot last night."

I remember being struck by the words "Senator Kennedy." They felt so official and distant. Teddy was a senator too, but I knew he meant Bobby.

"Is he dead?" I asked.

"No," said my dad, "but they're not sure he'll live."

I looked away. I wanted them to leave. I wanted to get some breakfast and start watching television. I knew they were sad and wanted to share their sadness with me, but I was mad at them for not having told me the night before when I got in from the party. We had a basement garage, and its automatic door shook the whole house when you opened it. There was no way to sneak in. They had known I was back but hadn't come down to tell me.

But really I was mad at myself for having been out at a party instead of checking the late returns from California. I should have turned on the radio while driving home instead of listening to my carload of drunks as they sang Motown a cappella and teased the first-timer who'd thrown up.

Sirhan Sirhan shot Bobby Kennedy three times point-blank with a little .22-caliber pistol. A young Palestinian immigrant, he had seen Kennedy on TV wearing a yarmulke outside a synagogue and vowed in his notebooks to shoot him by June 5, the first anniversary of the Seven Day War between Israel and the Arab states. The worst bullet hit Kennedy behind his right ear. The mastoid bone slowed it down and broke it up, but pieces of bullet and bone continued into his brain.

For a while, I held out hope. I had worried—everyone had—that he would be shot, but our experience was with the powerful, quick-killing sniper shots that had hit his brother, and King, and Medgar Evers. This was different. There had been a four-hour operation. Now there was a long deathwatch. The doctors at the hospital explained that the bleeding and damage were extensive. The TV reporters interviewed neurosurgeons about these kinds of injuries. If he survived, they said, he would not be himself. I remember being struck by that euphemism. I knew what they really meant. He would be a vegetable.

Finally, his press secretary, Frank Mankiewicz, announced Kennedy's death. He delivered the statement deliberately, haltingly, trying not to break down. He gave the time of death and named all of the family members who had been with Kennedy when he died—his wife, his sisters, his sister-in-law. At the end he said simply, "He was forty-two years old." Then he waited a minute, apparently thinking there might be questions, but there weren't. With a dazed look on his face, he walked away from the podium.

In September, when I flew away from Indiana to start my freshman year at Harvard, life seemed to be presenting me with the rare opportunity of a clean slate. Through most of the fall, that feeling persisted. I read like a bandit, played on the football team, and glowed with pride that I was actually at Harvard.

My mom and dad came out on Parents' Weekend to see me play in the Brown game, but their plane was delayed and they didn't get to the stadium until the second quarter. My dad came down from the stands and leaned over the fence behind bench to let me know they were there. I told him I'd been knocked out making the tackle on the opening kickoff and I wasn't sure who we were playing let alone whether I'd be back in the game or not. Even in my fogginess the situation seemed like a joke that pointed toward what lay ahead—confusion, change, and a breach between us. My parents were tangled up in their messy, haunted lives, and I was heading out toward something new, though I had no idea what it was.

The differences between us became clearer when I flew home for Christmas. From the moment my parents picked me up at the airport in Indianapolis, I felt myself sinking back into the bog of my childhood. Driving up U.S. 52 toward West Lafayette and home, we passed the familiar string of landmarks—an abandoned pink motel at Lebanon, the Thorntown Dairy Queen, the billboard with the cartoon catfish urging you to eat all you can eat at Miller's in Colfax. I sat in the back seat waiting for them to start fighting.

My mother turned around to look at me. "I am so-o-o glad you're home," she said for the third time since we'd been on the road. Her hair was bouffed and the lenses of her cat-eye glasses magnified her eyes disturbingly. The holidays and my homecoming were shoving her into an upswing. She was headed toward the manic side of her bipolar disorder, talking on and on about how I stepped in the cake on my first birthday, came down with the mumps on my fifth, got a BB gun for my seventh. Then she launched into the jingle that appeared on my birth announcement, filling the car with her song, or rather, my song:

> I was born on George's birthday,
> So I cannot tell a lie.
> Nine full pounds of brand-new French,
> I'm really quite a guy.

This was an old pattern. Her nickname since college had been Diz, short for Dizzy. I knew these upswings, and they scared me. They made me think of a kid I knew in grade school who, as legend had it, worked a swing set so hard during recess, pumping and pumping his legs and urging on a team of run-through pushers, until he finally stopped at the top before crashing down in a tangle of chains.

My mother began singing again:

> I chose the name Ned Carleton,
> So now our family is
> Not just Charles and Dolores
> But Ned and Chuck and Diz.

I took a deep breath, exhaled slowly through my nostrils, and stared at my mother and then down at the piping on the back of the front seat where the fabric joined the vinyl.

"Mom... please."

I was trying to be gentle but firm, as if I were the parent. It was a familiar role, but I didn't like it and hadn't had to play it since August. I looked to my father for help, but he was checking his side mirror, deliberately avoiding my eyes. His hair was full of Vitalis, with a wave piled high in front in the fifties style he still favored. I noticed for the first time that his temples were graying. He had said nothing since we left the airport, but his loud, frequent sighs made it clear he was exhausted and turning my mother over to me. I'd had four months off, but now I was being called on again to deal with her, to calm her down, to love her. It was as if he and I were in a tag-team wrestling match with her, and now, just north of Thorntown, he had slapped my hand and crawled out between the ropes. I was back in the ring.

Outside, the air was heavy with mist, just short of a drizzle. Every so often my father flicked on the windshield wipers for a single sweep, pretending that it took all his concentration to do so. If this had been just the two of us—driving home from a Cardinals game, for instance, or a fishing trip—he would have chatted freely, draping his right arm across the top of the front seat and steering nonchalantly with his left hand. But now he sat silent and squeezed the wheel at ten and two. From the back seat, I could see the tension knotting his neck, feel the tension in his forearms. Something had to give. I'd been expecting him to get into it with my mother, or with me, to mention the length of my hair or blame Humphrey's defeat on McCarthy, but so far, he'd been mute. My mother, on the other hand, careened through a repertoire of stories about my childhood—how the paper boy had to help her get me off the window ledge when she was pregnant with my brother; how when I was three I stuck a bobby pin in a wall socket and was blown onto my back in a flash of blue light; how when I was sick with the flu in the top bunk I threw up on my sleeping brother down below. Her nest was emptying; she was terrified.

I looked past her and out the window. A light fog hung above the fields, drifting through the cornstalks and over the soybean stubble. The sky was low and gray, the way it would be from now until April or even May. Up ahead a black crow rose reluctantly from some gray roadkill. Large clods of mud that had flopped off a tractor tire littered the road.

My mother continued to talk until, finally, she reached the present. "Scott Allman is already home from IU," she said. "He called to ask when you were getting in. And Joanie Bain said Don is coming in tonight. I am so glad, so glad you're home." And then, in a burst, she grabbed my father's right arm. "Ned's here, Chuck. He's home."

He flinched away from her and barked, "I know that, but I'm trying to drive."

"I'm just glad he's home."

"Yes, dear, we all are." They might be glad; I wasn't. He had almost blown up but had caught himself.

Though I was just beginning to realize it, Boston was lost to me now, like a piece of luggage left back in Indy on a carousel. Harvard, poetry, and the student movement were just hallucinations. In Boston, I had been reading four or five hours a night while the fluorescent lights in the library buzzed and vibrated—Montesquieu's search for justice, Hobbes's cynicism, Sartre, Euripides. Oh, I was busy. *The Great Gatsby* a second time, and then a third. I spent each day in classrooms and only now and again did I focus my eyes as far away as the other side of the street.

Now, in the car, I could look only from him to her, from her to him. What had they been talking about before they'd picked me up? When would the fight erupt? Their thoughts were filling my head.

I looked across the fields to where the beech and maple trees stood wet and dark along the fencerows and the creek beds. The blackness of the woodlots and the grayness of the sky were broken only by the white streaks of sycamore trunks, standing upright like bones stuck in the ground.

In third grade, Mrs. Peterson had inducted us all into the Junior Audubon Society, in which on a field trip we had learned that some of these woodlots were relict groves left over from a period after the last glacier when Indiana had been covered with trees. These groves, isolated within more modern vegetation and lingering after the climate that had produced them, seemed to me even then to be both sad and admirable.

My best friend in third grade was Donnie Bain, whose parents had an American eagle on the wall above their garage. Third grade was the year he and I hid a cache of hickory nuts in a woodlot near Blackbird Pond. We were pretending to be Tom and Huck—he was Tom, debonair and civilized; I was Huck, rough and ready, ready to live off the nuts when we lit out for the territory. It was a fantasy we were proud of—something more interesting than the Davy Crockett stuff everybody else was doing. We never actually ran away, and in any case the woodlot was only a couple of acres, hardly enough to sustain us if we had. Now Don was in the Naval ROTC at Indiana University and married to our geometry teacher's daughter. She had played Dorothy to his Scarecrow in the spring musical our senior year. He was hurrying toward an adulthood which I did not approve of, or feared, and we no longer knew what to say to each other.

Outside, the mist and drizzle of the afternoon had given way to a cold rain, the kind that feels as if someone is throwing handfuls of pea gravel at you.

In the front seat, my mother had faced forward again but was still talking.

"You'll never believe what happened to the Wallaces." She paused to see if I was listening.

"What?" I asked, though I couldn't remember who the Wallaces were.

"She's filed for divorce. He was late every night at the office. You can hardly blame her, can you?"

I knew that to ignore her question would be cruel, but to answer it would be foolish. I gazed out the car window. The landscape looked mysterious and inviting. I wanted to throw myself out across the fields and join the troops of sumac assembling themselves at the edges of the forest. I wanted to be a part of their slow and peaceful march. King and Kennedy were dead, but something had to be done. We, the sumacs and I, would lead a succession of oaks and hickories out into the open, and Indiana would be forest again.

Rowing

My father grew up fishing muddy farm ponds in Missouri. He used worms, a cane pole, and bobbers, and caught gunnysacks of panfish—bullheads, bluegills, and crappies—which he kept wet and in the shade.

Years later, when he married my mom, who grew up in Minnesota, her uncles took him up north to fish. My mother was the daughter of a dairy farmer and her uncles were German Moravians—big, hard-working men with large hands and broad smiles. My grandfather, Fremont, the shortest of the brothers, was over six feet. By the fifties, when they took my father to the cold, clear lakes between International Falls and Ely, my great-uncles had all returned to the area around Dundas in southern Minnesota where they had grown up. They had come back from World War I and their rambunctious, oat-sowing times on the road, and now they all owned rich land left by the glaciers and large, productive herds of Holsteins or a lumber yard or part of a bank. But in their youth, they had been wild, or so my cousins and my father said. Clarence had been a bouncer at a roadhouse. He could lift two drunken men at a time off the dance floor and carry them to the parking lot. Harold had worked as a poacher for a mining camp in Colorado, keeping the men in elk and venison. Evidence of their youthful indiscretions remained. On Sundays, for instance, the communion decanter had to be refilled after traveling down their pew. Their sister Harriet, a widow for forty years, milked a full herd, sometimes with the help of a hired man, sometimes without it.

My father was a short man—5'7½"—and he grew up in a large and devout Methodist family. He and his six brothers and sisters were not allowed to drink, smoke, or dance. He could play only euchre because it didn't employ the full deck so it wasn't considered "cards." Early in the Depression, the family lost their farm to the bank. They worked and saved to buy a second, and then continued, always, to live carefully, even fearfully, to keep it.

Minnesota is the land of ten thousand Iowa jokes. The Iowan who threw back the northerns and kept the bullhead. The Iowan who looked into the minnow bucket and asked if we were going to fillet 'em or scale 'em. My mother's uncles told these jokes, and then laughed—bellowed really. My dad always laughed along with them, but I wondered if he was just being polite, Missouri being, if anything, less Minnesota than Iowa was. Missouri has small, red, dilapidated barns instead of big, white new ones; hogs instead of dairy cattle; yellow clay instead of black loam; farm ponds instead of lakes. My father genuinely liked my mother's uncles—they were kind, lively men—but when I look at old black-and-white snapshots of my father with them on fishing trips, he stands there among them looking slightly bewildered and out of place, sunburnt and blinking into the flash, helping hold up the catch of the day. He looks like an outsider, a sidekick, a kid brother along for the first time and not sure how to act.

Late in the summer of 1976, my dad and I headed up to Canada for a fishing trip. Just the two of us. My grandfather Fremont had died eight years earlier, and then water-skiers appeared on the Minnesota lake we had always fished, so we had moved further north to fish. I was living in Boston and my dad was living in Washington, DC. We were both tired of the bicentennial that had been dragging on. My parents' divorce had been finalized that spring. I was breaking up with my first serious girlfriend and dropping out of graduate school. We were both more than ready to hide out for a while and go fishing in the backwoods of western Ontario.

There, in the boat, the world seemed pared down to its essentials—the blue of the water, the green of the forest, the blue and white of the sky. We avoided the sticky issues—politics, my mother, my "career" plans—and talked instead about fishing and fishing tackle. Our toughest decisions were whether to use minnows or spoons, whether to fish sandbars for walleyes or weed beds for northerns.

The week was filled with familiar smells and sounds. The cough of the outboard motor as my dad fiddled with the idle, the frantic scurry in the bait bucket as you dipped for another minnow, the hesitant tug of a walleye or the slam-bam of a northern—these were old and certain images, refrains which, while heard only once a year, had played every year for as long as I could remember. We had been to this lake before, but this year was different. My brother wasn't there, and neither were any of my dad's colleagues or my mother's uncles. There was no carousing, no Canadian Club and lake water at sunset on the end of the dock. The fishing wasn't even very good.

The previous night, tired of fried fish, we cooked hamburgers, and told stories. The time Uncle Clarence found a muskie floating dead on the surface and cut it open to discover that it had choked on a beer can. The time Uncle Harold stuffed a minnow with snuff and tossed it up to the sea gulls, who coughed it up in an instant. The time Ray Wilson was showing his son Bill's big northern to another boat and accidentally dropped it over the side. The stories distracted us from the nagging fact that we would soon be heading back to the world, where we would have to rebuild our lives.

Our last day had started before dawn with bare feet on cold linoleum. Slowly, at the breakfast table, over coffee and cold cereal, we woke up. We each slurped a second cup of coffee and then went outside, where it was just getting light and the moon was setting. It was cold. Our tackle boxes were still in the trunk of my dad's rented car. We drove a bumpy twenty miles down lumber roads to the lake. Curtains of mist rose off the water. We didn't talk as we loaded and launched the boat.

That morning we caught a few fish, and then, around noon, we spotted a bull moose swimming across an inlet. We were able to get so close to him we could see the cloud of blue flies above his head and the annoyance in his eyes, which were as big as plums and as black as obsidian. The afternoon passed at a crawl. We alternated trolling slowly for walleyes and fast for northerns. Sometimes, we'd shut the motor off and just drift. The only sound would be a soft series of whirs and kerplunks as we cast red-and-white Daredevils or silver Johnson spoons toward the reeds along the shore. Late in the afternoon, we worked our way up and back down a little river lined with pickerelweed and granite. As we came back out into the lake, we got a long, quiet look at a bald eagle. The eagle, an adult, was perched high and still in a dead fir tree. It looked like the focal point in a precise Flemish oil. My dad said, "That's a pretty view to end on. I guess we ought to head on in."

Though my dad was short and solid, I am tall and wiry, more like the men in my mother's family. I am almost 6'2", and passed my dad in height when I was in the seventh grade. But I always thought of my dad as stronger than I am. I remember asking him once during the summer before junior high why he was stronger than I was. We were nailing twenty-penny nails through two-by-fours into the trunk of an oak to make the braces for a tree house, and I couldn't do it. My dad looked at me with surprise, his hammer caught in midswing, wondering why I was asking, I guess. Then he answered that he was older and that I would get stronger and that he had lifted things a lot when he was growing up—baskets of eggs, buckets of coal, hay bales, sacks of grain, fence posts.

He was also an athlete when he was younger—a pitcher in American Legion ball, a long jumper in track. His high school football team was undefeated his senior year. He was a pulling guard and middle linebacker, and though he was good enough to get some scholarship offers at little colleges in his part of Missouri, he followed his older brother to the University of Missouri. He was too small to play football there, of course, but he took up handball and won the intramural championship. He was also a good student, and his grades, along with his eyesight and reflexes, got him into the Army Air Corps during World War II. He flew P-47 Thunderbolts in Europe before coming home to Missouri to finish his studies and meet my mother. I was in my twenties before I beat him in a round of golf.

The early seventies were hard on our relationship. We'd had arguments about the standard issues of the times—Vietnam, marijuana, hair length. Once, as I stormed out of the family room, he yelled after me, "You wouldn't have that stereo if it wasn't for capitalism!"

Ours weren't the only fights in the house. My mother filed for divorce five times during my adolescence before finally following through with it. My brother and I shared a bedroom right next to theirs. I had a shortwave radio with headphones, not spongy little Walkman earphones, which hadn't been invented yet, but hard, black Bakelite jobs that looked like two telephone receivers held together by a metal strap that fit over the crown of my head and always caught in my hair. At night in the top bunk I'd listen to WLS out of Chicago and read under the covers so that I didn't have to listen to my parents fight, though to be honest, even the headphones didn't help that much.

When I was in high school, my dad started spending less time at home. He'd work at the office until 11:00 and then come home, falling asleep in front of Johnny Carson. He traveled out of town, consulting for businesses or delivering speeches. He even missed one of my football games senior year. He came by the school the following week to watch the game films with one of the assistant coaches, but it wasn't the same as replaying everything with him at breakfast on Saturday.

The year before our Canadian fishing trip, in the spring of 1975, my parents finally separated for what would be the last time. My father moved into an apartment and then, in April, his father was killed in a farming accident. My grandfather had been out checking on some hogs when he hit a soft spot on the bank of a pond and his tractor turned over on him, pinning him under the muddy water, where he drowned. My uncle Don, my father's youngest brother, found him and pulled the tractor off with his own tractor, but it was too late.

I was backpacking in the Blue Ridge Mountains with my girlfriend when the accident happened, and though my dad had the Virginia State Police looking for me, they couldn't find us. A week later, when I got home to my apartment in Boston, I found out what had happened. It was five days after the funeral, but I flew out to Kansas City anyway to visit the grave and see my dad.

I sat away from the table and listened while he and his brothers and sisters talked about what to do with the farm and with my grandmother, who had Alzheimer's. Could someone from town be hired to move in with her? I kept Grandma occupied while her kids planned the rest of her life. Sometimes she understood what had happened, what was happening, and she would cry; other times, she would say she saw Charley out by the hog barn and that she needed to get his dinner ready.

My aunts cleaned out the bedroom closet, my grandpa's drawers, and the medicine chest. I helped my dad in the garage, boxing up rubber boots, work gloves, overalls, and tools. In one corner there was a cane pole, two spin-casting outfits, and a beat-up tackle box. I held the poles in my left hand and the tackle box in my right, and turned to look at my dad. He was staring at me. The door was up and he was standing half in, half out of the garage.

"I'm sorry I couldn't get here until now," I said.

"That couldn't be helped."

"I wish I could have been with you at the funeral."

"I know you do." He was looking at the spinning rod in his hand. It was outfitted, pitifully I thought, with a little hook, a bluegill hook.

"I was on automatic at the funeral anyway. Thursday evening was when I grieved. I went out to the big pond to think about your grandfather. There are some pretty big bass in there now. I didn't take a rod with me. I just walked around the pond a couple of times by myself. We all fished that pond a lot. It's a pretty place.'

I didn't know what to say.

"The accident wasn't there, was it?"

He had stepped into the driveway and stood in the light, looking across the yard toward the barn.

"No, it was at the east pond, the little one."

"I used to gig frogs there."

"So did I. Don said there's nothing but bullheads and leeches in there now. It's really just a stock pond, but it always had big frogs."

I put the poles and the tackle box with the other things we had set in the driveway, and we finished cleaning out of the garage.

The year after my grandfather's death, the year I met my dad for the Canadian fishing trip, I spent most of the summer bumming around the country—backpacking, spending my savings, looking up old friends, and trying to figure out what I wanted to do with the rest of my life.

Two weeks before getting together with my dad, I was about to run out of money, and so I headed back east from California, where I had been sleeping on my sister's floor for a week. I had to hitchhike. I had some long waits between rides—a day in Fresno, a day in Bakersfield, another outside Falstaff.

It was late afternoon, almost evening when my ride, an army vet, and I finally crossed into Texas from New Mexico. Outside there was nothing but sagebrush and tumbleweed as far as you could see, but in the road ahead I kept noticing what looked to be leaves or wads of paper blowing across the asphalt. I kept looking, and saw that whatever it was, it wasn't blowing. It seemed to be hopping, clearing the two lanes in just three or four hops. I asked the trucker what it was.

"Tarantulas."

"I didn't know they could jump like that."

"Oh yeah, they can hop onto your shoulder."

"Shit."

The rest of the ride all I could do was watch the big, hopping spiders, which were now quite obviously what they were. It was like looking up a word and then seeing it everywhere you turn.

Outside Amarillo, where 287 headed south toward Wichita Falls and then Dallas, the trucker let me out. All I could think about was the tarantulas. I danced around in the sunset, singing and talking to myself to ward them off, and waited for a ride; I wanted to get one before it got dark. I was sure that a tarantula would hop out of the dark and onto my shoulder. In about half an hour, a Volkswagen van stopped to pick me up. The woman who was driving was a hippie. She was pretty, with long, straight brown hair, faded jeans, and an embroidered peasant blouse. There were already two other hitchhikers in the back—a young couple she'd picked up in Taos. She said she was heading back to her commune in North Carolina and could take me all the way to Alabama, where a friend of mine from college was living and where I could crash for a few days before heading back to Boston. Everything seemed cool. We talked for a while. I was beat. No problem, she said. I stretched out in back and crashed.

I woke up later when the van stopped. There were murmurs in the dark. I lifted my head into the beam of flashlight. A cop.

"Everybody out," he said, "and let me see your hands. Put them on your head."

The four of us assumed the position along the side of the van. The cops frisked us, then one cop covered us while another searched the van. He didn't have to search long. He found a baggy full of dope in the glove compartment.

Jesus Christ, I thought, here she is driving through Texas with North Carolina plates, love beads hanging from the rearview mirror, a beat-up old van, and she's got it in the glove compartment.

We ended up spending the night in the Quanah county jail, halfway between Amarillo and Wichita Falls, in the middle of the Texas Panhandle. The men's bunks had no sheets and were right below a full-blast air conditioner that you couldn't turn off or down. I woke with a crick in my neck. I didn't know how long I would be there, and I was mad I was there at all. A deputy brought us breakfast on styrofoam plates. The coffee was instant. The cream was Creamora. First-world problems, I know, but everything felt like a personal slight.

We waited all morning in the cell, playing solitaire or leafing through girlie magazines, while they searched the van, checked our records in their computer system, and quizzed us one by one.

Finally, unable to find anything on us, the cops led us into the judge. The driver, to her credit, had explained during her interrogation that morning that the rest of us were just hitchhikers. There was nothing incriminating in our backpacks, and so the judge, after a short lecture about America and our responsibilities, let the couple and me go.

I thanked the driver, got her address, and promised I'd write. I was wrung out, but hitched straight through to Indiana so I could rest up, wash my clothes, and let my mother feed me. My dad had moved to Washington, DC, where he was starting a new job at the Department of Agriculture. I phoned him from what was now just my mother's house.

His life had changed. He was divorced, his kids were raised, and he was living, for the first time in his life, in a city. Washington must have been crazy that bicentennial summer, though when I called, it was late August and the fireworks were over. The bureaucracy inched along through the swampy heat. Every day the offices closed promptly at five and Dad went home alone to his apartment. Most of this, however, had not dawned on me yet when he picked up the phone.

"How's your mother doing?"

I hesitated, unsure whether he was being polite or really wanted to know, whether anything specific would be a betrayal of her confidence, unsure whether I even knew how she was.

"All right, I guess. I just got here. How's Washington?"

"Hot."

"Yeah, it's hot here too."

There was another pause, magnified by the phone lines, and then finally he said, "Would you have time for a quick fishing trip? I could send you a ticket."

"Sure, I guess.... I mean, I'm a little short on money right now, but no ... I mean, yeah, that would be great."

He called me back in an hour. We made arrangements to meet in Thunder Bay in two days. I didn't say anything about the Quanah jail.

The eagle lifted slowly from its perch and we watched it fly away from the still, perfect painting it had seemed to be inhabiting. Then my dad opened the throttle on the Evinrude. We had a lot of water to cover. We were probably forty miles from our cabin when we started back—twenty miles on the lake, twenty more on the lumber roads.

Over the roar of the motor, Dad yelled, "Hope we didn't wait too long. I don't want to drive that road at night. Too many deer."

I nodded, pulled on my jean jacket, and turned to look ahead for rocks and landmarks. I rode the bounces and watched the late afternoon unwind in front of us. I'm slightly color-blind in my left eye, and I was playing with the shades of blue and green by looking through one eye and then the other when suddenly the engine sputtered and died.

In the sudden quiet, Dad said, "All that trolling really burns up the gas."

He disconnected the rubber feed hose from the now-empty five-gallon can, stood up, and reached for the reserve can. He expected it to be full, and when it wasn't, he sat down hard and fast, almost going over backward and overboard.

"Damn it," he said. "Damn it, the guides are supposed to keep the cans full. Damn it."

Then softer and mostly to himself, "Shoulda checked it this morning. Should always check."

We did the only thing we could—we started to row. It was hard work, and we weren't even sure where it would get us, because we weren't sure how far we had to go. We kept switching off. He'd row and then I'd row. We rowed and rowed.

The light faded, and the inlets and the bays and the bluffs began to look alike. The tree line grew darker. Time slowed down and distances stretched out. The quiet was eerie. We checked the map we'd got at the lodge from time to time, but it told us only what we already knew—we were lost and a long way from the outfitter's dock where our car was parked.

Finally, we accepted the fact that we weren't going to get back that night. A thunderstorm was building to the north. Then we saw some lightning. It was far enough away that we couldn't hear its thunder. Our new goal was to get to the southern shore and set up a camp.

My dad was rowing.

"Maybe you ought to take us in from here," he said. "This would be a lousy place for a heart attack."

I didn't know what to say. I waited for him to get up off the middle seat where our oarlocks were and make his way to the back seat. Then I got up from the front seat, sat down in the middle, took the oars, and started to row.

I felt ashamed that I hadn't even thought about a heart attack. I had never thought of him as having reached an age when you need to think about your heart. He was the one who had carried the grain sacks and the coal buckets. He was the strong one.

As I rowed, I thought of telling him I was sorry I hadn't thought about a heart attack, but decided we both might find his mortality embarrassing. I thought too that I should tell him about what had happened in Quanah, Texas, and that I was sorry about the divorce and that I had missed my grandfather's funeral and the fishing trips with Mom's uncles, but I didn't say anything. I just rowed.

In half an hour we reached a granite point, where we pulled the boat out of the water and split a salami sandwich and one of our two apples, all that was left from the lunch we'd packed. We sat for a while, mentioning from time to time how tired we were, and watched the storm moving east up past the north shore. And then the sun set.

We had no sleeping bags, but because the woods were dry, and we knew there was a no-fire watch, we didn't build a fire. We were tired anyway. We peeled thick slabs of moss off the rocks to make a kind of mattress. The rock was Canadian shield greenstone, the oldest rock in the world. Most of the slabs of moss were six inches thick and as big around as the lids of garbage cans. We had only my father's trench coat for cover. During the night, we kept waking up cold. We didn't sleep much. Without saying anything about it, we snuggled up together to try to stay warm. Finally, we used some of the moss as blankets.

In the morning, we ate the second apple and fished a little bit, but mostly we just waited, watching for planes and listening for boat motors. Around noon, the owner of the lodge where we had been staying and some of his guides found us. They had been out in two boats since 6:00 that morning looking for us. They gave us some coffee from their thermos, teased us a little bit, pretty gently, really, and showed us on the map where we were.

That summer, the summer of 1976, was the real end of the sixties for me. They were over for good, and so was my parents' marriage. I'm married now myself, and my father is remarried. Five years ago he had a heart bypass, and two years ago he retired.

The past two summers, my wife and I have spent a week in August on a lake in northern Minnesota with my dad and stepmother. My wife and I go for boat rides. My dad and I go fishing one day, and the rest of the time the four of us sit around the cabin, reading, playing solitaire, and talking about families, books, and the lake. We talk a lot, but there are things we don't talk about, and I may be wrong, but I think some things don't need to be talked about. Often during the last two summers in Minnesota, I have yanked the starting cord of a boat motor till the engine catches and roars, or I have stood on the dock and focused the binoculars on an eagle, and then I have thought about snuggling up with my dad under his trench coat and those slabs of moss and not being able to sleep because I was cold. I think about how he had to ask me to row.

Mass General

In the fall of 1976, I lied about my background to get a job as a janitor at Massachusetts General Hospital. On the personnel application I left out the fact that I'd gone to Harvard, claiming instead that I'd worked for several years as an oil field roughneck, a carpenter, and a groundskeeper. In fact, I had done all those things, but I stretched summer jobs to cover entire years and gave references that couldn't be traced.

For the next ten years, I worked at Mass General as a janitor and communist organizer, living a schizophrenic, semisecret life. I had friends from work and friends from the communist movement. The core of my world split and shrank down into my communist cell and the MGH emergency ward. I was a member of a Marxist-Leninist organization called the Boston Organizing Committee, or the BOC, which was, in turn, a part of a national network of local organizing groups that were trying to build a new communist party in the United States. The BOC was composed primarily of young, white, middle-class activists who had been politicized in the antiwar, student, and women's movements of the 1960s. We had cadre working throughout the Boston area—in the Quincy shipyards, the Lynn GE plant, the Framingham General Motors plant, a meat packing company, a steel fabrication place, and various community organizations.

The cell I was in was trying to organize a union at Mass General, Boston's largest hospital, then negotiate a breakthrough contract and set an example that would inspire the unionization of the rest of Boston's hospital workers (only 3 percent of whom were organized). With four medical schools, eighteen teaching hospitals, and 72,000 employees (7,500 working at MGH alone), health care was the city's largest industry. We in the BOC were coordinating our work with hospital organizers in other cities. We would launch a revolution.

It was an odd and jostling life. During the day I was a janitor, moving from spill to coffee break to pay check. At night, I went to meetings geared to analyze my work at the hospital in terms of the class struggle.

My first day at work I was assigned to the emergency ward. The EW was a busy, noisy, and confusing place, a swirl of people doing different jobs. Triage nurses snapped out decisions about stretcher patients. Clerks with clipboards asked for Blue Cross/Blue Shield numbers. Security guards in blue blazers floated through with time on their hands, chewing gum and flirting with nurses. Dispatch workers pushed gurneys, picked up blood samples, and dropped off test results. Nurses scurried everywhere with thermometers, IV bottles, meds, and bedpans. IV techs drew blood. Doctors took histories and ordered tests. Family members cried. The intercom barked commands constantly.

My job was to mop floors, wipe walls, empty the trash, and clean beds. The EW included four hallways of examining rooms, an overnight ward of ten rooms, an overflow ward filled with cots, a lab, two admitting desks, a waiting room, two trauma rooms, a minor surgery room, an orthopedics room, a nurses' lounge, and a doctors' lounge. With two other janitors and a maid I spent the day edging in and out of these areas, cleaning them during the intervals when they were vacant.

The senior, or lead, janitor was Al Carrington, a fifty-year-old

Black man from Barbados. Soft-spoken and careful, Al would be made a supervisor two years later.

The maid, Theresa Natkus, had been at the hospital twenty-seven years. She had a funny-looking 1940s hairdo that harked back to the McGuire Sisters, as well as a wandering eye, a speech impediment, and a hand that had been mangled in a street car accident so that all that was left was her thumb, part of her index finger, and her pinky. She loved to gossip, sometimes losing herself in it with such intensity that she sputtered a bit and you had to lean back to keep from being sprayed. Despite her disconcerting manner, Theresa sought out and won intimacy. Her confidence was manifest in the way she unselfconsciously laid her scarred hand on your own while talking to you intently about love, justice, or infidelity. In the daily battles for respect with doctors, nurses, and supervisors, she took very little crap. She'd lived all of her life in South Boston, the Irish neighborhood that, at the time, was resisting the school busing that they felt had been unfairly forced on them but not on the wealthy suburbs. She rode to work with our supervisor, who lived on her block. He knew that if he gave her trouble at work, he'd hear about it later in their carpool, if not then and there on the spot.

The third member of our crew was Pedro Gonzales. It was Pedro who was assigned to train me. He was my age, twenty-six, but about a foot shorter. He had a thin little caterpillar of a mustache, but it wasn't enough to make him look grown-up. He was outgoing and relished cutting through tension with a wink or an inside joke. The nurses loved him like a kid brother.

My first morning, after I had filled out my tax form and endured an orientation session with the rest of the day's new hires, the supervisor dropped me off in the EW, where Pedro took me under his wing. He showed me how to mop with my back straight so it wouldn't get sore, warned me about backing into shelves of IV bottles, explained that Room 3 was the "heart attack room," told me which nurses were grouches, and finally, to break the ice, did his imitation of Curly from *The Three Stooges*.

"You ever watch the Stooges on the Spanish channel?" he asked. "They are really funny in Spanish." And then he paused and waited until I grinned, letting him know I realized that even if the Stooges were dubbed, it didn't make much difference with humor that depended on poked eyes and rubber chickens. Satisfied I was not a total fool, he left me to mop a few rooms solo.

I worked the middle corridor with my "mop bucket," which was actually two five-gallon buckets mounted on a stainless steel cart—disinfectant on one side and rinse water on the other. I mopped a couple of rooms, and then headed back to the janitor's closet and its slop sink to change my water. I moved gingerly, my eyes on my bucket. I was still trying to figure out how to keep its four little roller skate wheels going the same direction so that I didn't splash water all over tarnation. I hadn't found out yet that pushing a mop bucket is like carrying a cup of coffee—to avoid spilling it, you shouldn't look at it.

As I inched down the hall, the already regular litany of the intercom and the hallway chatter was suddenly broken ten feet behind me with a shout: "Coming through! Trauma one. COMING THROUGH!"

I jumped back and looked behind me to see two EMTs pushing a gurney with an olive-skinned mustachioed man on it. They were coming straight at me. I yanked my bucket to the side, sloshing water on the floor, and plastered myself to the wall. As the gurney went by, the dark-haired patient screamed in what might have been Greek or Arabic and rolled his head violently from side to side. He looked like a construction worker. He had broad shoulders and was wearing muddy steel-toed boots and a hooded sweatshirt. His jeans were soaked black with blood from his waist to his knees. A triage nurse trailed the stretcher at a near trot. When she hit my puddle, she skated about sixteen inches, caught herself on my arm, and spat a "Godammit" right in my face. She let go and caught up with her patient just as the EMTs took the turn into Trauma Room One, twenty feet or so down the corridor.

I quickly wrung my mop dry and, as best I could, got up the water I'd spilled. Then I stepped back and stayed out of the way as some doctors scurried by. When things seemed to have settled down, I returned to my water-changing mission and headed once more toward the slop sink. As I passed the trauma room, I took a look, rubbernecking at the commotion. The nurse who had slid through my puddle looked straight at me and yelled, "Building Service! We're sliding in here. Get this floor for us." I couldn't believe I'd heard her right. But I looked at the floor and it made sense. It was covered with blood and they were slipping. And she was in charge. I wasn't.

I wrung my mop dry, went in, and worked as best I could around the feet of the three doctors and four nurses. The patient had stopped screaming. He must have been in shock or sedated. I tried not to look, but I couldn't help myself. His pants had been cut from him, leaving him naked from the waist down. There was a large, raw hole in the top of his right thigh, just below his hip, just outside his groin. His eyes were open and staring at a spot on the ceiling. He still had on his sweatshirt and jacket. I could see his chest rising with each breath.

A woman's voice came over the intercom with a restrained but definite urgency: "Code 3. Code 3. Cardiologist to Room 3, please. Cardiologist to Room 3." One of the doctors said, "Shit. Gerry, you and Mike get that code. We're OK here. It missed his femoral. Cindy and I'll get some blood in him and send him up to the OR.'

In an instant, our drama had paled. The spotlight shifted. Room 3 became the center ring. I was left in Trauma Room 1 with one doctor, two nurses, and the man on the stretcher. I picked up his torn, bloody jeans and, not knowing whether I should throw them away, laid them in the corner. The doctor said to the nurse, "This guy's lucky. Can you imagine? Fell forty feet onto a fence post. I can't believe it missed his pelvis and his artery."

I couldn't believe I was here. I dragged a pile of gauze pads, paper wrapping, and plastic syringe caps out of the way with my mop. And then, from behind me, I heard someone laugh and say, "Compañero, perhaps you need a broom and a dustpan." I turned to see Pedro, Al, and Theresa standing in the doorway, smiling.

I had plunged directly into a sea of oddness and confusion, where I would swim for a decade. The world of the hospital was an inversion of my previous life. I had gone to college with several of the MGH doctors (one had been in my biology class), but now I was invisible to them, just a mop, never there when I was needed, in the way the rest of the time. I answered to foremen and supervisors who had never been to college.

But the emergency ward, if weird and otherworldly, was also excruciatingly real. So charged with reality, in fact, you could not allow yourself to live entirely within it. While patients squirmed and bled and died, doctors, nurses, and even the rest of us joked and bickered. Hawkeye and Trapper John had been right—you have to laugh to keep from crying. The gore, the death, and the sadness sneak up on you if you don't protect yourself with humor. I remember early one Sunday morning, mopping on the other side of a screen from behind which I could hear, but not see, a daughter bringing her mother in to see the dead father. At some point I realized I was crying silently along with them, not sure how long I had been standing there, mop in hand, staring at the screen.

Day one was traumatic and bloody, but my life in the emergency ward soon settled into a routine. I had a job to do. Each day I focused on the same brown-and-white floor tiles, the dirty orange Naugahyde of the waiting room chairs, the eighty-seven waste baskets, and the endless spills and leaks and tracked-in snow, the broken IV bottles, and puddles of puke. Time slowed down and stretched out and, as in every work place, came to be marked off by going-away parties, Christmas parties, and retirement parties. At these get-togethers, secretaries and technicians, nurses and maids, even doctors stood and chatted in shifts, eating cake, drinking punch, and trying to relax, all the while listening for ambulances and wondering what the world might send through the swinging doors. Even at the parties, we talked shop, reminiscing about the nut case who bolted from his stretcher and chucked IV bottles at the head nurse. Someone bemoaned the patient's poor aim and weak arm, and we all laughed. We were reminded of another crazy guy, who, though tied by his wrists and ankles to his stretcher, had somehow worked an unconfiscated cigarette lighter from his pocket and managed to set his mattress on fire. Saturday nights were the worst, and if you had seniority and were smart, you didn't work them, especially during heat waves or a full moon.

Despite all of this, I found it easy to be a janitor. Not much was expected of you. I stayed out of the way and did what I was told. It was harder to be a communist. Being a communist meant pushing myself to meet new people, listening for issues, not keeping my mouth shut when somebody was getting taken advantage of, and yet, at the same time, picking my battles strategically. It meant translating theory back into practice. It meant figuring out who was respected, who the potential leaders were, and then trying to convince them that it was worth the risk to talk up the union or come to a meeting. It meant learning how to recognize stool pigeons and avoid them.

Two years of mopping, organizing and meeting went by and then, in 1979, the hospital introduced its new merit plan. This policy meant that raises throughout the hospital, even for people working the same job, could vary between 0 and 5 percent, depending on one person's evaluation of your work. Traditionally, people had been able to count on annual step raises, and so this new plan was very unpopular. The anger was slow to build, however, because people were evaluated not all at once but individually throughout the year on the anniversary of the day they had started working at the hospital.

Throughout this period, our BOC cell met weekly. Every Wednesday night, thirteen of us crowded into the third-floor living room of our cell leader, a nurse who worked in the operating room. With a concern for security that now seems self-important and comic, we staggered our arrivals over a half an hour or so. Seven women and six men, we included two RNs and an LPN, two nursing assistants, a supply room clerk, a secretary, an IV technician who took blood, a guy who worked the loading dock, a woman who filed medical records, a maintenance man, an orderly, and me. All of us were college-educated. None of us was yet thirty-five.

Each week we made progress reports, discussed timetables, drafted leaflets, and analyzed the consciousness of individual contacts. In addition to cell meetings, we attended study groups, meetings of the entire BOC, regional meetings with other groups from our tendency of the new communist movement, national conventions, and fraction meetings with Marxist-Leninist health-care workers from other cities. These communist meetings were in addition to our trade union work, which consisted of meetings with staff organizers from the union, with groups of workers from our departments, and with individuals who were willing, over a beer or coffee, to listen to our pitch. During the late seventies and early eighties, I probably averaged three or four meetings a week.

We were sustained by a fervid belief in Marxism-Leninism, the true version of which we felt could be found somewhere between the revisionism of the CP-USA and the left deviationism of the Maoists. The former were lackeys of the Soviet Union, the latter blind followers of China. We were looking for a correct and creative middle way that would be internationalist but homegrown.

Wednesday after Wednesday, our cell talked and talked about the merit plan. Sometimes we submitted written reports to ourselves and discussed them. I see now that this was what we'd learned to do in college—write papers, study, talk—and we did it to avoid taking direct action. In cell meetings, we went round and round about whether our fledgling union drive, still just a scattering of departmental committees, was ready to go open and fight back publicly. Finally, national leadership intervened. Two steering committee members from Philadelphia come to town to assess the situation. The merit plan is a class issue, they said. It affects every worker in the hospital and provides an opportunity you might not get again for years. Go open, they said. They were probably right, or at least as right as anyone could be at the time. Some of the workers and the staff people from the union were saying the same thing. But it wasn't the analysis of the out-of-towners that moved us, I think; it was their credentials. One of them was a young, fast-talking Italian American woman who had grown up in the working class, and the other was a laconic Black man, whose brother, we had found out, had just died of cancer caused by exposure to Agent Orange in Vietnam. These people were not petit bourgeois pretenders like ourselves, they were real, working-class communists, people who had paid a price, and we listened to them. They told us to fight the merit plan, and so we did.

But it wasn't easy. In the day-to-day routine of sour mopheads and boring coffee breaks, I found it hard to roust myself and have the conversations I should have. Instead of trying to get a respected, older worker, someone like Theresa or Al, to talk to others, I would spend my coffee break reading the newspaper. At Wednesday night meetings, our cell chair tried to hold us accountable for staying in touch with key contacts, often invoking the analysis of the Philadelphia leadership, but we could tell she had to push herself to push us. We all knew that even if the workers at Mass General were upset about the merit plan, they were also afraid. This was going to be a long march, not a prairie fire.

In October, I received a 5 percent raise when I came up for evaluation. Our supervisor, Frank Creighton, was a stocky, gray-haired ex-marine in his late fifties. He had a penchant for loud, ugly sports jackets and anything, well . . . Irish. He liked me because I could talk knowledgeably about the Red Sox and the Celtics, and because I "showed a little backbone." He respected the fact that I complained to him when doctors were particularly rude to us or when a head nurse had ignored TB precautions, allowing Theresa to be exposed.

A year earlier, when Al had been promoted, Creighton had assigned me to take his place as lead janitor in the EW even though Pedro had seniority. Creighton ignored and intimidated Pedro. He had no respect for him and called him "Pablo" as often as not. Theresa called Pedro "Petro" but that was was because she couldn't pronounce "Pedro," and besides, they liked each other. Pedro was not the type to hate people, but he didn't like Creighton one bit.

Early in December, Pedro was evaluated. When he came back from his meeting with Creighton, he avoided Theresa and me, and went off by himself to buff the main waiting room. Theresa found him, made him unplug the buffer, leave it there, and follow her. She closed her bad eye and with her good one and a sideways nod of her head directed me to a stairwell where we could talk but still hear the intercom if needed.

As usual, she didn't mince words. "What'd they give you?" He looked at the floor like a little kid called into the principal's office. "Three percent."

"That's bullshit." She turned to me. "You gotta talk to Mr. Creighton about this."

"How about you?" I said, "You ride with him." We had talked in cell meetings about building working-class leadership.

"No way. He can't give in to me. Besides, you're the lead man now."

She was right. There was no way out of it.

When Creighton made his rounds later in the morning, I asked him why Pedro got a 3 and I got a 5.

"Those raises are supposed to be confidential." His defensiveness surprised me.

"Well, he told me."

"Look, to tell you the truth, I just can't rely on him the way I can you."

He looked puzzled, even hurt, by the fact that I was bringing this up. I almost felt sorry for him. The merit plan wasn't his idea, and like a cop who has to fill a quota of tickets, he probably had to give some 3s and some 5s. But still, it wasn't fair and he knew it.

I went on. "He trained me. Half the nurses don't call for 'Building Service,' they call for 'Pedro.'"

He tried a different tack. "There's the language problem too. He doesn't always understand me."

"He translates for doctors in emergency situations."

He was still off guard. "Well, you know and I know, he's not that strong. There are things he can't do."

That was ridiculous. He was trying to make use of the fact that Pedro had a heart murmur and had had a pacemaker installed, but that was of no consequence. We didn't do any heavy lifting. It wasn't like we were working construction. I smelled blood and decided to challenge him directly. "That's bull. I mop one day, he does trash, then we switch."

"Look, you can think what you want, but don't cuss me. It's my decision, and I've made it."

He looked at his clipboard and up at the blackboard above the nurse's station to check the discharges. In essence, I'd called him a liar, and I would be in deep shit if I pushed any harder. He wasn't going to change his mind. He couldn't. I made one last stab anyway, though I knew it was futile.

"I want you to ask Miss Smith if Pedro and I can split the difference and each get a four."

"Well, that's very noble of you," he said sarcastically, "but you've got different base pays, so it wouldn't work. I've got to get up to the sixth floor, we're stripping and waxing a room up there."

Creighton knew the merit plan was bullshit, but he also knew that I was playing the martyr and that my "4 percent compromise" was a posture. It was not so much solidarity as altruism. Noble, as he said, but hardly a threat to the status quo.

My 5 percent and Pedro's 3 percent stood, but discontent with the merit plan spread. Our communist cell met and decided it was time to pull the small secret departmental groups together into one big meeting of all union supporters.

Planning for the big meeting energized the departmental committees. No longer were they just gripe sessions, now they were planning sessions—who would invite whom to the big meeting, who should speak at it, what they should say, how to follow up, refreshments, songs, rides.

The night finally came. I even bought a new shirt for it—a conservative plaid button-down I ordered from L. L. Bean. Pedro wore a sport coat. Theresa had on a red flowered dress with padded shoulders. She had dyed the skunk stripe that reappeared every other month along the part in her hair. I had been talking to the two of them about the drive for months, but this was the first meeting for both of them. Because Theresa was from South Boston and rode to work with Creighton, some of the Black women were uneasy with her presence, but Pedro stuck right with her while people arrived. Finally, a Trinidadian woman named Julie, who was a maid in the OR, made a point of coming over to talk to the two of them.

There were over a hundred people in the union hall that night. The room was adjacent to a set of offices on the sixth floor of a building overlooking the Boston Common. Some of the people had to sit on windowsills or stand along the sides of the room. Departmental committees gave progress reports. Some young white guys from central supply performed a skit that mocked an especially hated supervisor and included some slightly off-color bedpan jokes. The staff organizer from the union explained the election process and told us about the raises and benefits that unionized workers had been able to negotiate in other cities. A nurse and a secretary both spoke against the merit plan, and finally, Sylvia Vales, a Jamaican woman who had helped organize the big hotels in Kingston and Montego Bay and who had been a traveling speaker for the Salvation Army in the Caribbean, delivered the grand finale. She gave us a rousing vision of struggle and turmoil, full of call and response. She described the travail ahead. She took us through the land of frogs and snakes, through the parted waters, and on to victory.

But it wasn't to be. The hospital dropped the merit plan, gave a Christmas bonus, and set up a committee to investigate the feasibility of a dental plan. But while they dangled these carrots, they also dropped a big stick. We had known all along that they had a union-busting outfit from Chicago on retainer, but now they brought these consultants in full-time and gave them full rein. These "experts" met with supervisors in key departments such as building service and dietary, demanding profiles of every worker. They found out who had a drinking problem, who had dated a foreman, who talked back. At great risk, a friendly supervisor who worked nights in the OR kept us briefed on these meetings, which must have been like the flip side of our BOC cell meetings. Soon, union activists started to receive trumped-up warnings. Supervisors began sitting with workers at break time. The specter of affirmative action and lost jobs was injected into the all-white maintenance shops. Some workers who had been involved in the drive from the start began to miss meetings. Even people who weren't BOC members were red-baited. Some of our key young nurses took better jobs in suburban hospitals.

At the same time, the union's Washington office was impatient. They had a lot of staff and resources tied up in the drive, and wanted to go ahead and petition the National Labor Relations Board for an election. We tried to get the necessary cards signed, but the hospital was ready for us. Workers got letters with their paychecks warning them about exorbitant dues and undemocratic union bosses. From past experience the union said they would not petition for an election unless at least 65 percent of the potential bargaining unit signed show-of-interest cards. The union said we could expect delays, as appeals would be filed by the hospital's lawyers once we petitioned for the election, and that there would be additional intimidation tactics leading to 10–12 percent attrition in support during that period. Mass General now had the offensive. We couldn't get even 40 percent of the cards signed, and so the union withdrew its support. We never even had the election.

I stayed at the hospital for five more years, while the BOC and the new communist movement cannibalized themselves in internal debates. Then, in 1985, I finally left the hospital and moved back to Indiana to teach high school.

Marx adopted the proverb, "The way to Hell is paved with good intentions," and most everybody would still say he was right. But were my intentions even good? I think so. I wanted to have the answers that Marxism-Leninism seemed to provide and socialism seemed to promise. I wanted to be a part of the world's turn toward its new future. But if all that sounds grandiose, I was also pissed off on the day-to-day level. Creighton was unfair, and the union busters were scum, bullies who played on people's fears. By leaving my class, if only for a while, I learned lessons that can be learned no other way. I learned what it is like to become invisible because your uniform is blue. I learned that a 3 percent raise has more to do with self-esteem than with dollars.

When I finally decided to leave the hospital and move back to the Midwest, I thought that perhaps the race baiters and red baiters in the MGH personnel office had been right when they had said, "Ned's an outsider. He's not one of you." I felt that the East had beaten me and that I was copping out. While at the hospital I always had a safety net that the people I worked with didn't have—I was white, male, middle-class, and college-educated. Sometimes I still feel guilty and buy into that "outside agitator" slur. In such moments, I sum up my nine years at the hospital as petit bourgeois tourism, an extended posture, just something I could write about later. Connected to this self-doubt are bigger questions. Just as 1968 changed everything for my generation, so now have 1989 and 1991. The collapse of Eastern Europe and then the Soviet Union have forced us to question socialism in a new and unavoidable way. Scientific socialism is no longer scientific. At the very moment when I was questioning my time at Mass General and asking "What went wrong?" and "What next?" history forced me to ask those same questions about socialism. I spent almost ten years as a communist organizer, and so take personally the smug "I told you sos" of Bush and Reagan.

I still believe in socialism, because for me the socialist vision is one of peace, opportunity, and equality. To me, it is still the only vision that is hopeful and makes sense, and it has as much to do with fishes and loaves as a chicken in every pot, as much with Thomas Paine and Harriet Tubman as with Marx and Engels.

But the questions don't go away. They squat in the corner instead, like hobgoblins, no less scary for being theoretical. Can socialism be made to work? Can people learn to put cooperation ahead of competition? Such questions can get away from you. If they are posed too theoretically, they can move far from one's own experience and memories and fly out of control. I try instead to keep them concrete and personal, as concrete and personal as they must be for the people of Romania and Russia, for the people I worked with at Mass General. At the same time that I ask these bigger questions, I also ask myself, "What can I learn from my time at Mass General?," "What do I do now?," "When and where do I get involved?," and "How do I make my own work meaningful?"

Sometimes I think of Mass General as my *Down and Out in Paris and London*, a time in my life I want to remember as a kind of reality test, as George Orwell remembered his time in the sick ward and on the streets. I try to write and teach for the right reasons, to live a life that bespeaks a unity of motive and effect. I went to Mass General as a janitor and tried to "proletarianize," just as Orwell "went on the bum," but it is not enough to go through the looking glass and come back out each night. The struggle is to accept one's self and one's limits while pushing to extend beyond them. This feels contradictory, but as far as I have found, it is the only way forward.

It's fashionable now (as it was when Orwell published *Animal Farm*, as it was at the time of the Hitler-Stalin pact, and at the time of the Twentieth Party Congress) for leftist intellectuals to bail out and then swing the other way, to talk with rediscovered certainty about "material incentives," "profits," and "pragmatism." There is nothing wrong with pragmatism, if it means realism, but too often it means endorsing capitalism as it is. In 1992, Richard Rorty, who was the leading neopragmatist of the time, wrote in a *Yale Review* article titled "The Intellectuals at the End of Socialism" that "Western left intellectuals" must accept the fact that "bourgeois democratic welfare states are the best we can envisage," and that one must be willing to "concede that you need capitalism to ensure a reliable supply of goods and services, and to ensure that there will be enough taxable surplus left over to finance social welfare. The only hope for getting the money necessary to eliminate intolerable inequities is to facilitate the activities of people like Henry Ford and Steve Jobs, and even Donald Trump and Armand Hammer." He might add H. Ross Perot to his list, I suppose. Lots of people have conceded that capitalism is the best we can do, but I can't accept that the incentives necessary to prime the pump must include the possibility of becoming a billionaire.

Marx also wrote that the ideas of the ruling class are ever the ruling ideas of the age. Rorty may find it hard to "envisage" anything more than a "bourgeois democratic welfare state," but we must. We must do more than rationalize capitalism for the likes of Donald

Trump. It is time once again to buck up and remember what a classless society might look like.

I'm not sure how much we have been cheapened by leaders who, to quote George H. W. Bush, speak of the "vision thing." There is a difference between dreams and visions. If you sit high on the hill next to your pool and behind your security gates, L.A. (or Bucharest) is a bad dream. But if you are poor and exploited, your one privilege might be a vision of a better future. "From each according to their own and to each according to their needs" is not around the corner, and the Soviets were liars to say so, but in the context of Mass General, my 3 percent and Pedro's 5 percent was an "intolerable inequity," and in the context of our "bourgeois democratic welfare state," the difference between what you and I make and what Trump or Perot takes home is intolerable and not, as Rorty argues, "necessary."

Socialism (like capitalism) is, on one level, a theoretical construct. As such, it can easily be watered down into a term like "pragmatism." It can become airy and useless if not grounded in the experience of people's lives. Certainly, distortions and lies have robbed the word of much of its meaning, but if we force the issue back down to basic injustices, some of the meaning returns. Many of those who have called themselves socialists had good intentions but botched the job. Others have called themselves socialists but were opportunists and murderers who committed some of the century's worst crimes. But there are still other socialists who have waged the difficult battle to keep alive a faith in the future and a belief in equality, and in so doing, held capitalism in check. Without them, the capitalist state would long ago have jettisoned both democracy and welfare. Socialist theory remains elusive and undeveloped, and that is why a word like "pragmatism" is so easy to embrace.

The socialist vision, however, remains at the core of every struggle for peace, justice, and equality. It is the long view that motivates many small, good acts. The socialist vision is neither wrong nor outdated, and it has everything to do with why a college boy in possession of all the right words might complain (unsuccessfully) about an unfair raise. The socialist vision has to do with why, when a larger cause is at stake, a Puerto Rican janitor will stand next to his friend, an Irish woman with a funny hairdo, a penchant for gossip, and a willingness to say what is right. Then, sensing the importance of that example, a Trinidadian maid might conspicuously find her way across a crowded room to stand there with the two of them, knowing that the Irish woman can be trusted even though she carpools with a supervisor and has neighbors who throw rocks at school buses full of children.

Walking the Tracks

It is the end of May, and Elizabeth and I are taking a walk, as we do most evenings after dinner, along the railroad tracks out of town. Here, on the Indiana prairie, we can see for miles. The sun is setting behind a wall of clouds. The clouds are cumulus, heaped and boiling. A front is coming in from the northwest.

As we walk down this abandoned spur of track, I think about what I will be teaching my high school juniors tomorrow. We'll start with a minilesson on dangling modifiers but spend most of the hour on Huck Finn, and I'm not sure how to teach it. The students are tired of their small towns, and so was Huck, but their options are different from his. There's no "territory" left to "light out for." They will end up in Indianapolis, Chicago, or California, if they leave at all.

Elizabeth and I joke that these nightly walks are our "constitutionals," meant to help our digestion, and while they undoubtedly do, we know they are for our minds as much as our bodies. We grew up in Indiana, but before we met, we both lived and worked out East. I was a union organizer in Boston, Elizabeth a social worker in Virginia Beach. Three years ago, we came home to Indiana and met. On our wedding invitations we quoted *The Great Gatsby*: "So when the blue smoke of brittle leaves was in the air and the wind blew the laundry stiff on the line I decided to come back home."

While my mind wanders, I kick at the rocks and absently survey the ground. My boot hits something lighter than stone and it makes an odd, hollow click. The dry, white skull of a groundhog and part of his skeleton are scattered along the ties. He must have been killed by a fox or a hawk and then picked at by crows. How many times have I walked past here and not seen it? Tomorrow I'll bring a cigar box and gather up the bones, a prairie memento. I walk on, skipping rocks off the right-hand rail, making it ding. Elizabeth is to my left and down the embankment. She is at work with our field guide, trying to identify the new wildflowers that have appeared since last week so she can add them to her list: winter cress, crown vetch, elderberry, jimsonweed. She is tall, but the golden alexander in which she is standing is well above her waist. Her brown hair is sun-bleached. While I was poking at the bones, she put her hair up in a French braid to keep it out of her face while she bends to her flowers.

I throw a few more stones and Elizabeth makes another identification, then we leave the tracks and cross the fields, stepping deliberately over the little corn plants until we get to our destination—an abandoned silo that stands by itself like a bunker. We climb the forty-foot ladder carefully. The ladder is a series of U-shaped steel rods that run up the outside of the silo, the ends of each U embedded in the concrete. At the top we perch ourselves where we can see forever, or at least almost to Illinois. Elizabeth says what we always say, "It flattens out real nice, doesn't it?," and we laugh. The breeze gusting in ahead of a front gathers force and blows our voices away, so we just sit and look. Dust devils scurry across the field. A cat is hunting in the shadows along a fence row. Swallows and purple martins swoop below us, harvesting mosquitoes and gnats.

As the sun sets, lights come on in the farmhouses—here and there, all the way out. The closest one, maybe a half a mile from here, is the Gephart's place. Sally Gephart is in my third period journalism class. Her father farms the land between here and Little Pine Creek. I think the light I see is coming from the window above their kitchen sink. It's fluid and green, as if from an aquarium. Farther out, most of the lights are brighter and have a blue or an orange tint.

They are halogen security lights hanging from the eaves of barns or mounted on poles above gravel driveways. Some of them probably shine down onto basketball hoops. My students always ask why I left Boston for Indiana. If I could move class up here, maybe I could show them the beauty of their cornfields, train tracks, and farm lights.

The dots of light farthest away flicker and disappear and flicker on again. I imagine they are kerosene lamps setting aglow the mica windows of sod huts, or even the cooking fires at the hunting camps of the Sioux who followed the buffalo down from the Dakotas. Thickets of underbrush and scrub oak that mark the peat bogs into which mastodons stumbled and sank are disappearing now into the darkness. In the sky, Venus appears and then, one by one, the stars.

In a few minutes, we'll climb down and walk home. Perhaps, like Elizabeth and me, my students will have to leave before they can return. The past is hidden and the future is vast, but now, in the darkness, I can throw my thoughts at least a season ahead. If our summer sunsets are big and spectacular, like symphonies, in the winter they will be slow and simple, like piano music. It will snow and we will ski out across the fields and past this silo. If there is enough snow and it has drifted and crusted, we'll be able to ski right over the fences. The weeds will rattle on the snow and we'll find animal tracks—now and then the passing through of a deer or a coyote, but mostly the little busyness of rabbits and mice.

PART 2

The Edsel Farm

The ashes of my friend Brent Beebe have been scattered a few places—Massachusetts, Indiana, maybe Washington—though none in Hamilton, New York, as far as I know, but it's there on a hill behind Colgate University that I'd like to throw a handful to the wind.

My claims to upstate New York seem tenuous. I did live there once—in Canton, where the Canadian Shield juts past the Saint Lawrence into the Adirondacks—but only for a year. It is not, however, Canton during the year my wife and I taught at St. Lawrence University that defines the region for me. Instead, I think most often of Colgate and the Chenango River valley near Hamilton during the years between 1968 and 1972, when my friend Brent was a student there and I visited him regularly, and the two of us left stories and memories like so many traces of ourselves.

A place asserts itself into our lives in its own ways, depending on who we are at the time we inhabit it. Each day is a stream of impressions and experiences, but most of them fade away, then we find ourselves in love or on our own for the first time and suddenly every moment becomes charged with meaning. In an instant, our experience of the land around us fills us with the memories that make us who we are.

Brent and I grew up in an Indiana college town—West Lafayette, home of Purdue University, where both our fathers taught (his English, mine agricultural economics). West Lafayette was and is a small, stable community, and most of us had known each other since elementary school. In 1968 two of my best friends from high school and I were heading east for college. Brent was going to Colgate; his girlfriend, Mary Worth, was headed to Swarthmore; and I had gotten into Harvard. Graduating from high school and going away to college is by definition dislocating, but leaving our cozy little town to go east during the chaos that was 1968 felt especially unsettling. The spring of our last year of high school was marked by the Tet Offensive, the Soviet invasion of Czechoslovakia, the Paris uprising, protests at Columbia University, and the assassinations of Martin Luther King Jr. and Bobby Kennedy, this last occurring on the night of our commencement ceremony.

All three of us had grown up ambitious and bookish in a small but competitive high school. Mary and I were on the student council; Brent edited the literary magazine and wrote a humor column for the newspaper. We all read together, historical thrillers like *Seven Days in May* and *Fail-Safe* in junior high, and then, bored with the Ethan Fromes and Silas Marners being thrust upon us, more exotic fare during high school—the Beats, Richard Brautigan, Donald Barthelme, and D. H. Lawrence. One night, Brent and I, high on Ovid, whom we'd just been translating in Latin class, traipsed through the snow-filled ravines of Happy Hollow Park pretending we were Jason and the Argonauts.

During our four years of college we did battle not with harpies, sirens, or a Minotaur but with Nixon, McNamara, and other nightmares. In those years between the fall of 1968 and the spring of 1972, the United States invaded Cambodia, students were shot and killed at Kent State and Jackson State, the draft was reinstituted, college administration buildings were occupied, cities around the country were burned in antiwar and race riots, Woodstock exploded with music and transgression, astronauts walked on the moon, and I traveled often to visit Brent in the sleepy little upstate college town of Hamilton.

During my first semester at Harvard I played football, reread *The Great Gatsby* three times, and felt homesick. Then, in the spring, the Students for a Democratic Society occupied the main administration building demanding the university kick the ROTC off campus, stop evicting working-class families from property it wanted to develop, and create a Black studies program. A mixture of solidarity and curiosity took me into the building for a few hours that afternoon, but I was asleep in my dorm room the next morning when the Cambridge police, called in by the Harvard administration and brimming with longtime town-grown resentment, stormed the building, clubbed the occupying students, and bounced them down the steps to paddy wagons, arresting over two hundred and injuring thirty-seven. Campus reaction to the bust was swift. Ten thousand students, faculty, and staff met in the stadium and called a strike. I got involved, did press for a "moderate" group, and began attending society meetings.

Meanwhile, Brent had found himself in a place that was, in some sense, a step ahead of Harvard. The previous year, four days after the assassination of Martin Luther King Jr., when Brent and I were still in high school, Colgate students had had their own sit-in after some wise guy in the Sigma Nu house fired a starter pistol as two Black students walked past. Black students confronted the brothers of Sigma Nu, whose membership policies were explicitly all-white, and a few days later occupied the administration building. The faculty and student senates voted to revoke the fraternity's charter, the Colgate president negotiated a settlement, and the Black students, along with four hundred white supporters, ended their occupation.

The actions of the Colgate students were admirable, to be sure, but at Harvard we saw ourselves as the real thing—urban revolutionaries. From our ultraserious, have-you-read-Mao-for-yourself vantage point, scuffles about fraternity houses seemed quaint. During the spring of my sophomore year, thousands rioted in Harvard Square to protest Nixon's invasion of Cambodia. At first we were sitting down in the street, blocking traffic and protesting peacefully, but then some people began to throw rocks, and the police made their move. I got trapped in the crowd for a while and was hit once across the back with a billy club. In time I made it back to the safety of my dorm room, where my roommates and I took in a stranger who had been bloodied and knocked unconscious. Others stayed in the streets and fought the cops. Stores were looted, police cars were overturned and set afire, and the air was cloudy with tear gas. Over three hundred people, including fourteen policemen, sustained injuries, many of them serious.

In Hamilton, employing a calmer set of tactics, students argued that women should be admitted to Colgate, which had been all-male since its founding as a Baptist seminary in 1819. The administration experimented at first by allowing a few female transfers, and then in 1970 the school went coed.

Mary, who was still Brent's girlfriend, joined that first wave of women and transferred to Colgate her sophomore year. Over the next three years, she and Brent fought and she returned to Swarthmore; then they made up and she transferred back to Colgate. Brent had a Volkswagen bug they used to shuttle between the two schools. A spliced decal in the back window read "Swarthgate."

Visiting Colgate felt like traveling back in time to the nineteenth century, when colleges trained the sons of the well-to-do to become doctors, lawyers, or ministers. The school called itself a university but it felt like a college, with only 1,800 students, almost all of them white men. Harvard, of course, was also brimming with blue blood. When I got a work-study job as a janitor at the end of freshman year, for instance, each Wednesday I cleaned the bathrooms of William Randolph Hearst III and Joseph Pulitzer IV, both of whom lived in the dorm where I worked. But Harvard really was a university. It had graduate programs and professional schools, was in a city, and had admitted women since 1879 (though there were still only a fifth as many women as men and some old Harvard men may still have considered Radcliffe "the annex").

During Brent's first year at Colgate he lived in West Hall. It was the oldest building on campus, built with stone quarried by faculty and students in 1827. His roommate was a redheaded guy named Rick Everett from New Jersey, with a bushy mustache and a pack of Camels. Rick, it turned out, was a distant relative of Edward Everett, the senator (and Harvard president) who delivered the long, boring speech that preceded Lincoln's address at Gettysburg. Brent and Rick's room overlooked the main quadrangle, kitty-corner from the chapel.

Once, in October, when I visited Colgate, Brent took me to see where the quadrangle's stone had come from. The quarry, he promised, "was full, *full*, of fossils." It was also small, at least by Indiana standards—just a big room, really, maybe the size of a high school gymnasium with one wall left open. The quarries in southern Indiana were much bigger—huge in fact. After they had supplied the stone for the Pentagon or the Empire State Building, these holes filled with green water and became gigantic rectangular lakes. Their bottoms supposedly hid the bodies of murder victims in stolen cars, and their cliffs seemed to kill a drunken, high-diving teenager every summer. The Colgate quarry was small, crumbling and old by comparison, its floor littered with broken flagstones—blue-black shale and gray limestone.

Brent had admitted to me earlier that he'd had no idea where he wanted to go to college and had put off applying anywhere. Alarmed, his dad had finally taken matters into his own hands. Brent had been born in Ithaca when his father was finishing his PhD at Cornell, and now his dad, moved perhaps by fond memories of that time in his life, had begun to scout out liberal arts colleges in upstate New York. Cornell's application deadline had passed, but Colgate, which was being billed as a "hidden Ivy," apparently had some space left. Colgate, Brent admitted, had been a good choice—small, excellent academics, decent sports, beautiful setting.

And it was beautiful. Behind us the forest opened out from the quarry into a little meadow, and at the far edge of the meadow the Colgate ski slope dropped into the Chenago River valley. Across the valley we could see the hills beyond. Hickory, chestnut, and maple trees burned yellow, orange, and red.

Brent and I split up to look for fossils. I thought about how even as a kid Brent had been an entrepreneur, writing and selling a neighborhood newspaper to make comic book money, and later collecting fossils and geodes, which he sold to kids at school. He and another friend had searched the creek bed in Happy Hollow, where they found the fossils of ferns, snails, and, sometimes, wonderfully, a trilobite—a miraculous horseshoe crab the size of your thumbnail.

In no time I found the fossil of a complete bivalve, a little clamlike creature a couple of inches long set perfectly in a flat piece of shale, and I showed it to Brent. It was, I found out later, a brachiopod, the order Mucrospirifer to be specific. Its shell gives it away. It extends out along the hinge-line, ending in winglike points. Some people call them "butterfly shells." They were bottom-feeders, filtering water for food during the Devonian period. The layers of rock we were standing among are called the Hamilton group and date from the Devonian period. They spread horizontally across the entire upper Appalachian and vertically down through the Tully limestone, which is 350 million years old, into the Marcellus shale, which is almost 50 million years older than that. The Tully was a time of large inland lakes, when waters warmed and lost oxygen, leading some fish to develop lungs and crawl out onto the banks to breathe. They were the first vertebrates on land.

On that day when we were both young college students, Brent and I didn't know anything about the Devonian period. We knew only that the fossil I'd found was very, very old and that time was passing.

For years the fossil decorated my aquarium.

Sometimes I showed up at Colgate with one or another of my Harvard friends. We'd hitchhike across two states and arrive at all hours, having perhaps been stranded at the Rome and Verona exit of the New York thruway, where we stomped our feet in the cold and snow, sang Beatles songs, attempted to stay warm, and waited in the dark for the next ride.

During those visits I always tried to take a reading of what Brent was reading. It wasn't hard to do. He loved to talk books. "I'm taking a contemporary literature class with Fred Busch," he said one time. "He's great. He brought Ted Hughes here for a reading; after the reading, we all had a big snowball fight. Hughes seemed like a really good guy." Brent leafed through his fresh copies of Hughes's *Wodwo* and *Crow*. He exclaimed about the poems, asked me to read this one or that, and pointed to Leonard Baskin's beautifully spare illustrations. They were, he said, the kind of books he wanted to make. I'd read *Ariel* by then, knew about Sylvia Plath's suicide, and had my doubts, but I didn't know what kind of books I wanted to make or even what I wanted to do with myself, so I looked at the books, remarked on their beauty, and kept my thoughts to myself.

At about this time the content of some of Brent's reading turned religious. Though his father was an adamant atheist who groused when his second wife brought a Christmas tree into the house, Brent, like me, had always been a troubled but essentially doubting agnostic. Now he seemed to be taking a second look, apparently trying to see if he could convince himself to believe. He was reading, he said, Nikos Kazantzakis's *The Last Temptation of Christ*. I was tacking in a different direction, toward political involvement, Marxist criticism, and my own brand of atheism. Brent and I knew, without saying so, that we needed to find some common ground. We ended up talking about *The Sound and the Fury*.

At the end of that school year, our sophomore year, I hitched home to Indiana for the summer. Mary had transferred to Colgate by then and was living with Brent. I showed up at their apartment unannounced and dribbling a basketball, with a backpack on my back. Mary answered the door and screamed, "Oh my God, I can't believe it. Brent, it's Ned!" As we walked down the hall, I could see Brent smiling on the couch, books and notes scattered across the coffee table. "This is so weird," said Mary. "We're studying for a religion exam and were just talking about you. We decided your eschatological position is one of surprise." I laughed but I had no idea what she meant. When the end comes, a God in whom I don't believe is going to play tricks on me? Or am I going to play them on him?

Junior year Mary went back to Swarthmore, and Brent moved with Rick and some guys to a farm near Poolville, one valley east of the Chenango River. In the spring I hitched out to visit their weird hippie enclave. It was weird not so much because of the hippies as because of their landlord, who collected Ford Edsels. There were Edsels in the barn, Edsels in the front pasture, Edsels under the trees in the side yard. Two-tone Edsels. Edsels with white sidewalls. Even a station wagon. Novelties certainly, odd and wonderful in their own way with their silly horse-collar grilles, but every one a reminder of the commercial failure the car had been; every one, it seemed to me, an eyesore turning the valley into a junkyard. There were eighteen Edsels altogether, Brent told me. Why? I asked. He didn't really know. The guy just collects them, Brent said. He doesn't sell them. He just likes them. The landlord told Brent that the ones in the barn were in pretty good shape and one day soon he was going to get them running.

Then what? I wondered.

Later that day a bunch of Colgate guys drove out to the Edsel farm to enjoy the first stirrings of spring. After a few joints, we clambered up the bluff behind the farmhouse and on top we played touch football in a field by an apple orchard. We joked that our two teams belonged to the Mohawk Valley League. After the game, as we were walking back across the field, one of the guys from the other team came up behind me, slapped me on the back, and said, "Number twenty-seven? Hey, good game." He stuck out his hand. I took it straight-faced, nodded, and shook it. "You too," I said and we both laughed. We might have had long hair and John Lennon glasses, but underneath it was still Friday night, the cheerleaders were cheering, and we could smell the popcorn at the concession stand.

Later, Brent and I had a beer, just the two of us on his front porch. Getting out of town to the farm had seemed like the right idea, he said, but the winter had been relentless and now they were short a roommate—a guy I had known only by the name of Doc. He had been there when I had visited back in the fall, but he wasn't there now. During that first visit, the Dave Mason album *Alone Together* had just come out. It was a good album—Mason, formerly of Traffic, would soon be popping up everywhere: George Harrison's Bangladesh concert, Derek and the Dominos, Fleetwood Mac—but I remembered thinking at the time that Doc was going overboard about it. This album is important, Doc told Brent and me several times. This album is going to change everything. I didn't know then that it was his mental illness talking.

Brent took another drink from his bottle of Genesee. "He started eating acid like candy. He took it every day. Wanted us to take it with him. When he did go to classes, he insisted on walking, snowshoeing across that field and then across a bunch more after that. It's six miles to Colgate from here. Then he decided we all rely too much on our sense of sight and he started to snowshoe blindfolded. He never slept. We had to call his parents."

Brent looked across the road toward the field on the other side and sat silent for a while. I could tell that he still felt guilty and disloyal, but I didn't say anything. No one could know how cold and dark the winter had been in that farmhouse. I looked at the weird yard in front of us with all its abandoned Edsels, thinking that they probably hadn't helped the situation.

I wasn't really sure what Doc's situation had been, but I knew Brent's situation. His own relationship with Mary was falling apart, and his father and stepmother were divorcing.

On February 20, 1969, two days before my nineteenth birthday, when Brent and I were halfway through our freshman years in college, Denny Cripe, the older brother of our high school friend and classmate Larry Cripe, was killed in Vietnam. Denny, who was a year ahead of us, had been a lance corporal in the marines and in Vietnam only a short time. All four of us had played high school football together—Larry, Denny, Brent, and me. Sophomore year, I played defensive end, and Denny played next to me at tackle. We had to work together, callings stunts and reads, different defensive sets.

The season had started poorly, with some losses, but we won our last four games to pull out a winning record and begin what would be a sixteen-game unbeaten streak. Denny won the Most Improved Player Award.

I was against the war when Denny was killed, which seemed at the time to make it all that much harder to write the letter I wrote to Larry and his parents, but I don't know that it really did. How I felt about the war didn't affect how I felt about Denny and his family.

Brent wouldn't have written a letter, I don't think. He called himself shy, and maybe he was, but he was also careful and hid his emotions. His mother had left their family one afternoon when Brent was in fourth grade. She ran away with a graduate student she'd met doing theatre at Purdue. I don't know if Brent's dad saw it coming, but it definitely blindsided Brent and his two younger brothers. Brent's dad drank. He may have drunk before, and that may have led to the split up, I don't know, but when we were in high school, he definitely drank.

Brent and I were lucky to go away to school, to have draft deferments, to be able to grow our hair long and study what we wanted. But we didn't always feel lucky. My own parents were getting a divorce and I'd had to adjust to Cambridge, with its crowded streets and old money. Brent had to deal with Hamilton—the claustrophobia and long winters. We both broke up with girlfriends, had to pick majors and think about the future, and, during exam week, pull all-nighters, but finally we were lucky, and when we sat in our respective libraries and read the books that were important to us, I think we knew on some level just how lucky we were.

Brent and I grew up playing football together, but we also grew up playing golf. In the summer we played almost every day on the Purdue South, one of the university's two courses, so it shouldn't have surprised me during our senior year of college when Brent told me over the phone that he, Rick, and some other guys had started playing golf again, but it did. He must have known I was surprised because he said, "I can't believe it. The Colgate course was right here the whole time. I don't know what was wrong with us. It's beautiful—a Robert Trent Jones course. Water on twelve holes, big greens, great vistas. Rick and I are playing twice a week. And you know what? He's good."

Brent's decision to start golfing again seemed to me to mark another end to the sixties, which, at least since college had started, had not been about golf. They were instead about stopping the war and winning the future, or at least about going to Woodstock, which Brent and Mary had done, or driving out west in a converted school bus and limping back home in a VW bug, which all three of us had done. But if I disapproved a bit when Brent told me he was playing again, that disapproval was tempered with envy. I liked to golf and remembered a remark made by a friend of ours back in high school. This friend, himself an excellent golfer but also budding hippie, had said, "It's only a bourgeois sport if you're thinking bourgeois thoughts while you play it." I wanted to believe that, but it felt like an idealist error, and by now I was a Marxist.

Robert Trent Jones Sr. was born in England and grew up in Rochester, New York. An excellent golfer, he graduated from Cornell in 1930. While there he decided he wanted to design golf courses and put together his own course of study, taking classes in landscape architecture, agronomy, horticulture, surveying, and economics. Widely considered the greatest American golf course architect, Jones eventually designed or redesigned many of the country's championship courses, including Oakland Hills, Baltusrol-Lower Course, Southern Hills, Oak Hill, Congressional, and Augusta National. His sons Rees and Robert Jr. also became noted golf course architects.

One of Trent Jones Sr.'s first commissions was the Colgate course, which was named Seven Oaks after the English ancestral home of William Colgate, the soap manufacturer, Baptist deacon, and benefactor of the university that took his name. Jones designed the course in 1934, but a shortage of funds during the Depression kept the course from being built until 1954.

The last time I visited Brent at Colgate was at Rick and Mary's wedding. During the final unraveling of Brent and Mary's relationship, Rick and Mary had fallen in love. They were already close friends, of course, from all that time spent together, but this new development surprised me. I think it surprised them. When I asked her how it happened, Mary said simply, "He's always been kind to me."

By the time of the wedding, Brent was already with a Colgate woman named Kathleen. Both couples had graduated but were still hanging around Hamilton, negotiating the new alignments, and figuring out what was next. Before long, Brent and Kathleen headed out to the Pacific Northwest, where Brent's father had grown up and Brent had spent summers as a boy. Brent went to architecture school and then dropped out to start his own carpentry business, which he called Wodwo Productions. He and Kathleen broke up, and he met and married his second wife, Penny, and finally landed in Wisconsin, where he designed and built houses, including a beautiful one in a small valley outside the town of Barneveld. He and Penny had two children, a daughter and a son. Late one night in 1984 Barneveld was hit by an F5 tornado. It killed 9 people and injured 200 out of a population of 580. Brent, a carpenter, and Penny, a psychologist, helped rebuild the town.

I came back to the Midwest from Boston fairly often to visit, varying my route through upstate New York so I could bring Brent a new story about the area where he had lived and I had visited. Once I stopped in Hamilton and played Seven Oaks. Another time, I visited the Baseball Hall of Fame in Cooperstown. I went to the Museum of Waterways and Industry and the Women's Rights National Historical Park, which are both in Seneca Falls, and I drove along the shores of three of the Finger Lakes—Cayuga, Seneca, and Canandaigua.

Brent remained entrepreneurial, always willing to take a risk. I liked the security of a paycheck, so it was ironic that when I did take a risk, I had to call Brent for help. To get a job as a janitor at a big Boston hospital (where my new communist comrades and I were going to organize the unorganized) I needed to lie about Harvard and graduate school, and somehow fill in those years with something more proletarian. I called Brent to ask if I could put Wodwo Productions down on the job application. "Sure,' he said. I'm sure he was grinning. Another time, during one of my visits to Wisconsin, he was telling me about his plan to make a better golf bag. He and a friend were already looking for investors. I started to brainstorm with him—more velcro here, extra padding on the shoulder strap, maybe some Day-Glo nylon for highlights, a special pocket so you wouldn't lose your wallet and keys under the clutter of old scorecards and tees, market the whole thing with one of those little ads in the *New Yorker*. I had been going on and on. Finally, Brent smiled and said, "For a communist, you sure know how to think like a capitalist."

I laughed and said, "Well, you gotta know the enemy, and anyway, I imagine you and I will be petit bourgeois intellectuals to the end."

Barneveld, like Hamilton, was a nice place to visit. They're both at about 43 degrees north with secluded valleys and good cross-country skiing. They felt the same. Being with Brent felt the same too.

The union drive floundered and my communist organization dissolved into sectarian squabbles, so I left Boston and moved back to Indiana to get a job teaching high school and lick my wounds. It was then that I met my wife Elizabeth. She had been a social worker for six years in Virginia but was back in Indiana as well, recovering from a divorce and toying with the idea of writing fiction. Her father was an English professor at Purdue and even served a stint as editor of *Modern Fiction Studies*, the journal Brent's dad had founded thirty years earlier.

Over the next few years, Elizabeth, Brent, and I all began writing and went back to graduate school—she and I to the University of Iowa, and Brent to U Mass. Elizabeth and I had our daughters, Flannery and Phoebe, and landed our first teaching jobs at St. Lawrence University, a Colgate-like liberal arts school in upstate New York, before taking better positions at Florida State.

Brent and I drifted apart, staying in touch mainly through tongue-in-cheek holiday letters and occasional book recommendations (Richard Ford, Raymond Carver, Anne Tyler). Sometimes he'd send me something he wrote—a funny story about an imaginary round of golf with William Faulkner, a sad story about making it home too late to say goodbye to a dying father.

Our high school class has a quarterly online newsletter and each issue features a profile from one or another of us. I opened the February 2008 issue to find a profile by Brent. It was a chronology—a typically wry and honest list of accomplishments and failures, most of which I already knew about: marriage, divorce, marriage, carpentry, a son named Sam who went to Vassar and was now a song and short-story writer, a daughter named Casey who went to Evergreen College in Washington and was now married and an environmental activist, five pounds added here, five more there, starting AA, staying dry, and a plan to see us all at our fortieth reunion in the coming summer. But then it concluded with this disturbing entry: "2008 (February): found out suffered a heart attack in the past few months—oops, evidently my warning system (the suffering) is nonexistent. Quadruple bypass surgery pending *tomorrow*. Wish me luck!" The newsletter editor provided Brent's e-mail address and attached this addendum: "FYI—Brent's bypass surgery on 2/11 was successful, he is recovering in the hospital. Feel free to send him a get-well message."

I e-mailed immediately and tried to track down a phone number for the hospital, and then found out that Brent had gone into ventricular fibrillation and been flown by helicopter to a Boston hospital. He died five weeks later, having never regained consciousness.

That Brent went to school in Hamilton and brought me there with him seems, in retrospect, capricious, the result of his dad looking at the last minute for a hidden Ivy for his son, a place where Brent, now more or less on his own, might be able to figure out what to do with himself.

That Colgate was the place where Brent and I would help each other through the tumult of the sixties also seems arbitrary, and yet many of the names and stories and places that make us who we are seem arbitrary when we uncover their history. An epoch of sixty million years that is called Devonian because English geologists first hammered loose it rocks and studied them in the county of Devonshire. Layers of rocks spread across half a dozen states that is called Hamilton because of a hilltop quarry overlooking a little village named after a bastard son who became a Founding Father. A college and toothpaste named Colgate because a radical father fled imprisonment in the Tower of London and immigrated to the New World, where his son became a soap and candle maker, and made a fortune.

"Don't Be Cruel"
An Argument for Elvis

My wife Elizabeth and I went to Graceland for the first time twenty-five years ago, right after we married, and as the van took us back down the hill to the parking lot the driver asked his load of tourists if we had enjoyed our tour. One lady, a true pilgrim who had been sitting silently by herself, responded softly and immediately, "It was vury movin'." I looked at my wife and rolled my eyes.

I'm ashamed now of that response, for during the last few years I have rediscovered Elvis. Come home to the King, really. I always liked the early stuff, watched his first appearance on the Ed Sullivan show when I was a kid and the '68 Comeback Special as an adolescent, but now... well... now things are different.

It began when research for Elizabeth's most recent novel took her to Tennessee and some awful Cold War–era experiments on pregnant women at Vanderbilt. She needed the experiments, but not Nashville, and she'd been through Memphis a lot as a kid. She grew up in Indiana, and when her family went to Little Rock, where her grandmother lived, they always went through Memphis. So, being a fiction writer, she just moved the experiments from Nashville to Memphis.

Fifties. Memphis. Elvis was unavoidable, and soon we found ourselves at the annual Big E Festival in Cornelia, Georgia, with its T-shirts and "tribute artist" contest (don't call them impersonators). Then, almost before we realized what was happening, we'd visited the home place in Tupelo, begun buying CDs, watched bad movie after bad movie, put nothing but Elvis on our iPod, read and reread the biographies. But mostly we went to Memphis—a dozen times or so. Sometimes we took our daughters, sometimes Elizabeth went alone, but more often we went together—to Graceland, to the house on Audubon Drive, to Sun Studio, to Dixie Locke's house, to the band shell at Overton Park. One weekend we stayed in the Presley family's old apartment in the Lauderdale Courts.

But following Elvis around Memphis means going everywhere— to the city's blues clubs and bar-b-que joints (not the ones on the now gussied Beale Street—the real ones), record stores, the lobby of the Peabody Hotel, and Lansky's for shirts. Everywhere there is the residue of the past—a past still hoping for a future that hasn't arrived. Neon lights that seem to speak from the fifties—Prince Mongo's Planet, Walker Radiator Works, and a glowing shirt (with a bow tie) waving you into Happy Day Cleaners. Flaking painted signs on brick walls, palimpsests from another age hawking beer and tobacco products no longer available. A beauty shop that's become a restaurant called the Beauty Shop, its décor all Naugahyde and glass bricks. Sometimes, it seems, the whole city is done up in retro, right down to the Lorraine Motel—its balcony so familiar, its hopes undone.

Tad Pierson showed us a lot of this. He gives custom tours in his 1955 pink Cadillac, what he calls "anthro-tourism." He introduced us to Jimmy Denson, who grew up with Elvis in Lauderdale and whose brother, Jesse Lee, taught Elvis how to play guitar. Most of our friends think we've gone round the bend and are absolutely mondo, though one of them, the fiction writer Robert Olen Butler, gave us a beautiful portrait of Elvis made of candy wrappers and a certified piece of Elvis's hair.

I assure you there is very little irony in all this, and Bob's gifts are true sacraments, given and received as such. Yet I must admit I remain uncertain about this brave new world in which I find myself, and there are lines I still won't cross. I don't have an Elvis tattoo on my shoulder, for instance (though Elizabeth does). I believe Elvis is dead and isn't Jesus. He left the building and won't come back. And as much as I love his music, even the rhinestone ballads of the seventies, I see the skid of his last five years—the long, druggy depression after Priscilla left—as impossible to defend. Finally, however, I'm surprised at how willingly I've given myself over to the King.

I've thought a lot about the skepticism of my friends (save for Bob, who is always the enthusiast) and how in some corners of myself I share in it. I've looked hard at my residual anti-Elvisism and decided it's rooted finally in class bias. This makes sense given that most of my friends are, like me, white middle-class (or perhaps déclassé) intellectuals, who tend to sum Elvis up as white trash—rural southern white trash. "Trash," said Jim to Huck in *The Adventures of Huckleberry Finn*, when he had to set his friend straight for betraying him, "is what people is dat puts dirt on de head er dey fren's an makes 'em ashamed." Huck wasn't trash, but when he treated Jim badly, he acted like he was and that's why Jim called him out. To think you're superior in every way to a hillbilly who grilled his peanut butter sandwiches and wore rhinestone jumpsuits is a snotty attitude, and it's the attitude that was behind my eye roll on the Graceland minivan.

I want to look this attitude in the eye because it can lead to a facile dismissal of Elvis, and he should not be dismissed, for, as John Lennon famously said, "Before Elvis there was nothing." If you dismiss Elvis, you can't explore the truth behind Lennon's hyperbole. Dismiss Elvis and you cannot understand race, class, sex, and music in twentieth-century America.

I have run into several anti-Elvis responses. They are many and can seem sometimes to be shifting, veiled, and confusing, but I think they can be boiled down to the following seven:

- Elvis was dumb
- Elvis was racist, or at least a tool of racists
- Elvis was pathetic, not tragic
- Elvis sold out

- Elvis is not Sinatra, Dylan, or the Beatles (or alternately, he's not Jerry Lee Lewis, Carl Perkins, Johnny Cash, Chuck Berry, James Brown, or Little Richard)
- Elvis is for girls (or its corollary, Elvis was sexist)
- Elvis is not God

Let's begin at the beginning—*Elvis was dumb*. One of my best friends once put it to me exactly that way. She knew she was being harsh and perhaps even felt she was wrong because since then she's asked me a number of times, "Now *what* is it you like about him, exactly?" Maybe she keeps asking because I haven't explained myself well, but it's her faith in me, not in Elvis, that led her to ask in the first place. In any case, we started with the issue of Elvis's intelligence. As evidence that he was dumb, she cited a story she heard years ago from the late Mildred Dunnock, an actress who possesses—for both my friend and me—massive credentials. Dunnock was a teacher before she became an actress, received two nominations for an Oscar as Best Supporting Actress, and played Big Mama in the original Broadway production of *Cat on a Hot Tin Roof*. My friend knew her personally.

In *Love Me Tender*, the Civil War drama that was Elvis's first movie, Dunnock played Martha Reno. Elvis was Clint Reno, the youngest of Martha's four sons and the only one who doesn't go off to war. Dunnock told my friend (herself an accomplished playwright who attended the Yale School of Drama) that in one scene her character said to Elvis, "Put that gun down, son," and though he wasn't supposed to, he did. The director fumed and Elvis apologized. My friend saw the mistake as confirmation that Elvis was lacking and just didn't get it, but when Dunnock told the story to Peter Guralnick, Presley's biographer, she added, "For the first time in the whole thing he had heard me, and he believed me. Before, he'd just been thinking what he was doing and how he was going to do it. I think it's a funny story. I also think it's a story about a beginner who had one of the essentials of acting, which is to believe."

Flubbing the scene with Dunnock might have been an instance of method acting gone wrong, or, as some on the set suspected, maybe

Elvis was just fooling with the director, who had been emphasizing motivation, but in either case, I don't think it confirms stupidity. Our tendency to sum him up as dumb is, I think, a comment on us, a result of not recognizing the varieties of intelligence and of confusing intelligence with education or experience.

Sam Phillips, the founder of Sun Records, who (along with his assistant, Marion Keisker) discovered Elvis, was unequivocal about these kinds of errors. Phillips had been looking for a singer who possessed an understanding of southern music and its roots, or, as he put it, an understanding of "the elements of the soil, the sky, the water, even the wind, the quiet nights, people living on plantations, never out of debt, hoping to eat, lights up the river—that's what they used to call Memphis. That was where it all came together. And Elvis Presley may not have been able to verbalize all that—but he damn sure wasn't dumb, and he damn sure was intuitive, and he damn sure had an appreciation for the total spirituality of the human existence, even if he would never have thought of the term. That was what he cared about."

Whether Elvis understood the South and "the total spirituality of the human existence" brings us to the second response I've run into with regularity: *Elvis was racist, or at least a tool of racists.* Chuck D of Public Enemy put this case most plainly in "Fight the Power," the anthem that runs through Spike Lee's *Do the Right Thing*, when he refers to Elvis as a "straight up racist," along with John Wayne. My white friends soften this criticism a bit. "Elvis was just singing blues," they say. "Black artists like Chuck Berry and Little Richard were there first."

Well, yes and no. Even Chuck D circled back to explain that it wasn't Elvis he was after but the white power that crowned Elvis king, thereby whitewashing rock history. "Elvis' icon status in America," he explained in a 2002 *Newsday* interview, "made it like nobody else counted."

For his part, Sam Phillips believed rockabilly and blues came from the same place, and that both forms of music celebrated individualism and rebellion, as well as the possibility of integration and equality. Phillips produced Elvis Presley and Johnny Cash but also

B. B. King and Rufus Thomas. For him, crossover acts were about making a living *and* making a change.

It's this mixing of money and politics that's confusing, and leads many to the claim that Elvis is merely derivative and lucky—lucky to be born white. To his detractors Elvis was not an original talent who synthesized gospel, rockabilly, and blues into a new thing called rock 'n' roll so much as he was just Sam Phillips's tool, one more greaser with a guitar, lucky in a way that Carl Perkins, for instance, was not. The real innovators were the African American blues musicians whom Phillips robbed and Presley copied.

In her story "Nineteen Fifty-Five," Alice Walker creates a young, white character named Traynor who becomes rich and famous recording songs written by an older Black woman named Gracie Mae Still. Still is clearly based on Willie Mae "Big Mama" Thornton, whose 1953 hit "Hound Dog" Elvis covered with astronomical success in 1956. Feeling empty and guilty, Traynor returns to Grace Mae Still time and again ("hounding" her as it were) in search of answers, because, as he admits, "I don't have the faintest notion of what that song means."

This short summary of Walker's story cannot do it justice (you should read it yourself), and certainly there's a critique to be made of racism in America and its music industry, but the implication that Elvis (as Traynor) did not have the "faintest notion" of what he was singing about is wrong.

"Hound Dog" is often cited as a gross example of the way in which white artists and producers have ripped off Black artists, but the real history of the song complicates that interpretation. Jerry Leiber and Mike Stoller, two Jewish teenagers from Los Angeles, wrote the song, or at least the law says they did. They were working at the time for Big Mama Thornton's Greek American bandleader, Johnny Otis (formerly Yannis Veliotes), providing him with material and even producing a few of his sessions. Otis liked "Hound Dog" and proposed some changes, and Thornton may have as well. When the record came out, Otis shared the rights with Leiber and Stoller, who, because they were both nineteen at the time, had to have their mothers sign the contracts for them. Thornton's record took off, topping *Billboard*'s "Rhythm and Blues" chart for several weeks, and was covered that same year by five other artists, but when Elvis's version exploded three years later, Leiber and Stoller took Otis to court and won sole rights to the song.

Elvis was familiar with Thornton's record, but even more taken with a version done by Freddy Bell and the Bellboys, whom he heard in the lounge at the Sands during his first visit to Las Vegas in April and May 1956. Their "Hound Dog" was more up-tempo and less growly than Thornton's, and Bell (aka Ferdinando Dominick Bello) had added the lyric "You ain't never caught a rabbit / You ain't no friend of mine." Elvis and his band, the Blue Moon Boys, liked the song and put it into their repertoire as a novelty number they figured might work well on stage. Of the Bellboys' version, Scotty Moore said, "We stole it straight from them," though Moore soon added a modest guitar solo and D. J. Fontana put in a little drum roll between verses. Elvis himself added new inflections and, of course, the bump and grind that got him into trouble when he performed the song on the *Milton Berle Show* later that summer.

By the fall of 1956 Elvis was a national phenomenon, and when he returned to Vegas in November he found that now he was being copied. Jackie Wilson had recently replaced Clyde McPhatter as lead singer for Billy Ward and the Dominoes, and Ward's band did an Elvis medley as part of its act. Elvis was especially taken with the way Wilson sang "Don't Be Cruel," and he went back four nights in a row to catch the act. Elvis was famously caught on tape recounting the experience to Carl Perkins and Jerry Lee Lewis during the Million Dollar Quartet session. He didn't know Wilson's name at the time, but says the "colored guy" was "doing a take off of me. He tried real hard 'till he got much better, boy, much better than that record of mine.... Man, he sung the hell outta that song. I was under the table, looking at him, [thinking] 'Get him off, get him off!'" From then on, when Elvis did "Don't Be Cruel," he did Jackie Wilson doing Elvis, slowing it down, making it bluesy, and adding Wilson's footwork and his pronunciation of "tellyphone."

When we talk about high art, we use terms like "intertextuality," "appropriation," and "anxiety of influence," but with popular music, similar processes are disparaged as "covering," "copying," and "doing knockoffs." T. S. Eliot's comparison in *The Sacred Wood* of the forgotten Philip Massinger to Shakespeare, for instance, is memorable for its unusual candor. "Immature poets imitate," said Eliot, "mature poets steal."

This question of maturity brings us to the third of our seven complaints: *Elvis was pathetic, not tragic*. Maybe the kind of stealing Elvis did was artistic and, in Eliot's sense, figurative, but Colonel Tom Parker was quite literally a thief. In the paternalistic turn the anti-Elvis argument takes at this point, Elvis may have been getting rich, but he can't be really held accountable for the way in which the lucre was acquired or the decadence it led to because he was passive and naive, a pawn in the Colonel's game. Or if he wasn't passive, we slide into the fourth complaint, namely that *Elvis sold out*. I have a lot of unity with both of these positions. Sometimes I get mad at Elvis. Why did you waste a decade on those shitty movies? Why the sappy Glen Campbell ballads of the seventies? Why the deadly cycle of extravagant spending and endless touring? Why all the drugs and the sordid bathroom overdose? Why the jumpsuits? Why, Elvis, why?

Sometimes this downfall problem is posed as early Elvis versus late Elvis. "Oh, yeah," my friends say, "I like the early stuff—*Elvis '56*, even the Comeback Special—but when he gets to Vegas and starts all that karate posing, it's all over for me." The problem with this thinking is that it leads almost invariably to a summing up of Elvis in terms of his last five years and even a simplifying of that time. Most tribute artists, for instance, wear the rhinestones, scarves, and TCB sunglasses of the last years instead of the gold lamé of the early years or the black leather of '68. Maybe this is because so many of them are overweight and middle-aged. Jumpsuits are more flattering.

The real problem, it seems to me, is not the wardrobe but rather that Elvis was caught between generations. He'd be seventy-seven now and was always closer in age to the parents of the baby boomers than to the baby boomers themselves. This in-betweenness always presented problems in career trajectory and repertoire. You can feel the dilemma in the Nashville sessions Elvis did right after coming back from the army. These sessions were great but uneven. They generated an odd run of singles as well as the album *Elvis Is Back!* The sessions took place on March 20 and April 3, 1960, and include a weird and wonderful potpourri of songs: Leiber and Stoller's rocking "Dirty, Dirty Feeling"; the lilting and suggestive "Such a Night"; the doo-woppy ballad "Fame and Fortune"; a sweet cover of The Shirelles's swoon song "Soldier Boy"; but also the sappy "Are You Lonesome Tonight?" and the grandiose "It's Now or Never," which was a rewrite of "O Sole Mio." It's a schizophrenic album—part Vegas lounge act, part Beale Street blues club, part Jersey street corner or stoop.

The Colonel knew that some of the core audience of bobby-soxers had grown up while Elvis was in Germany, and he was worried about what would happen after the layoff. Could Elvis come back or would he be just another teenage sensation, doomed to fade away as Frankie Avalon and Fabian were already beginning to fade away?

His answer to the problem was eclecticism, which held the potential of broad and lasting appeal but also the danger of leaving no one fully satisfied. Elvis needed little convincing, however. His first loves were blues, gospel, and rockabilly, but another part of him had always wanted to be Dean Martin or even Mario Lanza. The Colonel booked a guest spot for him on a Frank Sinatra special that was shot in Miami. Elvis and Frank both wore tuxedoes and shape-shifted into each other. Sinatra sang "Love Me Tender"; Elvis did "Witchcraft."

I graduated from college in 1972, and when I outed myself as an Elvis freak on the Class of '72 listserv, one of my best friends on the list, who is now a television writer in Hollywood, connected this generational problem to the downfall problem quite neatly. We came of age with the Beatles, he said, while Elvis was basically (and embarrassingly) a part of his older sister's world, but even more crucially, for him, Elvis couldn't say no. He let the Colonel plot the course and it finally killed him. Sinatra survived, my friend reminded me, partly because he liked booze better than drugs, but also because he possessed a more vicious ambition and tighter focus than did Elvis.

Here the Elvis-was-pathetic response and the Elvis-sold-out response begin to morph into the complaint that *Elvis is not Sinatra, Dylan, the Beatles, or somebody else*. Another friend expressed his surprise about my Elvis love by remarking, "I'd always thought you were more a Beatles guy." There is truth to that (I saw them live at the Indiana State Fair in 1964) and my immediate response was that I can be both (and that I can also like Dylan and Sinatra), but after I sat on it a bit, I realized that was an easy answer. I gave it in part because I think Elvis recorded plenty of good material after 1968—the Memphis sessions, for instance, but also the early Vegas performances collected on *Elvis—That's the Way It Is*. I do think rock singers should be leery about doing albums of standards. Witness what has happened to Rod Stewart. That way can lead to Barry Manilow, Wayne Newton, or even—heaven forbid—Engelbert Humperdinck. But Elvis always made blues a part of his Vegas shows. "Suspicious Minds," "In the Ghetto," "Patch It Up," and "Polk Salad Annie" are great; so are neglected treasures such as "Wearin' That Loved on Look" and "Long Black Limousine."

What concerned me more, however, was why my friends felt—why in part I still felt—the need to choose Elvis over the Beatles or Sinatra or Dylan. The choice is a false one. It is also unfair—unfair because it is based, often at least, on the assumption that there is but one Elvis—sequined jumpsuit Elvis—but many versions of the others. We parse those artists—preferring *Rubber Soul* to *Revolver*, rhapsodizing about the Capitol sessions, continuing to argue about the electrification at Newport in 1965.

The reason for this, I think, has to do once again with the belief that Elvis was passive and without irony, or, less kindly, that he was stupid, at best naive. The others, we say, were not. Dylan was a smart middle-class Jewish kid who wrote his own stuff and bowled over the New York folk scene in the course of a single summer. Sinatra may have been, like Elvis, working-class and "merely" an interpreter, but he was also urban, street-smart, worldly wise, or even a wise guy. The Beatles too were working-class, or so John claimed, though I think when he says "A working class hero is something to be / If you want to be a hero well just follow me," he doth protest too much. His Aunt Mimi's house, where John lived from the age of six and in which he first heard Elvis records, was decidedly middle-class. Paul, George, and Ringo were more thoroughly working-class, but, like Sinatra, all the Beatles were urban and hip. They were also English, and versed in music hall parody and a distinctly British brand of art school Wildean wit. In addition, Sinatra had the Rat Pack, and the Beatles had each other—cohorts with whom they could work up banter and routines. Elvis had to go it alone (or essentially alone—the Colonel was neither collaborator nor buddy, and the bands were always backup bands). Hell, he had to hire the Memphis Mafia just to have "friends."

Elvis was a polite Christian boy, an only child from Tupelo; smart aleck wasn't really what he did. He was, as Jimmy Denson told me over and over, a momma's boy, a sissy. He looked like a greaser and he knew he was sexy, but he was always more comfortable singing in a gospel quartet, and part of him longed for the early days when he, Scotty, Bill, and DJ were a unit.

Keith Richards said all those other boys (by whom he meant Mick) wanted to be Elvis, but he wanted to be Scotty Moore—sideman to the boy singer. According to Scotty's 1997 autobiography, *That's Alright, Elvis*, when he and Keith met at Levon Helm's studio in Woodstock in 1996, "Keith pointed out that they both had worked with front men their entire careers, [and] his front man was still alive. 'What's his name?' asked Scotty, a glint in his eye. 'I don't remember,' deadpanned Keith. Then, after a pause, he added with a hint of resignation in his voice; 'We all need one man.'" If the rewards are greater for the front man, so are the pressures, which is why Elvis claimed to the end he wanted to be Jake Hess of the Statesmen, or even just a soloist at his mom's Assembly of God church. Of course, fame, which he also wanted, took that dream away. No one can be anyone else, but Elvis perhaps did not even get to be himself.

Which brings us to our last two complaints: *Elvis is for girls* and *Elvis is not God*. It's true that Elvis was a mama's boy. Gladys invested everything, too much perhaps, in this boy whose identical twin was stillborn. She convinced Elvis he had special powers and a special calling. Within that intense relationship, as Elaine Dundy and others have shown, Elvis developed the potent mix of responsiveness and confidence he projected onstage. Men want to be wanted by women in the way Elvis was wanted by women, but they don't want to have to act the way he acted—all that flamboyance, vulnerability, and showiness. The pink-and-black pants, the sideburns and hair, the pouty lips, the eyeliner, the dancing—it's all too ambiguous and too geared to please women, women who know your secrets, women who will take you in, women who will mother you. If you're not careful, you find that you're Liberace playing to tables full of blue-haired old ladies under a tent on Cape Cod.

Elvis was not gay and so remains threatening in a different way as well. The squealing teenagers are grandmothers now, and in my experience men still feel the need to mock women's devotion to the King. One colleague told me that he had found out Elvis had died from the lady working behind the counter when he picked up his dry cleaning. Her face was tortured with pain, he said, and then he rolled his eyes just as I rolled mine at Graceland twenty-five years ago. A friend of my wife's warned her that this Elvis obsession meant she was just reliving her youth, trying to be a teenager again. One of my friends told me how his mother, who had seen Elvis several times in Vegas, dragged him to one of the farewell concerts in the summer of 1977. He went but found it silly. Boiled down to its ugly essence, the underlying theme in these dismissals, including my own that day in the minivan, is that Elvis is really meant for dumb, white, southern chicks.

"Yes, I'm gonna tell my mother howdy when I get home," sang Elvis in the gospel number "Milky White Way," and I hope he has, though I don't believe in heaven and so don't think he and Gladys are up there. When I tell my sophisticated friends that I'm making yet another trip to Memphis or just read another Elvis book, I joke as I did at the outset of this piece that there are lines I still won't cross, about how I don't think Elvis is God. I mean to let them know that I've retained some skepticism and have inoculated myself with irony, but I can tell they're worried.

They needn't be. I'm just trying to move closer to Elvis in order to move further away from Martin Amis, who when it was suggested to him that Elvis was complicated, was even a paradox, replied, "Oh no he wasn't. Indeed, in the circumstances it is hard to imagine a character of more supercharged banality. Elvis was a talented hick destroyed by success: what else is new? All that distinguished him was the full-blooded alacrity of his submission to drugs, women, money and megalomania, and the ease with which these excesses co-existed with his natural taste for spiritual conceit and grandiose Confederate *machismo*."

Well, there you have it, all seven forms of resistance tied up in one neat paragraph, a human being as the sum of his weaknesses, his strengths and his accomplishments ignored. I'm not here to condone the Jungle Room, the gun collections, or the womanizing, the lost way, and certainly not the sorry end on the bathroom floor, but I do think Elvis was anything but banal. If you dismiss him as trash, you can't understand what he brought to America—sexuality and a release from the buttoned-down world of the 1950s, certainly, but something more, a new kind of music and a voice that recovered lost emotions, celebrated submerged cultures, and took us toward possibilities we had forgotten or never known, toward Memphis, toward the "lights up the river."

Thank You, Jon Gnagy

Growing up in the early 1960s I watched a Saturday morning television show called *Learn to Draw*, hosted by a man named Jon Gnagy. He sported a neatly trimmed Vandyke, exuded a comforting mix of calm and enthusiasm, and was artistic but not too artsy. Each show he taught us how to draw something new: a clown, a snow scene, or an ocean liner at dock. His hands flew as shapes and outlines turned magically into pictures. He laid the chalk on its side to achieve "effects" and talked continuously, identifying the light source and explaining the vanishing point.

I tried to keep up but never could. At the end of each show, Gnagy would slap a frame on his drawing and declare it done, but I had to keep going, working on my version of "Mountain Lake" or "Boy Sledding" into the afternoon, sighing, starting over, and trying again and again to get it right. Hoping it would help, I convinced my mom to order a Jon Gnagy *Learn to Draw* Art Kit that included a tablet, pencils, charcoal, kneaded eraser, and guidebook.

I never became an artist, but I like to draw and so does my ten-year-old daughter, Phoebe. Recently, when she and I were poking around on YouTube, I remembered Gnagy, searched his name, and, though he died in 1981, there he was once again. We clicked "play" and it all flooded back. Strauss's bouncy "Künstlerleben," or "Artist's Life," is still the opening theme. Gnagy is wearing his plaid shirt, goatee, and ready smile. Today's scene of a boy sledding might look complicated, he says, but it isn't. If you can draw four simple forms—the ball, cone, cube and cylinder—you can draw anything.

Phoebe loved it, and I could see my old desire in her—to emulate Gnagy and learn to draw, to acquire his sharp eye and his quick, smooth lines.

I've also been writing a book about middlebrow culture, and just as when you learn a new word and suddenly see it three times in print over the next week, so have I been seeing middlebrow everywhere. Or at least I think I do. Nicola Humble, one of middlebrow's historians, has said, "'Middlebrow' has always been a dirty word."[1] Because it's so dishonored, middlebrow tends to hide and pass itself off as something else entirely—children's television, for instance. It is sometimes hard to spot. Yet here, in Jon Gnagy's earnest efforts, middlebrow was undeniable. Self-improvement, democratic access to the humanizing possibilities of art, the promise of new and easily acquired skills, an original and effective marketing scheme that made use of the latest mass media, the invocation of past masters—it was all there.

And now it's gone. The Age of Middlebrow has passed and Jon Gnagy would be gone with it except his shows have been digitized and saved in the museum that is YouTube—a handful of artifacts, nine-and-a-half-minute clips from 1950s and 1960s America.

Jon Gnagy was born in Pretty Prairie, Kansas, in 1907, and displayed artistic skill early in childhood.[2] His Mennonite family valued pacifism, simplicity, and craftsmanship but forbade portraits as idola-

1. Nicola Humble, *The Feminine Middlebrow Novel, 1920s to 1950s: Class, Domesticity, and Bohemianism* (New York: Oxford University Press, 2001), 1.

2. Gnagy's daughter maintains an excellent website about her father's life and work with links to articles about him and videos of the original shows. See Polly Gnagy Seymour, "The World of Jon Gnagy," October 20, 2006, http://www.tseymour.com/gnagy.html. The best print sources on his life are a brief biography from *An Ex-*

try, so his first drawings were landscapes. When he was thirteen, he won a ribbon for one of them at the Kansas State Fair. He kept winning and while still a teenager began to get and accept job offers. The first took him to Tulsa to create posters for the International Petroleum Exposition, then it was on to Wichita to do designs for aircraft companies, and finally, to Kansas City, where he worked for an ad agency and took courses at the Art Institute (where Walt Disney had studied a few years earlier).

But then the Depression hit and in 1932, armed, as he put it, with "ignorant nerve plus enthusiasm," Gnagy took his wife and young daughter to New York City. Things went well at first—he landed a job doing full-page ads for ALCOA in *Fortune* and the *Saturday Evening Post*—but soon the freelancing dried up, the couple added a son, the young family was forced into a cheap apartment over a steam laundry in Queens, and Gnagy suffered a nervous breakdown.

A job offer in Philadelphia and a move to the perfectly named town of New Hope, Pennsylvania, saved him. New Hope's Mennonite community felt familiar, but Gnagy was most invigorated by the town's growing group of artists. Lured by ads in the *New York Times* for cheap properties, Gnagy's neighbors in the Bucks County "Genius Belt" included (middlebrow) artists such as Dorothy Parker, S. J. Perelman, Oscar Hammerstein, James Michener, George Kaufman, Moss Hart, and Pearl S. Buck.

For a decade, Gnagy commuted to Philadelphia, reading and sketching three hours a day on the train. After Pearl Harbor he picked up extra work showing army recruits techniques in camouflage and creating posters for war plants; then, as the war wound down, he did some workshops for local colleges, women's clubs, and art centers. He found that he loved teaching and decided it was what he wanted to do.

---

hibition of *Paintings and Litho-Drawings* (Idyllwild, CA: Idyllwild Arts Center, 1964); Susan Morgan, "Each and Every One of You," *Real Life Magazine* 18 (Summer 1985); and Bill Eihorn, "Did You 'Learn to Draw' from Jon Gnagy?," *Reminisce Magazine*, November 22, 1997. Full citations from Michele H. Bogart, *Artists, Advertising, and the Borders of Art* (Chicago, IL: University of Chicago Press, 1995), 404.

On May 14, 1946, sporting an artist's smock and a beret, he opened the first show NBC broadcast from its new sixty-one-foot tower atop the Empire State Building. It was called *Radio City Matinee* and featured a comic, a cooking demonstration, and a woman who modeled hats. When Gnagy picked up his crayon to begin, he found the lights had melted it into a useless glob, so he switched to a piece of chalk. For seven minutes, the chalk squeaked across the paper as he showed his viewers how to draw an old oak tree.

There were only about three hundred television sets within the tower's eighty-mile range, most of them owned (as the first radios had been and the first personal computers would be) by buffs. Maybe half of them were tuned to WNBT that day, but the creators of television knew Gnagy was onto something. Vladimir Zworykin, one of the inventors of the TV tube, rushed over to shake Gnagy's hand. RCA and NBC president David Sarnoff called to congratulate him. The show's producer exclaimed that his segment was "pure television."

Pure television was going to save American culture. In 1941, Sarnoff predicted that television would introduce the country to opera, dance, literature, and art so that Americans might "attain the highest general cultural level of any people in the history of the world."[3] After the war, Sarnoff hired Sylvester "Pat" Weaver, a wealthy Phi Beta Kappa Dartmouth graduate, and the two of them launched "Operation Frontal Lobes" to produce the programs they thought America needed. "Television is a miracle," said Weaver. "It is going to change social history" and "create an aristocracy of the people, the proletariat of privilege, the Athenian masses—to make the average man the uncommon man."[4]

To the defenders of high art such grandiose claims were disturbing. The art establishment, schooled by New York intellectuals such

3. David Sarnoff, "Possible Social Effects of Television," *Annals of the American Academy of Political and Social Science* 213 (January 1941): 152, quoted in Pamela Wilson, "NBC Television's 'Operation Frontal Lobes': Cultural Hegemony and Fifties' Program Planning," *Historical Journal of Film, Radio and Television* 15, no. 1 (1995): 89.

4. Weaver as quoted by Thomas Whiteside, "Profiles: The Communicator (Part I)," *New Yorker*, October 16, 1954, 39.

as Clement Greenberg, who had recently railed against the "insidiousness" of middlebrow culture and accused it of "devaluating the precious, infecting the healthy, corrupting the honest, and stultifying the wise," knew middlebrow when they saw it and moved quickly to censure Gnagy.[5] Victor D'Amico, the education director of New York's Museum of Modern Art, convened a special session of the Committee on Art Education, a national commission of art educators. The group drafted a resolution and sent it to WBNT: "Television programs of the Jon Gnagy type are destructive to the creative and mental growth of children and perpetuate outmoded and authoritarian concepts of education. Creative education is based on the development of each child's individuality, the opportunity to use his own experience and to explore new media and techniques. The use of superficial tricks and formulas, found in the Jon Gnagy type of program, destroys this objective."[6]

The *New York Times* picked up the story and interviewed Gnagy, who displayed a winning self-deprecation even as he skewered the committee with irony: "I dream of the day when I can feed the viewers more and more esthetics.... I'd like to sell the same thing the Museum of Modern Art is selling." In the meantime, he allowed, the market wouldn't bear it, so he'd just keep trying "to get as many people as possible to sketch on their own and to be observant of the things around them."[7]

Viewers agreed, and Gnagy won the day. His show remained on network television until 1971 and in syndication on PBS beyond that. He received no royalties but had a platform from which to promote his lesson books and art kits. Doubleday sold a copy of his book to one out of every fourteen television set owners in the United States. His art supply company moved fifteen million art kits.[8]

5. Clement Greenberg, "Symposium on 'The State of American Writing,'" *Partisan Review* (August 1948): 879.
6. Quoted in Val Adams, "Art Instruction for the Masses: Jon Gnagy Combines TV Entertainment with Drawing Lessons," *New York Times*, January 20, 1952, X11.
7. Adams, "Art Instruction for the Masses," X11.
8. Cecil C. Hoge Sr., *Mail Order Moonlighting*, rev. ed. (Berkeley, CA: Ten Speed Press, 1988), 44.

But if Gnagy's success was undeniable, so also was the pained mix of anger and apology lurking in his witty response to the committee. Clearly he wanted to be taken seriously by the tastemakers, and it hurt that he was not. Yes, he could sniff out pretension in others and in himself—he kept his goatee, for instance, but got rid of his beret and artist's smock after the first show—and he would make a good living doing what he did, but he knew where he stood with the critics. "Let's not call my program art," he told the reporter from the *Times*. What he did, he admitted later, was just a "fence-straddling combination of entertainment and education."[9]

I am middle-class and middlebrow, a product of mid-twentieth-century American middlebrow culture. My family's journey parallels that of the country's new middle class. It begins with my grandparents on both sides, who were Midwest farm couples, moves through my mother, who was a Book-of-the-Month Club member and over whose shoulder I read, and my father, a GI Bill intellectual and college professor, to my wife and our daughters with our ranch house, our Volvos, and our Jon Gnagy *Learn to Draw* Art Kit that we ordered online.

9. Quoted in Adams, "Art Instruction for the Masses," X11.

The Book of Knowledge
Essays and Encyclopedias

Recently, I was reading chapter 87 of Roland Barthes's *S/Z: An Essay*, "The Voice of Science." In the previous chapter, "The Voice of Empirics," Barthes argued that narrative, like Sarrasine, will die; now he adds that cultural codes "will also be extinguished." There is, however, one small difference. The narrative will come to an end, whereas the references will be used up. "The Voice of Empirics" is silenced when the end of the long chain of the "already-written, already-seen, already-read, already-done" is reached, when the last domino has fallen. At such a point, we are finally at the tail end of the tale. 1001 Nights minus one and counting.

"The Voice of Science," on the other hand, is paradigmatic rather than syntagmatic. Field theory applies, not linearity. The cultural or referential codes live in neighborhoods, not on the street. They are grouped in farragoes, medleys, or conglomerations, a little here, a little there. Or, alternately, one might say they reside in books—a "set of seven or eight handbooks accessible to a diligent student in the classical bourgeois educational system," says Barthes (though he then lists nine).

I was a diligent student—hardworking, curious—and when I was a kid, because I was their oldest child and so diligent, my parents bought me a child's encyclopedia. It was called the *Book of Knowledge*. For a long time, it was for me the "anonymous Book" to which Barthes refers, a kind of Platonic realm wherein all answers resided. I would ask my parents why cats had whiskers or the sky was blue, and they'd tell me to look it up in the *Book of Knowledge*. Soon, however, I found that I had to go beyond the *Book of Knowledge*, and so I moved down the shelf to my parents' *Encyclopedia Americana*, sure it would have the missing answers and that soon I would learn everything.

To be honest, I'm still possessed of some of that same pride, or at any rate, I still like to look things up. I own a *Columbia Desk Encyclopedia*, William Rose Benét's *Reader's Encyclopedia*, the *American Family Encyclopedia*, an *OED* (with magnifying glass), Will Durant's *The Story of Philosophy: The Lives and Opinions of the World's Greatest Philosophers from Plato to John Dewey*, a *Hammond's Natural Atlas*, several field guides, Jeremy Hawthorn's *Concise Glossary of Contemporary Literary Theory*, M. H. Abrams's *Glossary of Literary Terms*, and so on and so on. Part of me still hopes my reference books will join forces and become Barthes's "anonymous" or "anterior Book."

It's the same dream Diderot had in 1751 when he launched his encyclopedia. In the entry for "Encyclopédie" in the *Encyclopédie*, he wrote, "It would have been difficult to propose a more extensive object than covering everything related to human curiosity, duty, needs, and pleasures." Then, apparently having already caught some guff, he quickly added, "For this reason some persons accustomed to judge the possibilities of an enterprise by the limited resources they recognize in themselves have pronounced that we will never bring ours to completion." Diderot gave the project twenty-five years of his life, continuing on even when his coeditor (and now *former* friend) Jean le Rond d'Alembert dropped out in 1759. D'Alembert was discouraged because the government (in league with the Church) had banned their attempt to make all knowledge available to all people. But the *Encyclopédie* had become a big business, employing 140 contributors (including Voltaire, Rousseau, and the Baron d'Holbach) and scores of illustrators, engravers, typesetters, and printers. The sheer size of the project enabled Diderot to keep it going. It became a kind of open secret. He would eventually publish twenty-eight volumes, containing 71,818 articles and 3,129 illustrations.

To those limited persons who dared judge the possibilities of his enterprise, Diderot said, "They shall have as sole reply this passage from Chancellor Bacon, which seems to address them specifically: 'As for the impossibility, I take it for granted that those works are possible which may be accomplished by some person, though not by every one; which may be done by many, though not by one; which may be completed in the succession of ages, though not within the hourglass of one man's life; and which may be reached by public effort, though not by private endeavor." Diderot took this passage from Francis Bacon's unfinished *De augmentis scientiarum* (Partition of Sciences). We essayists are now, I think, mostly Montaigneans, and reading the passage, we're liable to dismiss it as typical of Bacon, who was, after all, a systematizer, originator of the scientific method, utopian novelist, and writer of closed, careful, didactic, aphoristic, and short impersonal essays.

But we might do well to remember that Montaigne, though certainly more hesitant, humble, and forthcoming than Bacon, was not without ambition. In his own way, he too was after it all. In the three editions of his *Essais* (1580, 1588, 1595), Montaigne rarely subtracted. Instead, he added—sometimes just a word or a sentence, sometimes a whole essay. He may have been less afraid of contradicting himself than Bacon was, but the fact remains that his book kept growing, and his search for what he knew stopped only with his death. *Essai* means "trial" or "attempt," and we usually characterize the attempt as provisional, but the root leads also to "assay," an analysis or trial meant to tell us once and for all whether we've been fooled or the gold is real.

The essay, split at its root between Bacon's empiricism and Montaigne's subjectivity, is still split, or at least its practitioners continue to maintain different relations to knowledge. These include generalists and specialists writing as generalists, all of them trying to figure out what they do and don't know. Scott Sanders, in "The

Singular First Person," has nicely called the essay "an amateur's raid on the world of specialists," but it's also the genre of choice for specialists who want to shake off their jargon and talk to the general public. Among twentieth-century American experts alone who were also essayists the list includes at least Aldo Leopold (MS, forestry, Yale, 1909), Rachel Carson (MS, zoology, Johns Hopkins, 1932), Loren Eiseley (PhD, anthropology, Pennsylvania, 1937), Lewis Thomas (MD, Harvard, 1937), and Stephen Jay Gould (PhD, paleontology, Columbia, 1967).

I'm no expert, but as I said, I do know how to look things up. The reference books on my shelves still get some use, but I'm no fool. I know that in the digital age publishers will no longer be printing dictionaries and encyclopedias. Why would they when a digital version is so much easier to search? We say Google makes us stupid, but our iPads and smart phones have resurrected Diderot's dream. All of us have all of the answers right at our fingertips. Google Books makes every book available to everybody, or at least it will, says Google, if we can loosen the copyright laws and usher in Lewis Hyde's gift economy. Then everyone will have borrowing privileges at Borges's Library of Babel, which contains every possible book.

But will we?

Google is trying to scan every book, but every book is not—as both Borges and Barthes knew—the same thing as every *possible* book.

Eventually, I outgrew my *Book of Knowledge*, then I outgrew my parents' *Encyclopedia Americana*, and then I went off to college and outgrew my parents. No one knows as much as a college freshman, or at least the college freshman that I was. I thought I knew everything, or at least, with the help of my college education and some new smarty-pants reference books, I soon would. Suddenly my parents seemed hopelessly middlebrow. My father the college professor might be an intellectual, but he was just a GI Bill intellectual, and my mother... well, she had only an associate's degree. She was just a Book-of-the-Month Club intellectual, which was no intellectual at all. Oh, I was full of myself.

I came home from college for the summer, but this time I didn't have a job lined up. June was edging toward July and my lollygagging was driving my dad crazy, so he hired me himself. Every year for maybe a decade he had written the *World Book Yearbook* entry on agriculture and now he was getting tired of doing it. Plus, he had a lazy ingrate in the house who needed a job. He handed me a file full of clippings and said, "Here's last year's entry, some articles, and the current data from the USDA. Update the entry. I need a draft in two weeks."

I did need the money. And how hard could it be? A GI Bill intellectual had done it on autopilot. Boredom would probably be the big challenge. But, I would come to find out, both encyclopedia articles and the middlebrow people who write and read them were more complicated than I had thought.

"'Middlebrow,'" according to cultural historian Nicola Humble, "has always been a dirty word." From the beginning, it has been equated with smugness and avidity, an unseemly grasping after status, the contamination of real culture. The OED says that the word's first appearance in print occurred in the December 23, 1925, issue of *Punch*, where it was used to describe "people who are hoping that someday they will get used to the stuff they ought to like." I'd not come across that reference yet, but already I knew that my parents were trying too hard and that as hard as they tried, they weren't quite up to snuff. After all, I'd gone away to college and was reading real highbrow stuff—Milton and Donne, T. S. Eliot and James Joyce, Shakespeare, for Christ's sake. Now, home for the summer, everything seemed thrown into high relief. My mom's Michener novels and Utrillo prints had become downright embarrassing.

I hadn't even read the New York intellectuals yet, but already they were warning me against my parents and their pathetic attempts to acquire cultural capital. The Revised Standard Version on Sunday morning and *Omnibus* on Sunday afternoons would no longer cut it. For twenty years, without me knowing it, Dwight Macdonald and his cohort had waged and won the Battle of the Brows. Clement Greenberg blamed middlebrow for "corrupting the honest" and "stultifying the wise." Robert Warshow labeled it the "mass culture of the educated classes" and warned that it was bringing about a "disastrous vulgarization of intellectual life." Macdonald called it "a tepid ooze" that was "spreading everywhere." He dismissed the Encyclopedia Britannica's fifty-four-volume *Great Books of the Western World* as nothing more than "The Book-of-the-Millennium Club." I didn't need to have read the New York critics on middlebrow: my college roommate's mother had done it for me and passed on their wisdom through him to me: "*Life* magazine is for people who can't read, and *Time* magazine is for people who can't think." My mother read *Time* cover to cover every week.

But here's the rub, essayists: Isn't the essay—that translator of specialized knowledge, that kissing cousin of the journalistic article, that product of memory and research rather than imagination and art, that service genre used to explain the more literary genres such as fiction and poetry, that fourth genre that, as E. B. White reminded us in the foreword to his collected essays, "stands a short distance down the line"—isn't it finally . . . I mean if we face facts . . . well, isn't it middlebrow?

And because contradictions abound, here's another rub: When I went away to college in 1968, at the same time as I was getting a heavy dose of high culture, my classmates and I were marching in the streets and occupying buildings, fighting not just to end the war but also to democratize culture. We were arguing for women's studies and African American studies programs, for a canon that included women and minority writers as well as dead Englishmen. Soon, we'd begin to read theorists of the French generation of 1968: Barthes, for instance, who in *Mythologies* took seriously such products of mass culture as professional wrestling, soap ads, plastic, strip joints, and Garbo's face.

It would be a while but in time these French critics would even take middlebrow seriously. Would take my parents seriously! For Pierre Bourdieu, the point was not that middlebrow taste is good or bad *as taste* but rather that it is indicative of one's position within class society. Middlebrow culture is caught in the middle. Its contradictions are of a particular kind. For Bourdieu, the middlebrow is a figure that is at once pathetic and noble, an earnest autodidact who never quite finds the "good" taste she is after. They are, he says, "divided between the tastes they incline to and the tastes they aspire to." The GI Bill intellectuals and their families were part of an expanding middle class, one that included my mom and dad as well as Ward and June Cleaver. They had acquired some new capital but did not have a lot of *cultural* capital. To fill that gap, they subscribed to what they thought were the right magazines, joined book clubs, and learned to play bridge. For Bourdieu, their rush to display their culture seems more tragic (or comic) than threatening. I still wasn't sure.

And then there's the question of the essay as middlebrow. In *Distinction* Bourdieu writes, "The producers . . . of middle-brow culture" who make up "the new cultural intermediaries (the most typical of whom are the producers of cultural programmes on TV and radio or the critics of 'quality' newspapers and magazines and all the writer-journalists and journalist-writers) have invented a whole series of genres, half-way between legitimate culture and mass production ('letters,' 'essays,' 'eye-witness accounts')."

Bourdieu's analysis would, in time, help explain *Omnibus*, Bernstein's Young People's Concerts, Eric Sevareid, the rise of PBS, *New Yorker* profiles, and even Terry Gross, but back in 1969, I still had a *World Book* entry to write. And little did I know that I didn't have to go to high falutin' French theorists to get a good take on encyclopedias. In fact, one of the best middlebrow critics, Carl Van Doren, had already written about "the idea of the Encyclopedia." Reviewing a new French encyclopedia in 1962, Van Doren wrote,

> The idea of the French work is also radical. It appears to be statable in five propositions, each of which may sound strange to the reader of an ordinary encyclopedia. The five propositions are these:
> 1. The primary aim of an encyclopedia should be to teach. It should only secondarily be to inform.
> 2. An encyclopedia should be primarily a work of art. It should only secondarily be a work of reference.
> 3. The point of view of an encyclopedia should be primarily hu-

man. It should be only secondarily historical and/or scientific and/or literary.
4. The ideal reader of an encyclopedia should be primarily the curious average man. He should only secondarily be the specialist and/or the high school student.
5. An encyclopedia should be primarily a document that hopes to change the world for the better. It should only secondarily be a document that accurately reflects the knowledge, opinions and prejudices of its time.

As I began to work on my *World Book* entry, I knew nothing of Van Doren's ideas, but I soon experienced something he had observed: "Most encyclopedias, particularly the American ones, have little or no idea of themselves. They just grow; they are not created." That is, the whole mystique of an encyclopedia, indeed of writing itself, began to fall apart for me. It was, as Barthes would say, demythologized. The *World Book*, which I knew stood on our shelves both literally and culturally between *The Book of Knowledge* and the *Encyclopedia Americana*, might be middlebrow, but it was also tricky and asking something new of me. Where once I had used it for my school reports, now I was writing it, or more properly, ghostwriting it. And that was both weird and a little unnerving. My dad had been contracted to do the job. They'd bought his byline, not mine.

But if I didn't get the byline, I did get some money. I don't remember how much now. It wasn't a lot, but it felt like a lot. It was the first time I'd gotten paid for a piece of writing, which was a big deal to me. Still is. My dad had trusted me to write the piece and then when I did, he took my draft seriously. He gave me criticism and asked for some changes—it was going out in his name after all. We revised, we collaborated, and when it came out, he sent me a copy. I've still got it.

Which is not to say everything was hunky-dory. When I told my high school buddy Brent Beebe about this job my father had given me, he in turn told me how his stepsister, Lou-Ann Smith, had set herself the chore the previous summer of reading the entire *World Book*. This revelation did little to lift the *World Book* in my eyes—

quite the opposite, in fact. Lou-Ann Smith seemed nice enough, if a little dorky (she played the pipe organ at the Episcopal church), but I didn't really know her. She was just Brent's stepsister. She, her mom, and her younger brother and sister had joined Brent, his father, and Brent's two younger brothers in a kind of odd and uncomfortable precursor to *The Brady Bunch*. The Beebe men had been on their own since Brent's mom ran off with a graduate student when Brent was in about fifth grade. Brent's father, a Joyce scholar, a real intellectual, drank too much. The basement was a man cave with a bar, a TV mounted above the bar, a pool table, and the boys' bedrooms. Lou-Ann's brother Clay fit in okay. He seemed thrilled, in fact, to have all of a sudden acquired some brothers, but even then I could tell that the girls found their new house to be less congenial. Lurlene, Lou-Ann's mother, had been married to an army man. She was a strong woman who corrected my grammar once and often stood up to Brent's dad. Once, I saw her try a few puffs of cigar. It was something I couldn't imagine any mom doing, certainly not my own. In any case, it pissed Brent's dad off.

"Who do you think you are? Amy Lowell?"

"Relax," she shot back. "Sometimes a cigar is just a cigar."

Brent and I laughed at Lou-Ann behind her back and made fun of her (apparently successful) attempt to read her way through the *World Book*. To our thinking, reading an encyclopedia from A to Z did not save you from being a dork; it confirmed that you were one. But we were adolescent boys who stupidly thought we knew everything, or at least we thought we knew everything about Lou-Ann, who was stupid enough to think she could read an encyclopedia and then know everything.

If, indeed, that is what she thought. Maybe she was bored. Maybe she was trying to escape the weird house of boys in which she found herself. Maybe she missed her father.

Of stupidity and the cultural codes, Barthes has this to say: "In fact, the cultural code occupies the same position as stupidity: how can stupidity be pinned down without declaring oneself intelligent? How can one code be superior to another without abusively closing off the plurality of codes? Only writing, by assuming the largest possible plural in its own task, can oppose without appeal to force the imperialism of each language."

Brent and I were right to think that not everything is in the encyclopedia, but we had no idea about what actually lay outside in the real world. Years later, I found out that at the same time Barthes was writing *S/Z* and I was writing my *World Book* entry, Lou-Ann's dad, major general Homer D. Smith, was serving as chief of staff of the First Logistics Command in Vietnam, the largest in the U.S. Army at that time. His operation, with an assigned strength of over one hundred thousand troops, provided logistical support to all the army, navy, air force, and marines engaged in combat in the Da Nang area. On February 20, 1969, about two hundred kilometers north of Da Nang, in Quang Tri Province, Denny Cripe, who played football with Brent and me, was killed by "an explosive device," one of 58,220 Americans and perhaps a million Vietnamese who died in the war. Six years after that, General Smith was still in Vietnam serving now as the defense attaché at the U.S. Embassy. As such, he was the senior military officer in the country and oversaw the evacuation of 1,373 U.S. citizens and 4,595 "Third Country Nationals and Vietnamese citizens" from Saigon.

General Smith was in one of the last helicopters to lift off the roof of the U.S. Embassy. The evacuees he helped escape included hundreds of Vietnamese and Vietnamese American orphans in what was called Operation Babylift. Unfortunately, on April 4, 1975, during this operation 138 people were killed in the crash of a C-5A Galaxy transport plane, including seventy-eight children and thirty-five defense attaché personnel.

To Barthes, the idea that there is something called life that we might know (or that, according to two know-it-all boys, Lou-Ann Smith might not know) is a mistaken one. For Barthes, even the word "Life" must be capitalized and put inside quotation marks. It is a creation of the "anterior book" that is at once a book of science, wisdom, and all "the didactic material mobilized in the text." All of these references, says Barthes in "The Voice of Science," these cultural codes, by "a swivel characteristic of bourgeois ideology, which turns culture into nature, appear to establish reality, 'Life.'"

Such setting in stone is what I was trying to do when I wrote the definitive article about U.S. agriculture for the *World Book Encyclopedia*.

It wasn't an essay.

PART 3

Our Queer Little Hybrid Thing

Toward a Definition of the Essay

What is an essay?

Well, it ain't a five-paragraph theme—tell 'em what you're gonna tell 'em, tell it to 'em, then tell 'em what you told 'em. The essay is bigger, messier, and more fun than that.

It's so big, in fact, that it is not so much a genre as a galaxy of subgenres. Over the years the word "essay" has collected its own passel of adjectives: "personal," "formal," "informal," "humorous," "descriptive," "expository," "reflective," "nature," "critical," "lyric," "narrative," "review," "periodical," "romantic," and "genteel." And it keeps collecting them. Now there are radio, film, and video essays. Maybe a map or field of Venn diagrams in which all these adjectives meet and greet would be the best way to describe the essay.

Further confusing the situation, however, are the aliases behind which the essay has hidden or been hidden: "feature," "piece," "column" (or, once upon a time, "colyumn"), "editorial," "op-ed," "profile," and "casual." The title of an excellent 1984 piece (or was it an essay?) by Phillip Lopate on the first page of the *New York Times Book Review* summed the situation up quite nicely: "The Essay Lives—in Disguise."

The essay has also gotten lost under the big tent of terms like "literary journalism," "new journalism," "literary nonfiction," and more recently, "creative nonfiction." All of these catchalls are problematic. They lump the essay in with things that it is not and in so doing make an already sprawling genre seem bigger than it really is. Here the adjectives serve not so much to stake out small claims as to pump up that poor, scribbled thing that journalism is said to be, or clarify and legitimize the vast wasteland that has been locked outside the fiction corral by the nondefiner that is "non-." Scott Russell Sanders is quite good on this. Nonfiction, he points out, is "an exceedingly vague term, taking in everything from telephone books to *Walden*, and it's negative, implying that fiction is the norm against which everything else must be measured. It's as though, instead of calling an apple a fruit, we called it a non-meat."

Adding the adjective "creative" may be well intentioned but is finally of little help. "Creative" as opposed to what? "Destructive"? And just how "creative" can we be? James Frey creative, or just John D'Agata creative?

All this fuzziness, but especially the essay's proximity to fishwrap journalism, leave it stigmatized as "the fourth genre." The critic Suzanne Ferguson has argued that "like societies of people, the society of literary genres has its class system, in which, over time, classes reorganize themselves, accept new members, and cast old members into the dustbin. It has its aristocracy, its middle classes, and its proletarians."

E. B. White longed to be a poet and is known for his children's books but was, above all, an essayist. He meant his essays to last, and they have, but they were written first on weekly deadlines for the *New Yorker*, then on monthly deadlines for *Harper's*, and finally again for the *New Yorker* when the mood struck him, but he always saw himself as a working journalist. In the foreword to his selected essays, he wrote, "I am not fooled about the place of the essay in twentieth-century American letters—it stands a short distance down the line. The essayist, unlike the novelist, the poet, and the playwright, must be content in his self-imposed role of second-class citizen. A writer who has his sights trained on the Nobel Prize or other earthly triumphs had best write a novel, a poem, or a play, and leave the essayist to ramble about, content with living a free life and enjoying the satisfactions of a somewhat undisciplined existence." Perhaps another reason for what David Lazar has called the "queering" or "definitional defiance" of the essay has to do with the fact that it had two parents and so was, in a sense, split at the root. Its first practitioners, Michel de Montaigne and Sir Francis Bacon, who wrote at the turn of the seventeenth century, conceived of the essay in very different ways. For Montaigne, *l'essai* was a means of self-exploration, an exercise in self-portraiture, and a way for him to explore, tentatively and skeptically, his own thoughts and feelings; for Bacon, it was a form of "counsel," a means of instruction, a guide to conduct, a way to test, recognize, and appreciate the "truth." Montaigne's essays are digressive and shockingly personal. They grew as he revised—elaborating, circling back, and constantly asking himself *Que sais-je?* or "What do I know?" Bacon's essays, on the other hand, appear complete and once and for all, polished as a billiard ball. They're short, aphoristic, tidy, and impersonal, though always brimming with opinion and even pronouncement.

Now we have two more adjectives for the essay—"Montaignean" and "Baconian"—which is fine, but if we're going to bring this queer little hybrid thing further into focus, perhaps we should talk about it in terms of two kinds of writing rather than in terms of two writers, whose work you may or may not know. Let's lay out a spectrum on which the essay sits (or hovers?) in the middle. This spectrum has nonfiction at one end and fiction at the other, or more specifically, given that the essay is short rather than long, it has the article at one end and the short story at the other. And yes, I understand I'm doing some negative defining of my own here. By saying an essay is neither story nor article, I'm still saying it's nonfiction and nonjournalism, but I'm hoping to be a bit less vague, a bit more compare and contrast, a bit more precise.

The article is researched, fact-based. It provides information and usually tries to make a point. It is True with a capital T. It tries to be accurate. Its details and quotations are verified and fact-checked. It is a product of interviews, field notes, and memory. As for its form, if it's a news story, it is likely organized by means of the inverted triangle, with its answers to the five Ws (who, what, when, where, and why) and the one H (how) front-loaded. Its intentions are announced in its headline and spelled out in its lede.

Or if, it's another kind of article—an academic article—it argues a thesis, and uses footnotes. It is organized by means of a preconceived outline, marching from I to A to 1 to a ... and so on. William H. Gass, one of our great essayists, has made his living as an academic, and so knows whereof he speaks when he contrasts the essay with "that awful object, 'the article,'" of which, he says, it

> pretends that everything is clear, that its argument is unassailable, that there are no soggy patches, no illicit inferences, no illegitimate connections; it furnishes seals of approval and underwriters' guarantees; its manners are starched, stuffy, it would wear a dress suit to a barbecue, silk pajamas to the shower; it knows, with respect to every subject and point of view it is ever likely to entertain, what words to use, what form to follow, what authorities to respect; it is the careful product of a professional, and therefore it is written as only writing can be written, even if, at various times, versions have been given a dry dull voice at a conference, because, spoken aloud, it still sounds like writing written down, writing born for its immediate burial in a Journal.

At the other end of the spectrum is the short story. Unlike the article, the short story is fictional, made-up, a product of imagination more than of research. Hell, it can even include unicorns or hobbits, and be set in the future or in a land far, far away. As for their structure, stories don't always march from "Once upon a time" to "happily ever after." They may turn metafictional, fold in flashbacks, and surprise in wonderful ways, but generally they follow a single traditional form, one that has been diagramed as an inverted check mark. A conflict is triggered and grows increasingly tense and complicated until it finally arrives at a climax, which is followed by a short unraveling, or denouement. Or, to put it another way: foreplay > orgasm > cigarette.

"One has a sense with the short story as a form," says Edward Hoagland, "that while everything may be been done, nothing has been overdone; it has permanence." It is tidy, original, elemental. It predated even cave painting, argues Hoagland, and is "the art to build from." It explores the love and grief that hold the tribe together, the war and betrayals that tear it apart. A story is also universal because it is made up and so could be about any of us. This is what Aristotle was talking about when he drew a distinction between poetry and history in the *Poetics*: "The true difference is that one relates what has happened, the other what may happen. Poetry, therefore, is a more philosophical and a higher thing than history: for poetry tends to express the universal, history the particular."

The personal essay appeared almost two millennia after Aristotle wrote the *Poetics*, and after several centuries of perhaps too much universality and church doctrine, too many answered questions, too much deferral of particularity and the self, and too little democracy. As a consequence, Montaigne flipped Aristotle's assertion, arguing instead, "*Chaque homme porte la forme entière de l'humaine condition*," or "Each man [or person] carries [or bears] the entire form [or impress, or stamp] of the human condition." For Montaigne, history isn't less than poetry, because history carries the universal within it. Any living individual can represent the whole of humanity, the possibilities within each of us. Montaigne did not apologize for himself and his new approach, but laid down a challenge instead: "If the world find fault that I speak too much of myself, I find fault that they do not so much as think of themselves."

The essay sits somewhere between an edited, organized, largely voiceless, researched, fact-based, history-based article and a narrated, made-up, speculative, climactic, imaginary story. It offers a third way, another way to find everyone's story in one person's story. The personal essay differs from the inverted checkmark story in that it doesn't tell (or just tell) the story of an event. Instead it lets you into what a particular person thinks about an event... or a subject, person, place, or problem. It offers—or essays—an answer to a question, a question such as "What is an essay?" As a consequence, an essay is more digressive and meandering than a story. It may be a story, says Hoagland, but it is the story of a mind thinking.

Because we think in terms of narratives and tell stories regularly, an essay might well contain stories or even be organized around a single story. George Orwell's oft-anthologized and justly famous essays "Shooting an Elephant" and "A Hanging" are narrative essays. They slide toward the story end of the spectrum and live in what Doug Hesse has called a "boundary zone" that is adjacent to (or even overlaps with) first-person short stories. Some of this has to do with how we read, with the contract between author and reader, and with the context in which we are reading. Orwell's essays, for instance, have occasionally been anthologized in short story anthologies, where they are inevitably read differently than they would be in an essay anthology. "Reading a work as key to some more general truth," says Hesse, "involves a different set of perceptions than reading it as representing some action, however meaning laden. We expect an essay story to show the way things are, a short story the way things happen." Orwell's narratives, for instance, are usually read as essays because they use the stories they tell to explore colonialism, complicity, and capital punishment, as well as Orwell's own growing understanding of those larger issues.

Another way to put this is that essay can include an anecdote (again, one that actually happened), but to be an essay, it must rise above the anecdote and point us toward its significance. Fiction writers sometimes complain about being hounded in workshops by the show-don't-tell-police, but essayists are always trying to figure out how to show and tell.

A good way to begin drafting an essay is to explore a story that you yourself aren't quite sure about, a story that haunts you, a story you need to tell but you don't know why. Usually, the answer will come by slowing down and dramatizing the scene, by exploring what your thoughts were about the events at the time they occurred, and finally what you think about the incident now. The struggle is both to tell the tale but also to find your inner voice from that time (the voice of reflection) and your inner voice now (the voice of retrospection). In her classic essay "On Keeping a Notebook," Joan Didion has a nice passage about the emotional work this process can require: "I think we are well advised to keep on nodding terms with the people we used to be, whether we find them attractive company or not. Otherwise they turn up unannounced and surprise us, come hammering on the mind's door at 4 a.m. of a bad night and demand to know who deserted them, who betrayed them, who is going to make amends.' This essay stuff is getting complicated, isn't it? An essay recaptures the voice of a former self and in so doing enables one's current self to talk about that former self, and then one or both of them, though most likely just the current self, talks to the reader about the lives lived by both selves.

Got it?

Maybe this passage from Virginia Woolf's "The Modern Essay" (1925) will help. In it, she's talking about how effectively Max Beerbohm was at getting his voice (or at least a voice that we take to be his voice) down onto the page:

> He was himself, simply and directly, and himself he has remained. Once again we have an essayist capable of using the essayist's most proper but most dangerous and delicate tool. He has brought personality into literature, not unconsciously and impurely, but so consciously and purely that we do not know whether there is any relation between Max the essayist and Mr. Beerbohm the man. We only know that the spirit of personality permeates every word that he writes. The triumph is the triumph of style. For it is only by knowing how to write that you can make use in literature of your self; that self which, while it is essential to literature, is also its most dangerous antagonist. Never to be yourself and yet always—that is the problem. . . . Even things in a book-case change if they are alive; we find ourselves wanting to meet them again; we find them altered. So we look back upon essay after essay by Mr. Beerbohm, knowing that, come September or May, we shall sit down with them and talk.

It's slippery business. Our selves are and are not. They once were lost but now are found. But isn't this the way life is? You grow up and move on. You become someone else and yet are always yourself, just as my father, though ravaged by Alzheimer's, was himself even at the end. Woolf's passage is as slippery as its subject, and it must be. It deftly moves between Max and Mr. Beerbohm, between writing and talking, between never being and yet always being one's self.

The self of whom Woolf speaks is a written self but it must not sound written. It is created, as Woolf says, through the "triumph of style" and must sound alive, intimate, and spoken, or, as Gass put it, it must not sound "like writing written down, writing born for its immediate burial in a Journal."

But how to do this?

Hoagland, still comparing the essay and article, has an answer: "Essays don't usually boil down to a summary, as articles do, and the style of the writer has a 'nap' to it, a combination of personality and originality and energetic loose ends that stand up like the nap on a piece of wool and can't be brushed flat. Essays belong to the animal kingdom, with a surface that generates sparks, like a coat of fur, compared with the flat, conventional cotton of the magazine article writer, who works in the vegetable kingdom, instead." Notice that Hoagland does what he says an essayist should do. He enacts the theory he advances. His use of the term "nap" is an example of his own nap. Describing prose style in terms of fur is a metaphor that generates sparks.

Just being distinctive, however, is not enough. In Flannery O'Connor's "Everything That Rises Must Converge," Julian's mother thinks she's bought a distinctive hat, one in which she won't meet herself "coming and going" (though of course she does), but the hat is purple, feathered, floppy, and "hideous." A store-bought hat, like a machine-made T-shirt, can be ordinary or hideous, but so unfortunately can a hand-knitted and nappy sweater. You still have to have style, which is a result of hard work, much reading, ruthless revision, and a full closet of options, or as E. B. White puts it, "The essayist arises in the morning and, if he has work to do, selects his garb from an unusually extensive wardrobe: he can pull on any sort of shirt, be any sort of person, according to his mood or his subject matter—philosopher, scold, jester, raconteur, confidant, pundit, devil's advocate, enthusiast."

Do clothes make the man? Does prose style make the woman? Adopting a persona or playing a role is part of life. We are each mothers, daughters, sisters, and wives as well as scolds, raconteurs, and enthusiasts, but I am also Ned, just as you are whoever who you are. We are individuals who transcend our roles. Similarly, while we construct a self on the page, we should not, as essayists, overemphasize fabrication and push our written self too far toward the fiction end of the spectrum. White knew this, for right after he wrote the lines I quoted above he reminded us, "There is one thing the essayist cannot do, though—he cannot indulge himself in deceit or in concealment, for he will be found out in no time."

How do we avoid concealment and fabrication? An essay isn't cinema verité, and it certainly isn't reality TV. Openness in an essay doesn't result from having the cameras on all the time. Its dialogue isn't found on transcribed tapes. Which is not to say we never do this kind of thing. Nancy Mairs's great essay "On Not Liking Sex" is a rewriting of an earlier essay of the same name in which she quotes and criticizes what she'd written earlier. Didion pastes her psychiatrist's report and sections from some court transcripts into "The White Album." Research certainly has its place, but what essayists are really striving for is the candor, honesty, and intimacy shared between friends. The self on the page is a construct but it is also you. Scott Sanders again:

> The essay is not fenced round by [the same] literary inhibitions [as fiction]. You may speak without disguise of what moves and worries and excites you. In fact, you had better speak from a region pretty close to the heart, or the reader will detect the wind of phoniness whistling through your hollow phrases. In the essay you may be caught with your pants down, your ignorance and sentimentality showing, while you trot recklessly about on one of your hobbyhorses. You cannot stand back from the action, as Joyce instructed us to do, and pare your fingernails. You cannot palm off your cockamamie notions on some hapless character. If the words you put down are foolish, everyone knows precisely who the fool is.

So you pull on the right shirt and try to avoid getting caught with your pants down. You present yourself without making a fool of yourself—how hard can that be? Well, damn hard, as Sanders suggests. Ever go through a day without a fib? Come on... be honest.

Let me be honest. I don't think I've truly defined the essay here. I've tried... but I think pinning down a genre is as tricky as pinning down a self. Jacques Derrida said as much when he famously and ironically opened his essay "The Law of Genre" with the following declaration, the following false promise:

> Genres are not to be mixed.
> I will not mix genres.
> I repeat: genres are not to be mixed. I will not mix them.

And then in his essay (or was it an article? a manifesto? a parable?) he demonstrated that the law of genre is that there is no law, for the law will always be broken (which is the new law but not a law at all). All genres are contaminated by other genres, and taxonomy itself is a subjective and relativistic exercise.

I must admit, such poststructuralism makes me uncomfortable. I'd like something to hold on to. Maybe the best way to define the essay is simply to gesture toward it with a simile. At various times Montaigne called his book of essays a self-portrait, an autopsy, his child, a gift to a friend, an ongoing tale, a patchwork quilt, a fricassee, and a pile of crap. Hoagland calls the essay a greased pig, and far be it from me to assume I've grabbed it.

WORKS CITED

Derrida, Jacques. "The Law of Genre." Translated by Avital Ronell. *Glyph* 7 (1980): 202–32.

Didion, Joan. "On Keeping a Notebook." In *Slouching toward Bethlehem: Essays*, 131–41. New York: Farrar, Straus, & Giroux, 1968.

Ferguson, Suzanne. "The Rise of the Short Story in the Hierarchy of Genres." In *Short Story Theory at a Crossroads*, edited by Susan Lohafer and Jo Ellyn Clarey, 176–92. Baton Rouge: Louisiana State University Press, 1998.

Gass, William. "Emerson and the Essay." In *Habitations of the Word*, 9–49. New York: Simon and Schuster, 1985.

Hesse, Douglas. "A Boundary Zone: First-Person Short Stories and Narrative Essays." In *Short Story Theory at a Crossroads*, edited by Susan Lohafer and Jo Ellyn Clarey, 85–105. Baton Rouge: Louisiana State University Press, 1989.

Hoagland, Edward. "What I Think, What I Am." In *The Tugman's Passage*, 24–27. New York: Random House, 1982. Appeared originally in *New York Times Book Review*, June 27, 1976.

Lazar, David. "Queering the Essay." In *Bending Genre: Essays on Creative Nonfiction*, edited by Margot Singer and Nicole Walker, 15–20. New York: Bloomsbury, 2013. Published originally in *The Essay Review*, available at http://theessayreview.org/.

Root, Robert L., Jr. "Interview with Scott Russell Sanders." *Fourth Genre: Explorations in Nonfiction* 1, no. 1 (1999): 119–32.

Sanders, Scott Russell. "The Singular First Person." In *Essays on the Essay: Redefining the Genre*, edited by Alexander J. Butrym, 31–42. Athens: University of Georgia Press, 1989. Reprinted in Scott Sanders, *Secrets of the Universe: Scenes from the Journey Home*. Boston, MA: Beacon Press, 1991.

White, E. B. Foreword to *Essays of E. B. White*. New York: Harper Colophon, 1977.

Woolf, Virginia. "The Modern Essay." In *The Common Reader: First Series*, edited by Andrew McNeillie, 211–22. 1925; repr., New York: Harcourt. 1984.

An Essayist's Guide to Research and Family Life

When you have two writers in the house, research becomes a family project, a way of life. It seeps into everything the family does—the whole family. Family vacations, dinner parties, and birthdays are all bound up with our research. My wife and I give each other old books for Christmas. In the summers we have taken our kids to see Elvis tribute artists and the childhood homes of our favorite writers. Research is what we do even if sometimes we don't recognize it as research (though the IRS guidelines for tax deductions help remind us that it needs to be identified and labeled as such). Even our friends—most of whom are writers too—are pulled into this vortex of research. They throw us book parties featuring our obsessions: mermaids, Memphis, rockabilly, and Montaigne. They give me collections of essays and a history of Greenwich Village for my birthday. Our friend Bob Butler, who knows and shares our Elvis obsession, gave us an authenticated lock of Elvis's hair and a portrait of the King made from candy wrappers. At our house it's all research all the time.

Elizabeth is a fiction writer; I write personal essays and cultural criticism. She publishes with New York trade houses; I publish with university presses; we both collaborate with our friend Janet Burroway on a writing textbook published by Pearson. We both teach in the Department of English at Florida State University. Every day we write and talk about writing. Every day we do some kind of research. We are also both the children of writers. Elizabeth's father published poetry, short stories, and literary criticism; her mother wrote plays and children's books. My dad was an agricultural economist and academic who also wrote for popular magazines. Elizabeth's parents even gave her the middle name of Caroline, after Caroline Gordon, a friend of the family and the subject of a biography Elizabeth's dad published in 1972.

Now we have two teenage daughters of our own—Flannery and Phoebe. Can you hear the literary allusions in their names?

Soon after Phoebe was born and about the time Flannery turned three, Elizabeth and I landed our first full-time university teaching jobs. The academic life, especially because we teach at a research university, means we are expected to write books, stories, essays, and articles. It also means we have a lot of freedom to pick our projects and we get to work at home a lot. This is mostly to the good, of course. We have generous vacations and there's no need to use a sick day if one of the girls gets sick. It's easy to schedule parent-teacher conferences or doctor's appointments. It's a good gig. If there is a downside it has to do mainly with finding the time, the quiet, and the space within one's own home to do one's work. Research and writing don't always look like work, and sometimes we have to remind ourselves and our daughters that what we do is real work and should be treated as such even if we don't head to the office each morning like other parents do. At our house there is a lot of "I can't help you with that right now. I've got to finish this book review. You'll have to talk to your mother." Our house is small and the only real study we have is a converted garage in the basement, which we use sparingly. As a consequence, the wall we must build to establish our working space is largely a virtual wall. Elizabeth and I have to both pitch in to keep this wall from crumbling.

Take, for example, the fall of 2001. About the middle of August, Elizabeth's editor at Doubleday told her she had put Elizabeth's as-yet-largely-unwritten first novel in the spring catalogue, which meant Elizabeth would need to deliver the manuscript by the end of December. When in September al Qaeda started crashing planes into buildings our house had already been in panic mode for a couple of weeks. The girls were three and six at the time. I took them to the park a lot. I took them grocery shopping a lot. I took them to the library a lot. But sooner or later the three of us had to come home where Mom was trying to write. I remember fixing dinner, breaking up sibling spats, and watching the news about anthrax scares and sleeper cells while Elizabeth, exhibiting unbelievable powers of concentration, banged away in the next room. She made her deadline.

The novel she wrote is called *Mermaids on the Moon* and it's set at Weeki Wachee, a postwar tourist attraction created by a former navy frogman just north of Tampa. Elizabeth had visited Weeki Wachee with her friend Lu Vickers, who was researching an article on this clear-water spring where young girls have been dressing up as mermaids and performing before an underwater amphitheater since 1947. Lu's article was to be a paean to the old Florida and the wonderful kitschy attractions that seem doomed by Disney World and the centralization and corporatization of tourism in the Orlando area. In 1997 Weeki Wachee celebrated its fiftieth anniversary, and several of the mermaids who had performed there as teenagers in the 1950s and 1960s came back for the celebration. Some of them found they really missed the place and wanted to put their tails back on and perform again. A few still lived in the area, others subsequently retired to Florida, and before long the Mermaids of Yesteryear, or Merhags as they called themselves, were doing a regular Friday night show. Elizabeth got to know them and soon we were driving the three and a half hours from Tallahassee to Weeki Wachee whenever we could. It was, I realize now, our girls' introduction to research and writing.

My writing also took us at one point on a Georgia presidents' tour. We saw Jimmy Carter teach Sunday school in Plains and then traveled north to Warm Springs, the location of Roosevelt's Little White House, where he went for polio treatments and died of a cerebral hemorrhage while having his portrait painted. And lo and behold, the trip seemed to strike a chord with both girls. Flannery did a poster project on Carter, Sadat, and Begin at Camp David. Phoebe and a friend worked FDR into a history fair skit about Jonas Salk and polio vaccine. They even used Phoebe's vial of water from Warm Springs as a prop.

Elizabeth and I have also found that every year we each have to have some sustained stretches of uninterrupted, out-of-the-house writing time. Occasionally, again when book deadlines demand it of us, we've given over parts of our winter or spring breaks to our writing, but our regular plan is to each take a week or two during the summer at a writer's retreat, most often the Lillian E. Smith Center for the Arts near Clayton, Georgia, but also at the cabins of generous friends. This has worked out well for both of us. A week or two of single parenting is not too bad, certainly nothing like doing it fulltime. You end up having conversations with your daughters you might not have otherwise. You treat yourself and the girls to some meals out, even if it's just to Whataburger, figuring the three of you deserve it since Mom or Dad is up at the cabin "writing." (Elizabeth may have a different take on this, as it seems the tropical storms always hit Tallahassee and the basement floods while I'm in Clayton.)

Sometimes we take working vacations and the girls get dragged along. Elizabeth and I occasionally teach at the Iowa Summer Writing Festival, for instance. One of us does two weekend workshops sandwiched around the other one's weeklong workshop. The girls get to hang out with us, see where they lived when they were little, and visit old friends. One year, however, Phoebe got an infection in her hip and spent a couple of nights in the hospital, and then Elizabeth and her publicist got their wires crossed and Elizabeth had to fly to San Francisco and back in the middle of the week to do a reading, and the house the University of Iowa found for us to stay in had no air-conditioning and there was a heat wave and it was 95 degrees all week, but other than that we had a good time.

So why force this writing life on your innocent children? Why require them to traipse around the scuzzy ruins of an Indiana health spa that is the setting of a story? Why abandon your wife and kids for a couple of weeks to spend beautiful summer afternoons in Harvard's Houghton Library reading the letters between Alexander Woollcott and Harpo Marx? Why take the whole family to the Big E Festival in Cornelia, Georgia, with lawn chairs and T-shirts and "tribute artist" contests, to the home place in Tupelo, and finally to Memphis—a dozen times or more to Memphis—to see Graceland, the house on Audubon Drive, Sun Studio, Dixie Locke's house, the band shell at Overton Park, and the Presley family apartment in Lauderdale Courts? Why do all this seemingly silly research?

Well, because you're a writer, that's why, and writers have their reasons for doing research. Nine of them by my count:

1. Getting It Right

Fact-checking alone is reason enough to do research. One misstep and you can lose your reader. And this is true whether you're writing fiction or nonfiction.

The great fiction writer Tobias Wolff has also written two wonderful memoirs—*This Boy's Life* and *In Pharaoh's Army*. In a *Paris Review* interview, he talked about accuracy, honesty, and the different allegiance to reality the two kinds of writing have. He wrote his memoirs, he said,

> with the knowledge that they'd be read by people who lived through those times with me. I couldn't write down things that were simply untrue, that I knew were untrue, because I stood to be ferociously corrected—and embarrassed—by people who knew better. Now that doesn't mean there weren't differences of interpretation—I'm sure, for example, that my then-fiancée would have a very different take on what happened: He had it coming, he was a selfish brute, I needed to get his attention. She would, I'm sure, have an explanation for why she destroyed my car that night, but she wouldn't dispute that she did it. So, too, with the other book. My mother was very much alive when I wrote *This Boy's Life*, and my brother, and other people who saw those times with me. So I was answerable. It's different from writing fiction.

Which is not to say fiction doesn't also benefit from and even require fact-checking as well. When Elizabeth placed a story in the *Atlantic* for the first time, she encountered a different level of copy editing there than she had in the little magazines where she'd published previously. I remember the copy editor from the *Atlantic* calling with two questions: Was there really a circular public swimming pool in Ottumwa, Iowa? And were there tan Volvos in 1972? To the first, Elizabeth said, "I don't know, but I doubt it. I've never been to Ottumwa. I was thinking of my hometown in Indiana." The copy editor said they would get a lot of mail from people in Iowa. Soon they'd hammered out a solution. Invent an imaginary town in Iowa (Elizabeth called it Magruder) and put the circular pool there. To resolve the second question, the magazine's intern did some research and found out Volvo didn't make tan cars in 1972, so Aunt Merry's car turned gray.

As Wolff says, differences of interpretation are one thing (e.g., the difference between how he and his then-fiancée see her destruction of his car), but even with the seemingly objective there are shades of gray. Or perhaps, it would be more accurate to say some such issues are more important than others. Most readers, for instance, would read right past the Ottumwa swimming pool and the tan Volvo, but a writer's concern—whether he or she is writing fiction or nonfiction—must be with those few who won't, those residents of Ottumwa and Volvo aficionados. For them and for yourself, you have to get it right.

2. Adding Detail and Specificity

Not unrelated to getting it right is making it better, and specificity makes it better. There is, after all, a difference between "a beer" and "a Pabst Blue Ribbon" just as there is a difference between a PBR and a Sam Adams.

Picking the right beer is easy for those of us who drink beer, but what if your characters want to drink champagne? Anne Lamott in her wonderful book on writing, *Bird by Bird: Some Instructions on Writing and Life*, tells the following story:

> When I was writing my second novel, I got to the part where the man comes over for his first date with the woman and brings with him a bottle of champagne. He removes the foil. We get to see his hands, which are beautiful, long and broad with white moons on his big square fingernails, so lovely that they almost make up for the fact

that he is wearing a yellow polyester shirt. Also, it is in his favor that he has brought along a nice bottle of champagne; the woman loves to drink. So the man has peeled the foil away, and then he begins to remove that wire thing that covers the champagne cork.

Now, I've always thought of that wire thing—that little helmet—as the wire thing, and that is how everyone I've ever known refers to it: "Honey, will you take the wire thing off the champagne? I just had my nails done." "Oh, look, Skippy's playing with that little wire thing; I hope she doesn't cut her little lips on it . . ."

But it must have a name, right? I mean, boxes of them don't just arrive at wineries—five-hundred-count Wire Things. They have to have a label. So I called the Christian Brothers Winery, whose vineyard is near the Russian River. I got a busy signal. I really did.

Eventually Lamott gets through to the receptionist, who puts her in touch with an older gentleman in back, who, as Lamott tells us, "was so glad I'd called. He actually said so, and he sounded like he was." She explains her predicament, how she doesn't know what "the wire thing" is called, and he says, "Ah . . . that would be the wire hood."

And now we know.

3. Time Travel

My good friend and collaborator Janet Burroway says this about research in her book *Imaginative Writing: The Elements of Craft*:

> I once had the luck, just as I was starting on a novel set in Mexico and Arizona in 1914, to hear a lecture by the great novelist Mary Lee Settle. She offered three rules for historical fiction research:
> - Don't read about the period; read in the period. Read letters, journals, newspapers, magazines, books written at the time. You will in this way learn the cadences, the turn of mind and phrase, the obsessions and quirks of the period.
> - Don't take notes. If you save everything that interests you, you'll be tempted to use it whether it fits or not, and your fiction will smell of research. Immerse yourself and trust that what you need will be there.
> - Don't research beyond the period you're writing about. If you know too much about the future, your characters will inevitably know it too.

Now, these rules are particular to historical fiction, but I think the spirit of them is applicable to any sort of imaginative research.

I'm not sure I agree with every element of this—I'm an inveterate note taker—but basically, I think this is the right approach for historical research. I also agree with Janet's suggestion that this kind of immersion works not just for historical novels but also for other kinds of imaginative writing.

Take personal essays, for example. In "On Keeping a Notebook," Joan Didion says that one reason to write personal essays is "to keep on nodding terms with the people we used to be, whether we find them attractive company or not. Otherwise they turn up unannounced and surprise us, come hammering on the mind's door at 4 a.m. of a bad night and demand to know who deserted them, who betrayed them, who is going to make amends. We forget all too soon the things we thought we could never forget." What if the former self you must summon up is your fourth grade self? Fourth grade may not seem that long ago, but trust me, in my case, it is. What candy did I favor then and why? Was it Pez or Milk Duds? Slo Pokes or Atomic Fireballs? Was fourth grade the year you began playing Wiffle ball till the streetlights came on? The year you carried a squirt gun to school, listened to the *Lone Ranger* on the radio, and began longing for the day when you could be on safety patrol? It may not seem as ancient and exotic as the Mexico and Arizona of 1914 to which Janet traveled, but in its own way, it is. Retrieving the deep images of that time will require some research. You'll need to leaf through some old *Highlights* magazines, reread a few volumes of Ramona and Beezus, and watch some episodes of Captain Kangaroo (which, thank God, are archived on YouTube).

4. Enlarging Your Subject

When writing essays, I think it's best to start with yourself—your memories, concerns, stories, obsessions, all the images and snippets of dialogue that haunt you even if you aren't sure why they haunt you. I've begun essays by freewriting about that afternoon my parents told me they were going to get divorced, or the moment when I heard my dad cuss for the first time, or the night we were driving back from Minnesota and the fan belt broke in the early morning darkness of the South Side of Chicago. I write down the scene, usually in the present tense the first time because I find it gives me more ready access to the past. Then I let the pages sit for a while until I can listen to them with new ears and begin to figure out what the piece is about—*really* about.

It is only at that point that I think it's okay to plunge into some reading and generalizing and thinking about what others might have said about the issue that seems to lie at core of my essay. Only then do I feel ready to do a new kind research about my subject. Only then am I ready to read what Betty Friedan says about marriage in the fifties, what linguists say about swearing, what Isabel Wilkerson says about Chicago and the Great Migration.

Aldous Huxley sets up a nice system for thinking about essays in the preface to his *Collected Essays* that speaks to the relationship between memory and research, the personal and the universal: "Essays belong to a literary species whose extreme variability can be studied most effectively within a three-poled frame of reference. There is the pole of the personal and the autobiographical; there is the pole of the objective, the factual, the concrete-particular; and there is the pole of the abstract-universal. Most essayists are at home and at their best in the neighborhood of only one of the essay's three poles, or at the most only in the neighborhood of two of them."

Here, however, is the hitch. Just as Huxley tells us that most of us are good at only one or maybe two of these modes of writing, he then lets us know that the real goal is to become accomplished at all three: "The most richly satisfying essays are those which make the best not of one, not of two, but of all the three worlds in which it is possible for the essay to exist. Freely, effortlessly, thought and feeling move in these consummate works of art, hither and thither between the essay's three poles—from the personal to the universal, from the abstract back to the concrete, from the objective datum to the inner experience."

Paradoxically, an essay is most universal when it is most individual. Readers can see themselves in your work when you are giving yourself to them with the fullest honesty, particularity, and specificity possible. This is because what you're trying to do is lift your essay above your own life while never leaving that life behind. But lift it you must, for while we love you, we really don't want to hear you drone on about yourself unless there's a payoff and the piece has something to tell us. After all, we're as egotistical as you.

If all I'm telling you are anecdotes, then I'm probably stuck at the level of bar stories and not moving deeply into myself and out into something larger, something universal. Montaigne is good on this phenomenon: "Each man bears the entire form of the human condition."

5. Serendipity

Another great thing about research is that it can surprise you. You never know where you'll end up. One thing leads to another and then that thing leads to yet another, and pretty soon you're someplace you didn't plan to go but are meant to be.

I think this is especially true for the essay, a form that has always been digressive. For the last twenty-two years of his life, Montaigne worked continuously on his *Essais*, which were published in three editions (1580, 1588, 1595). He revised constantly and yet never took anything out. He only added, and he didn't just add new essays, he also added a word or a sentence here or there, or dropped a new passage, sometimes several pages long, into an existing essay. He did this even if the new bit seemed to contradict what he'd written earlier. As he put it (long before Whitman bragged about contradicting himself), "I cannot keep my subject still. It goes along befuddled and staggering, with a natural drunkenness. I take it in this condition, just as it is at the moment I give my attention to it. I do not portray being: I portray passing."

You know the experience. You're in the stacks looking for a book, but along the way your eyes fall on another title that looks interesting, and then another. Eventually, you circle back to the one you were looking for in the first place—the notecard in your hand with that book's call number on it reminds you why you're there—and you find it and check it out. But you'll also end up checking out some of those other books—wonderful, intriguing, beautiful books that will take you into some new direction, books that you weren't looking for but that seem to have been looking for you.

Of course, it's not just serendipity. As a friend of mine once said, his tongue firmly in his cheek, "Yeah, that Jack Nicklaus—luckiest golfer I've ever seen." Probably it's a little bit of both: skill and luck, preparation and opportunity. Probably it's a little bit like love. You've got to be alert, keep your eyes open, and be ready for that wonderful book to find you, though once it does, make sure to take it out for coffee so you can really get to know each other.

Serendipity doesn't happen only in libraries (though I think it happens in libraries more often than on the internet, where the frenzy of the search seems to induce ADHD and we're required to put ourselves at the mercy of what Google hands us and narrow our search to this or that key word, our eyes glued to a single screen). Serendipity also happens when you're out in the world doing fieldwork. Remember Anne Lamott and the wire hood on the champagne bottle? Well, there's more to that story. While she was on hold, waiting for the receptionist at the Christian Brothers Winery, she says she "sat there staring off into space." But she didn't just sit:

> I watched the movie in my mind of the many times I'd passed those vineyards and remembered how, especially in the early fall, a vineyard is about as voluptuous a place as you can find on earth: the sense of lushness and abundance; the fullness of the clumps of grapes that hang, mammarian, and give off an ancient autumnal smell, semiprotected from the sun by their leaves. The grapes are so incredibly beautiful that you can't help but be thrilled. If you aren't—if you only see someone's profit or that in another month there will be rotten fruit all over the ground—someone has gotten inside your brain and really fucked you up. And you need to get well so you can see again, see that the grapes almost seem to glow, with a light dusting of some sort of powdery residue, like an incredibly light snowfall, almost as if they're covered with their own confectioners' sugar.
>
> I wrote all this down and then called the winery again.

Serendipity? Sure, if she had got right through the first time she might not have daydreamed about the fields and the grapes, but she also made smart, efficient use of her time on hold and created some damn fine writing.

6. Adult Education

One reason I like to read essays is that I learn something new by reading them. One reason I like to write essays is that I learn something new by writing them.

Reading and writing exist in a kind of dialectical relationship, a Möbius strip of influence. When you read an essay you learn a little about this or that and soon you're at the library looking to learn more, then you bring that knowledge back to a rereading of the essay and the essay is the richer for it, revealing itself to you in new ways, and so on and so on. It's akin to that phenomenon we've all experienced when we look up a new word and then see it three times in print during the next week.

There's an excitement to such discovery. It's like the excitement you felt back in school when your teacher read *Tom Sawyer* aloud during afternoon rest time and you actually began to hear Tom and Huck talking, or when the cocoon your second grade class had kept all winter finally opened and a monarch came out, or when your small group presented its project on the Dred Scott decision and when you finished the class burst into applause. The only difference is now you are a grownup and you are your own teacher.

Essayists are teachers too. I think the genre is especially geared to introduce us to knowledge (which is not to say essays don't do lots of other things as well). An essay, according to Scott Russell Sanders, "is an amateur's raid in a world of specialists. Feeling overwhelmed by data, random information, and the flotsam and jetsam of mass culture, we relish the spectacle of a single consciousness making sense of a portion of the chaos." I agree, though I don't think either Sanders or I mean to suggest that creative nonfiction is the only genre that teaches us something, but I do think nonfiction is often more explicitly about the imparting of information and so has a special relationship to research. When we read essays we often hope to learn something. We're likely, for instance, to pick up an essay on mountain lions (I'm thinking here of Edward Hoagland's great "Hailing the Elusory Mountain Lion") at least in part because we think it might tell us something new about mountain lions; we're much less likely to pick up Willa Cather's *Death Comes to the Archbishop* because we know it's set in the Southwest and might by chance include some mountain lion information.

7. Connecting

It's a cliché to say so, but it's true: writing is a lonely business. It consists of long hours of facing a computer screen or scribbling on a legal pad, long hours alone with your imagination, and as a consequence, a writer can become a hermit.

Research, on the other hand, puts you in touch with people. This is less true of research on the Internet, though even there one can find ways to connect. Increasingly, I see writers on Facebook crowdsourcing. They ask the hive to suggest a good book about this or that subject, answer a question that has them stumped, or help them find the right word. But research can also help connect you to the material world. It can get you out of your study and down the street to talk face-to-face with a butcher about meat, a farmer about tractors, a research librarian about a special collection, or a wine master about the "wire thing" on the top of a champagne bottle (I know, I know, Anne Lamott called him on the phone, but you get the point). These conversations don't just yield information; they also introduce you to new people, help you build new relationships, initiate new projects, knit the culture together, and even promote your book.

8. Having Fun

This getting out into the world can even be fun. There's no reason research has to be a dry and boring province populated by eggheads and geeks.

Above I said Elizabeth and I drag our two daughters along with us on our research trips. Actually I don't think we really have to drag them, not usually. I think the girls enjoyed their several visits to Graceland, Sun Studio, Beale Street, and the Civil Rights Museum when Elizabeth was researching her last novel and I was working on an essay about Elvis.

It's even gotten to the point where it's not just the research of the parents that determines our family vacations. The girls make their preferences known too. When we went to New York, we took them to the Algonquin and the Strand and the dinosaur room at the Museum of Natural History, but they also put in their own requests. They wanted to have tea at the Plaza just like Eloise did, and take a hansom cab ride through Central Park to celebrate one of their favorite Seinfeld episodes, the one in which Kramer stupidly feeds Beano to the horse. Later, in our Times Square hotel, they rode the elevator up and down, taking notes as if they were Nancy Drew or Harriet the Spy:

"Young couple in room 714 may be on honeymoon."

"Old man alone in 651 seems sad."

"Family at end of the hall has left for the Empire State Building."

Our family also reads out loud a fair amount together, and on road trips we listen to books on tape. To me such reading and listening is also a kind of research. We've pretty much memorized our favorite Nancy Drew tapes (which, by the way, are read wonderfully by Laura Linney). Just as certain Seinfeld episodes have become touchstones for us (as they have for everyone) so have favorite moments from our favorite books. There is, for instance, always a point near the end of a Nancy Drew book when the semibad guy who is basically good but who fell in with the wrong crowd comes clean to Nancy and helps her solve the crime. For us, the line "Honest, Miss Drew" marks any kind of repentance or overeager earnestness.

Just as their parents did, our girls are growing up around writers, which I think is a good thing because maybe then they'll be less likely to romanticize writers, mystify the writing process, or see research as an onerous task. Elizabeth's father organized the visiting writers series at Purdue University for several years, and he and her mom hosted many writers. Some of them... well most of them... were pretty self-involved and felt they were above the cow town they'd found themselves in (the poet May Swenson was the notable exception). Elizabeth saw lots of writers off duty—drinking, cussing, and wearing out their welcome. She didn't know it at the time but it was research. It gave her some great and wicked lines for a story she wrote years later titled "Famous Poets."

Our own writer friends, of course, are much better behaved than those famous poets and, in any case, shall remain nameless here, but the girls have seen them all off duty and so they don't think being a writer is a big a deal at all. It's just what Mom and Dad and their friends do. Both girls, for instance, are Facebook friends with a friend of ours, who has called on them to critique chapters of a young adult book she's writing. And Phoebe and Flannery were once profiled themselves in *The Believer*. They still like to get that issue out and read it aloud from time to time so they can cackle about the antics of their younger selves.

9. Being Alert to Life

As you can tell, I define research broadly. For me it includes watching old Elvis movies, going to blues clubs in Memphis till four in the morning, and visiting Willa Cather's house in Red Cloud, Nebraska, as well as putting on cotton gloves to handle old manuscripts in the Beinecke Rare Book Library at Yale.

In fact, I'd go further. As I've already suggested, I think research often occurs when you don't even think you're doing research. When a draft is really cooking I find I'm alert to the world in way that I'm not otherwise. I don't mean to suggest that writing leads me into some sort of schizophrenic state in which I begin to see correspondences and messages everywhere, writing on the wall, as it were. What I mean is that writing makes me feel like maybe, just maybe, I am, at least now and again, the kind of artist Henry James described in "The Art of Fiction"—"one of the people on whom nothing is lost." When I feel like that kind of person, everything is research.

In "On Keeping a Notebook," Joan Didion talks about how she tries to systematize this process, admitting all the while that such systematization is difficult. She opens her essay by sharing with us an entry from one of her notebooks: "'That woman Estelle is partly the reason why George Sharp and I are separated today.' *Dirty crepe-de-Chine wrapper, hotel bar, Wilmington RR, 9:45 a.m. August Monday morning.*" Then Didion goes on to try to make some sense of the entry:

> Since the note is in my notebook, it presumably has some meaning to me. I study it for a long while. At first I have only the most general notion of what I was doing on an August Monday morning in the bar of the hotel across from the Pennsylvania Railroad station in Wilmington, Delaware (waiting for a train? missing one? 1960? 1961? why Wilmington?), but I do remember being there. The woman in the dirty crepe-de-Chine wrapper had come down from her room for a beer, and the bartender had heard before the reason why George Sharp and she were separated today. "Sure," he said, and went on mopping the floor. "You told me." At the other end of the bar is a girl. She is talking, pointedly, not to the man beside her but to a cat lying in the triangle of sunlight cast through the open door. She is wearing a plaid silk dress from Peck & Peck, and the hem is coming down.

The function of the notebook is both to preserve and to prompt. It is a way to hold on to a moment she suspects has meaning even though she has not yet figured out what that meaning might be: "Why did I write it down? In order to remember, of course, but exactly what was it I wanted to remember? How much of it actually happened? Did any of it? Why do I keep a notebook at all? It is easy to deceive oneself on all those scores. The impulse to write things down is a peculiarly compulsive one, inexplicable to those who do not share it, useful only accidentally, only secondarily, in the way that any compulsion tries to justify itself." Writers are people who notice things even when they aren't exactly sure what they're noticing. They are collectors. Unfortunately, they have to collect much more than they'll ever use because they don't know in advance what will be useful. Maybe "packrat" is a more precise and honest term than "collector". There are lots of ways to collect. Elizabeth keeps a journal that is not unlike Didion's notebook; I've got a gazillion folders on my computer.

Right now I'm living on New York's Upper West Side and teaching at Columbia. I'm only going to be here for a few months so I'm trying to make good use of the time, but again I'm not always sure what "good use" might mean. Earlier this week I read a piece by Jonathan Lethem about the Upper West Side. Lethem grew up in Brooklyn, but as a child he often visited his great-grandmother "Omi," a refugee from Germany, who had "landed in a residence hotel on Broadway and Eighty-something, in a small apartment full of lace and Meissen china." As Lethem explains it, "She spoke barely any English and expressed her affection for me by running her fingers through my hair while calling me 'Yonatan'—so, for me, a drive to the Upper West Side might as well have been a voyage to Europe." At the end of the piece he confides that he "still can't cross Broadway on foot, passing those traffic-island benches, little tulip beds stranded in taxi smog, and not be reminded of the Holocaust."

Lethem's essay, especially that closing line, caught my attention because most mornings I run in Riverside Park and to get there I have to cross Broadway. I run past just such a bench. Now and then there seems to be an Omi or two among the people who sit there, but more often, the old friends are African American. Last week, as I ran by, one woman shouted to her fellow bench-sitters, "My sugar was 69 this morning! Coulda died, went into a coma!" When I got home, I wrote down that line not knowing if it would work its way into an essay I've considered writing about being a member of the sandwich generation, those boomers with responsibilities to both their young kids and aging parents, or an essay about my time on the Upper West Side, or an essay about how to use research in writing.

So, research is wonderful. It enriches your writing, brings your family together, and makes you alert to the world you live in. Great! How wonderful!

Well, yeah, but as with anything, it's also got a downside. You can also overdo it, and so I feel compelled to sound a note of caution. For one thing, research, while necessary to writing, is also easier than writing. Reading, taking notes, searching the stacks, going through family photos, and doing interviews are all easier than facing a blank page or an empty screen. Research can become a way of procrastinating.

A related problem is that it's also easy to drop a piece of research indiscriminately into a draft rather than *writing* your way toward the moment where such a detail is really needed. In other words, you can add too much research. You can end up with too much of a good thing.

How do you avoid doing this? I'm not sure. I'm still working on it, though I do think experience helps. I've tried playing games with myself—working in some other part of the house so that I can't get at my books and my filing cabinets quite so easily, but to be honest that doesn't work too well. If I want to get at my research, I do. Such games sure as hell don't work with the research that I've put on my computer—all those files of notes, all those bookmarked sites, all that stuff Google makes so available. It's all just too easy to get at. I've heard of these applications that block you from the internet for a set period of time, but they sound gimmicky, too. I try instead to exert some self-discipline and just write, remembering that the goal is significant detail, not detail for detail's sake.

Let me close with one more personal story. As I mentioned, my dad was an academic, one of those GI Bill of Rights intellectuals that America created after World War II. He loved teaching and scholarship, he loved his family, and he felt there was something to learn everywhere. Our summer vacations took us to Old Ironsides, the Smithsonian, and Mark Twain's house in Hannibal. Sometimes, however, the lesson ended up being different from the one that was planned. I remember vividly spending several minutes opening a can of beans with that funny little hook on a Swiss Army knife while sitting on the tailgate of our Plymouth station wagon in the campground at Valley Forge while my mom held an umbrella over me in the pouring rain. I suppose that moment taught me to appreciate how rough the winter must have been for Washington and the troops, but what I remember most is how patient and careful I had to be with that knife and how on the next camping trip it would probably make sense to bring a real can opener.

That time the lesson was not what Dad had planned, but often he came up with some pretty innovative lesson plans himself. He knew well that there was plenty to be learned outside museums, libraries, and national monuments. His own field of agricultural economics, for instance, was for him much more than data and statistics. It was really about food and where it came from and how it was distributed, marketed, and sold. In ice cream parlors, for instance, he liked to meet the owner, blind taste the product, and guess the butterfat content. When we visited my mom's parents in Florida, he always wanted to go to the docks in the evening to see the fishing boats come in and talk to the captains about the day's catch. I remember him talking excitedly about an early morning trip to the produce market in Rio. He could even get wound up about a grain elevator or a new kind of silo.

It was all there in those moments with him: Accuracy. Detail. Time. Enlarging. Serendipity. Education. Connecting. Fun. Alertness to Life.

I thought of this one day, while waiting in line with my own children at the DMV. Phoebe, who was then about two, toddled over with a big three-ring binder in which the Motor Vehicles people had put a waiting-room magazine so no one would walk off with it. She held the notebook up and announced, "Look, Daddy, it's my manuscript."

The clerks and the people in line laughed in astonishment, and I had to explain that, yes, she comes from a family of writers.

"Dear John"

Facts and the Lyric Essay

Dear John,

I'm afraid it's over between us.

You know how important you've been to me. I've adopted *The Next American Essay* for classes. I reviewed *The Lost Origins of the Essay* and sang its praises. Carl Klaus and I have included your 2003 headnote about lyric essays, the one that introduced Jenny Boully to the world, in our new anthology, *Essayists on the Essay: Montaigne to Our Time*. I admire you, but admiration isn't enough, and now you've even undercut some of that admiration. It's over, John.

But, nevertheless, we should talk. I owe it to you to tell you what I really think.

What I think, John, is that you've fallen between two stools. You have, but the essay hasn't. Let me explain. When Karen Rosica called you a "journalist poet," indeed a "passionate journalist poet," you should have just gone with it. You should have thanked her and moved on. I know the word "journalist" bugs you. Don't let it. That's

This essay, adapted for *Brevity*'s Nonfiction Blog, was originally presented at "The Lyric Essay: A Collapse of Forms or a Form of Collapse," a panel discussion at the Association of Writers and Writing Programs (AWP) Conference in 2012. The satirical letter is addressed to John D'Agata, whose *The Lifespan of a Fact* (coauthored with Jim Fingal) had just been published, sparking a widespread conversation about the relationship between art and fact in literary nonfiction.

the way it is with our genre—by which I mean the essay, not the lyric essay, but of that, more in a minute. The essay has always been about facts *and* literature, about memory *and* imagination, about journalism *and* literature, about plain old truth (aka accuracy) *and* Truth with a capital T. But when she said "journalist poet," you apparently got your dander up. The adjective and the noun seem like they're in contradiction. So what? Contradict yourself, be large, contain multitudes.

Instead, you've turned it into a false either/or, John—Fish Wrap journalism versus Pure Poetry. It doesn't have to be that way. And I think you know it. That's why you went looking for an adjective yourself. "How about 'lyric essay'?" you said. And you were right and I like that about you, John. I really do. You and Deborah Tall were out ahead of us all, giving a name to those beautiful essays that weren't afraid to be beautiful, essays we were already reading and teaching—"Living Like Weasels," "The White Album," "Delft"—but not yet calling *lyric*. And then you went further. You went looking for new ones and found them—"The Body" and "Ticket to the Fair." Thank you for that. You gave those essays a name, you collected them in one place, you reimagined anthologies, making them almost essays themselves by writing your headnotes as one long narrative essay (yeah, a little self-satisfied sometimes and show-offy, but hey, that's you, John, and that's okay—the book worked, it really did).

You kept going and I was still with you when *The Lost Origins of the Essay* came out. Sometimes it did feel like you were pushing too far, but hey, that's what you do and we've all got to do. I understand. You're shaking things up. And even then some of it made perfect sense, right from the start. When you put it in this new context, "On Some Verses of Virgil" was immediately transformed into a lyric essay for me. Of course, I thought—it's not about Virgil and hexameters, it never was—it's about sex and lyrical digressions. I even liked, as a kind of thought experiment, the idea of reading "The Marriage of Heaven and Hell" and "*Tlön, Uqbar,* Orbis Tertius" as lyric essays, though I finally decided that the one is a prose poem and the other is a short story.

I have to say, John, you're an eight-hour day. You're learned and heavy. You really are. It's a lot of what drew me to you originally—all that learning, all that classical learning. I mean, you translated your own Latin *and* Greek in *The Lost Origins of the Essay*. The trip back to Mesopotamia and Heraclitus, the willingness to range across Europe and Asia in search of lyric essays was . . . well . . . a trip. Mind-boggling, really. Thank you. The book Carl Klaus and I edited is the better for it. You got us searching outside the Anglo-American tradition, and that improved our book, for we found new essays about the essay—lots of them—by Latin Americans, French Canadians, Germans, even an Australian. I don't think we'd have done that if you hadn't gone there first.

I understand why you went in search of an adjective to put in front of "essay." People have looked for adjectives for centuries. Before we had lyric essays, we had periodical essays, formal essays, informal essays, review essays, romantic essays, and, of course, personal essays. And, with your classical background, I know that you know that what that word "lyric" can bring is its classical Greek connotations—a solitary song, not a chorus, sung by a single musing singer to the accompaniment of a lyre (pronounced *liar*).

Well, we've ditched the lyre, but I know what you're going for with the term—the poetic, the densely figurative, the brief exploration of a mood or idea, and yes, a little looser connection to facts. It's a reaction maybe to that ugly, ugly term "creative nonfiction." Or, as Scott Sanders so nicely put it, "creative nonfiction" is "an exceedingly vague term, taking in everything from telephone books to *Walden*, and it's negative, implying that fiction is the norm against which everything else must be measured. It's as though, instead of calling an apple a fruit, we called it a non-meat."

So yeah, I understand, John. "Nonfiction" as a term sucks and you've got to dress it up with an adjective, but "creative" isn't much help. *Creative* as opposed to what? *Destructive?* And if "essay" as a term is pulled toward nonfiction and journalism, I can understand wanting to dress up "essay" with an adjective. But, you've got to be careful, John. In your hurry to get away from journalism and to get some of the cachet of poetry, you can go too far.

I like lyric essays but I don't think there is such a thing as pure poetry, at least not on this earth. Which is not to say pure poetry is not a worthy goal. It's a fine, but tricky, goal. Seeking after pure poetry can lead one to beautiful flights of language and high lyricism, indeed some of the best essays we have, but it can also lead to disengagement, solipsism, and art for art's sake. I think investigative reporting, the slick paper of commercialism, the hurry-up of deadlines, and the political engagement of journalism can be good things for an essay, even a lyric essay.

Look at your own anthologies, John. Take John McPhee's "The Search for Marvin Gardens," which is the first essay in *The Next American Essay*. I'm glad it's there in your anthology, but as Lynn Bloom has pointed out, "All anthologies . . . deracinate their material—old or new—from its original context and replant it in the anthologist's soil." McPhee's essay appeared originally in the September 9, 1972, issue of the *New Yorker* (though you messed up, John, and said 1975—probably could have used a good copy editor or fact checker). I love McPhee's essay—its braided narratives, its history of the Gilded Age, its ongoing Monopoly game, and its walking tour of Atlantic City in 1972 when racial strife, economic decay, and rampant drug use made it a bombed out shell of its former self. But the essay is also a comment on the *New Yorker*, the magazine that is its and McPhee's home. The essay's irony, indeed its lyricism, rings with a new sound when you read it next to the ads for Sony, Estée Lauder, Lord & Taylor, and L. L. Bean that surrounded it.

Or look at another one of your selections, another one of your lyric essays: Joan Didion's "The White Album," her famous disjunctive and helter-skelter goodbye to the sixties. Three sections of this essay appeared originally as installments of her "Points West" column in the *Saturday Evening Post*. The *Saturday Evening Post*, John! The *Saturday Evening Fucking Post!* Norman Rockwell's magazine! Didion discussed the context of these pieces in the *Paris Review* interview, in which she recalled how she and her husband John Gregory Dunne moved to California in June 1964. "I started doing pieces for *The Saturday Evening Post*," she said. "We needed the money because neither one of us was working." The *Post*, she explained, was "on the verge of folding" and so "would let you do whatever you wanted." What had once been the magazine of Norman Rockwell was now trying unsuccessfully to rebrand itself as some weird combination of *Esquire* and *Cosmopolitan*. The section of "The White Album" on Huey Newton and the Black Panthers appeared in an issue the cover of which promised to explain "How Barney Rosset Publishes 'Dirty Books' for Fun and Profit." The section about Jim Morrison and the Doors was illustrated with a photograph of the Lizard King without a shirt and had a cover that featured a teaser in which Vanessa Redgrave announced, "I've Always Known I Was Sexy."

Even lyric essays, even your lyric essays, were published first in general magazines, middlebrow magazines, political magazines, women's magazines, and even, heaven forbid, commercial or mass-market magazines. Writing to make a point or a buck certainly has its dangers, but it does not necessarily preclude one from writing lyrically or creating something of lasting literary merit.

John, you've ignored where at least some of your lyric essays came from and you've begun to draw too sharp a distinction between journalism and the lyric essay. And, as a consequence, you've ended up arguing too strenuously against facts and prose and journalism and mass culture and commerce. On the first page of *The Next American Essay*, you announced, "I want you preoccupied with art in this book, not with facts for the sake of facts." And in the opening of *The Lost Origins of the Essay*, you wrote, "I am here in search of art. I am here to track the origins of an alternative to commerce."

Well, all well and good, but you've gotten carried away, and I'm starting to distrust your motives. Don't write essays just so you can be a poet, John. Don't write essays just so you can wear a beret. Maybe it's time for you to come home to America, maybe it's time for you to stop being quite so high falutin'. I worry that you've gone so continental, so postmodern, so highbrow, so, dare I say, *lyrical* because you're running away from journalism.

Don't get me wrong. I'm not running to journalism and mass culture exactly, just not away from it. And neither am I arguing that Hollywood, television, slick magazines, and the lure of big book deals have not been treacherous in their own ways. Nor am I arguing that little magazines and alternative presses do not play a role, an important role, in the struggle against monopoly capitalism and for art. What I am arguing is that this is the way it is. We live in a world in which commerce touches everything and art is never pure. All of these things—slick magazines and little magazines, blogs and books, high culture and mass culture—make up the terrain in which art is made and read. I am arguing that we must proceed on all fronts and that there is also a role to be played by those who publish in mainstream magazines and get paid in cash rather than copies.

There's an American essayist on the essay I think you should read—Berton Braley. He's a funny guy who wrote a piece called "On Being an Essayist" for *The Bookman* back in 1920. In it, he said that the "elect" had become too protective of the essay, and of literature more generally. The essay, he said, was possessed of a "Little Lord Fauntleroy complex." It was too intent on being literary and had become "a precious, precious thing." The essay needed, said Braley, to romp around again and get "all mussed up with the butcher's boy and the rest of the crowd in Dugan's back lot," it needed "to play with the rough common boys of Popularity and Commercialism."

I know you'd like to do that too, John, and that a respect for, or at least attraction to, journalism is some of why you wrote *About a Mountain* and let Norton bill it as "an investigation of Yucca Mountain and human destruction in Las Vegas," a "bearing witness to the parade of scientific, cultural, and political facts that give shape to Yucca's story."

"Facts," John? Facts? I'm for facts. You're not. I understand there's a gray area. I understand memory must be supplemented by imagination. I understand we need, sometimes, to compress time and accelerate a narrative. I understand that the stage can get too crowded and we might need to delete a character or fold some others into a composite character. I'm not a dodo, and I love the idea at least of writing a book about the gamble that is Yucca Mountain and the pit of poison that is Las Vegas, about your mother's life and Levi Presley's death, but *geesh*, changing the timing of that poor dead boy's death. Necessary? I don't think so.

John, I don't think I've changed. I think you've changed. I still love lyric essays. But I don't love you anymore. I do hope we can still be friends.

Sincerely,
Ned

My Name Is Ned

Facebook and the Personal Essay

I want to talk about three things: first, what I think Facebook does well; second, what the dangers of Facebook might be; and finally, what the other panelists have already talked about—more eloquently probably than I will be able to—namely the difference between Facebook and the essay, and how essayists might be able to make good use of Facebook.

First of all, then, what does Facebook do well? Ironically, I found out about Facebook at a writers' retreat—not at Bread Loaf (like Jocelyn Bartkevicius) but at the Lillian E. Smith artists' retreat in north Georgia, where I had no access to the internet. Another writer there, named James Austin, a fine young novelist, was talking about Facebook and I asked him, "Why would anyone want to *be* on Facebook?" He said, "Well, it helps you to be in touch with your old friends; it's more efficient than e-mail." Often, he argued, there are times when you find yourself sending out basically the same e-mail to a number of different people but you want it to be different, so you don't just do a CC but instead personalize it slightly—a kind of mail merge in es-

This essay, adapted for TriQuarterly Online, was originally presented at "Status Update: The Personal Essay in the Age of Facebook," a panel discussion at the 2011 Association of Writers and Writing Programs (AWP) Conference.

sence, and Facebook makes it easy to do that. And, he added, you can include photos very easily, of your family and so forth. And I said, "Oh, so it's sort of like those Christmas letters that my mother used to send." "Kind of like that," he said, "but it's always up there and always available." And, you know, the rest is history. Of course, now I have several hundred "friends." And I'm on Facebook every day.

James was right. Facebook does help you keep in touch with old friends and family. It's a way of reestablishing contact with people and sometimes even a community that was once lost, almost like a high school class newsletter. That can function just at the level of nostalgia—sharing those YouTube videos of Sam Cooke performances, or early Van Morrison appearances, or old bits from *The Twilight Zone*. This is what we boomers do.

But more important, there are certain moments when that community is touched by loss, perhaps illness or death, when Facebook can rise to the occasion in an odd and wonderful way.

That has happened a couple times recently, actually, with friends of mine from high school: one who died after heart surgery, and another who is suffering from pancreatic cancer. Now those of us in these circles are talking a lot, reassuring each other, keeping in touch with family members, and getting updates. Facebook is good for this, I have to say.

The possibilities of Facebook in this area were brought home again to me last week, when one of my wife's high school classmates committed suicide, and people began writing on his wall after his death. They addressed him personally, as if he were still alive, and they addressed his family as well. I was struck by that—this use of the term "wall" resonated in a new way for me then, and I began to think about the Vietnam Veterans Memorial wall, and those impromptu memorials for 9/11 victims that were established along the fence outside the hole where the World Trade Center used to be, where people left messages for their loved ones. This man's bereaved family was then able to send out one post, one message to the people who had posted on his Facebook wall, communicating their thanks.

In addition to reestablishing old connections, Facebook can help us build new ones. As it happens, James Austin, the person who introduced me to Facebook at the north Georgia writers' retreat, lives most of the year in Egypt, where he teaches at the American University in Cairo. Of course, people have been talking about the role that social media, such as Facebook and Twitter, have played in the Egyptian and Tunisian revolutions. It's hard to measure their impact precisely, but certainly social media have helped organize people and bring about change. At the suggestion of certain Facebook friends, I began watching the live feeds from Cairo supplied by Al Jazeera in English, and I've recommended to others that they do the same.

Facebook can also be an important site for political debate. I'm Facebook "friends" with my fundamentalist, right-wing brother-in-law, and over time I've become friends with some of his friends. I enjoy butting heads with them. It's a way to be in touch with a group of people I might not otherwise be in touch with. As an English professor, I live in what you could call a narrow little crypto-Marxist community where everyone shares a certain set of allusions and agrees that we are all in the know. Phillip Lopate in *Against Joie de Vivre* talked about sometimes pushing a prejudice as far as you can, to find out the limits of what you believe. I think he is right about this, and we need to learn to be more honest about our beliefs. This is part of what I like about butting heads with my right-wing brother-in-law and his friends. I think that kind of debate helps me test my beliefs and be more honest with myself. I find myself stopping and wondering if I'm posturing a little bit or if I've gone too far. But don't worry—I'm not going to second-guess myself too much or go all the way to the dark side.

So, those are some of the things I think Facebook can do. There are dangers, however. Facebook's strengths, like all of our strengths, can also sometimes be its weaknesses.

Last summer I was teaching at the Iowa Summer Writing Festival, and one of my students was a psychiatrist. During an individual conference, I said something about Facebook. She responded, "Oh, Facebook, don't tell me about Facebook, it has destroyed so many marriages!" Many of her clients get on Facebook and reignite an old flame, she said, and then their marriage is gone. I didn't say this to her, but I thought, Well, I think you're blaming the messenger. But, of course, she was right in a certain sense, and speaking from much experience—people do try to get in touch with people on the sly, and when they do, hijinks ensue.

A second danger of Facebook is that it can be a time suck—a very addictive one. And yes, "My name is Ned and I'm an addict."

On weekdays I get up early, before my wife and my two daughters, to make the coffee and make sure that my oldest daughter is at the bus at 6:30, and while the coffee is brewing I check my e-mail, sometimes the *New York Times* online, and always Facebook. Then I leave it on during the day while I'm working. As I said, I've been on Facebook only for about the last eighteen months, and thus far I've been able to work while it's on. I've got two books coming out this year, and they're both in the final stages—copy editing and getting permissions to reprint and proofreading and indexing. I can do that kind of work and leave Facebook on. But I already know that if the next book is to happen, I'll have to either find one of those programs that allow you to shut off your internet for a set number of hours—which seems awfully artificial but also attractive—or head to north Georgia again to jump-start the writing without access to the internet. Because Facebook *is* addictive.

Related to the time-suck problem is the problem of the fragmenting of consciousness. It's the reduction of sentiment and thought to either four-hundred-and-twenty-character status updates or one-hundred-and-forty-character tweets. Facebook develops its own frenzied pace, and that's not healthy.

As Jen McClanaghan's proposal for this panel suggested, another danger of Facebook is its tendency toward voyeurism. Debra Monroe, who was going to be on this panel but for whom I'm filling in, was kind enough to share her notes with me. One of the things she talked about was the commoditization of private life. That can happen with Facebook, sparked by the same impulse that draws us toward reality TV. It provides us with a way of keeping an eye on other people. You can go to the Facebook page of someone you don't actually know and look at their family photos—say, their daughter's prom picture. It's creepy. But I think it's only creepy if you're a creep. Many of us might want to see what our own prom date looks like now after all these years, but it is the people who really do that *a lot* who are suspect, I suppose. You don't *have* to stalk people.

Yet as the title for this panel suggests, we are in the age of Facebook and there is no going back. The toothpaste is out of the tube. We need to learn to live with it. So the last question to address here is, can personal essays and Facebook peacefully coexist—and perhaps even fruitfully coexist?

First of all, how are essays different from Facebook? Alfred Kazin wrote, "In an essay it's not the thought that counts, but the experience we get of the writer's thought; not the self, but the self thinking." William Gass said something similar: "The hero of the essay is its author in the act of thinking things out, feeling and finding a way. It is the mind and the marvels and miseries of its makings, in the work of imagination, the search for form." And finally, in a similar vein, Edward Hoagland argued, "Through its tone and tumbling progression, the essay conveys the quality of an author's mind."

A personal essay offers us the tumble of the mind and is, at least potentially, a work of art. It may be brief by comparison to a memoir or a novel, and in its brevity more akin to a lyric poem, but it is longer, more sustained, more revised, more substantial, and more artistic than anything on Facebook. If an essay gives us the story of a mind thinking, Facebook gives us isolated thoughts. It gives us updates; it gives us fragments.

It can also be said, however, that Facebook gives us conversation, or at least exchanges. But the exchanges on Facebook are ephemeral, fragmented, interrupted conversations; that stream of Facebook updates keeps moving down the page and disappearing out the bottom. There's something sad about that. It's not a real conversation, because you pick it up only when you're in the room. It is more akin to those unsatisfying half-conversations we have at high school reunions or wedding receptions than it is to a full and filling fireside chat.

But a trope for the essay from the beginning has been that it is a conversation, or at least that it is conversational. Montaigne wrote, for instance, "I am not building here a statue to erect at the town crossroads, or in a church, or a public square. This is for a nook in the library, and to amuse a neighbor, a relative, a friend, who may take pleasure in associating and conversing with me again in this image." One of the important phrases in that passage is "in this image." An essay is not really a conversation; it's the image of a conversation, it's a simulation of a conversation. Certainly it uses familiar language; it can sound spoken rather than written—and often does. It can simulate, as Walter Pater first pointed out, a Platonic dialogue. But finally, it is—or at least it usually is—just one side of a conversation. It's a monologue. "We commonly do not remember," wrote Thoreau, "that it is, after all, always the first person who is speaking."

Facebook is something else entirely. It is a lot of people speaking. Sometimes it's a chat, sometimes a cacophony. But its conversations are overheard, busy, fragmented, and again ephemeral. It's akin to the crawl at the bottom of a news channel. By contrast, an essay, however occasioned and journalistic, is finally a revised and polished piece of art.

So how might essays make use of Facebook? I want to offer two possibilities. First, like any new mode of communication, Facebook can provide fodder for essayists.

It can enter the world of personal essays, become a subject for personal essays. Its language can be appropriated by essayists. If, for instance, as my psychiatrist friend at the Iowa Summer Writing Festival suggested, Facebook breaks up relationships, at least those breakups might become the subjects of essays.

Think of Katha Pollitt's essay of a few years ago, "Webstalker," which appeared in her collection *Learning to Drive and Other Life Stories*. It opens with a great sentence: "After my boyfriend left me, I went a little crazy for a while." Then it goes on to chronicle, in beautiful and excruciating honesty, the way Pollitt compulsively Googled her ex-boyfriend for weeks and months on end. For years in the column "Subject to Debate" that she writes for the *Nation*, she called him the Last Marxist. Her essay culminates in a wonderful, creepy scene, when the Last Marxist and his new girlfriend are putting his apartment up for sale. This gives Pollitt the opportunity, via his real estate agent's website, to take a virtual tour of his apartment. She takes an inventory of it, makes a nostalgic trip through her old haunt, the place of her old relationship, and even notices a few prints on the wall that the two of them had purchased together and he has kept. It was almost as if she were there on the wall herself and the new girlfriend didn't know it.

A former student of mine, a fine young writer named Mike Croley, has also taken a stab at this kind of essay. He wrote a piece, as yet unpublished (for any of you editors out there, I can put you in touch with Mike), about breaking up with his girlfriend on Facebook. The piece moves from a status of "In a relationship" to "In a relationship with" to "It's complicated" to "Single." At the end of the essay, they're still Facebook "friends," but you wonder if they're still *friends*. If you have seen *The Social Network*, you know that Hollywood has already got hold of this idea—it is used in the final scene of that movie.

There's a second way that essayists might make use of Facebook, and that is to create community and make connections with other essayists. Among writers I know, the person who I think is doing this best is Dinty Moore. Dinty is a master of the short, provocative, helpful status update. Often he does this with a quote about writing. Just as my seventh-grade English teacher, Mr. Tatlock, used to put a "quote of the day" up on the blackboard each morning and use it to start a discussion and remind us of the power of well-chosen words, Dinty copies a quote from Mark Twain or Richard Bausch or Joan Didion and puts it on his wall each morning. Often these lead to good discussions about writing and the writing life, but they also keep people tuned to Dinty's work, so that when he posts links to the latest issue of *Brevity*, his magazine, or to a new post on the *Brevity* blog, many of Dinty's Facebook friends click and take a look. There are a lot of us who participate in those discussions.

I close in the hope that we essayists might be able to use Facebook not only as material but also as a place to create a community. In that vein, I hope that by the time I get back to my hotel tonight, I'll have some new friend requests from a few of you.

WORKS CITED

Bartkevicius, Jocelyn. "Donna Brazile Loves Mud-Slinging, or Why We Need the Essay Now." *TriQuarterly Online* (Winter/Spring 2011), http://triquarterly.org/views/donna-brazile-loves-mud-slinging-or-why-we-need-essay-now.
Gass, William. "Emerson and the Essay." In *Habitations of the Word*, 19–20. New York: Simon and Schuster, 1985.
Hoagland, Edward. "What I Think, What I Am." In *The Tugman's Passage*, 27. New York: Random House, 1982.
Kazin, Alfred. "Introduction: The Essay as a Modern Form." In *The Open Form: Essays for Our Time*, xi. New York: Harcourt, 1961.
Lopate, Phillip. Introduction to *Against Joie de Vivre*. In *The Art of the Personal Essay: An Anthology from the Classical Era to the Present*, 713. New York: Doubleday, 1994.
Montaigne, Michel de. "Of Giving the Lie." In *The Complete Essays of Montaigne*, 503. Translated by Donald M. Frame. Stanford, CA: Stanford University Press, 1958.
Pater, Walter. "Dialectic." In *Plato and Platonism: A Series of Lectures*, 156–76. London: Macmillan, 1893.
Pollitt, Katha. "Webstalker." In *Learning to Drive: And Other Life Stories*, 21–34. New York: Random House, 2007.
Thoreau, Henry David. *Walden and Resistance to Civil Government*. Edited by William Rossi. 2nd ed. 1854; reprint, New York: W. W. Norton, 1992.

ACKNOWLEDGMENTS

I never imagined that I'd one day be writing acknowledgments for Ned's book—a book he worked on for many years but didn't get to hold in his hands. I can't express his gratitude the way he would, but I will do my best to speak for both of us.

Ned had friends from all parts of his life and was so good at keeping in touch with them. It was one of his many gifts. There are countless people he'd want to thank—so many that I can only mention a few here.

Special thanks go to Carl Klaus and James Peltz for their initiative, generosity, and assistance in proposing that this collection be published and for helping it to find such a wonderful home. John Price and I couldn't have done it without you, and we are grateful beyond measure.

The essayist friends Ned made while at the University of Iowa (and at writer's conferences, and, yes, on Facebook) meant so much to the development of his work and, most importantly, to him personally. Again, there are too many to mention here, but I hope you know who you are.

Thank you to our many brilliant, talented students, friends, and colleagues from Florida State who've enriched our lives. Because of you, Florida State feels like home.

Lisa Bayer and Elizabeth Adams from the University of Georgia Press—you are amazing. Thank you for helping Ned's dream come true. He'd be so pleased.

Thank you to the Albers family and the French family for all your love and support over the years.

Flannery and Phoebe French, you are an integral part of this book and a source of great joy for your father. He loved you more than anything. This book is dedicated to you.

Finally, thank you to our great friend John Price for getting this project going, working so hard on all aspects of it, and for seeing it through. The foreword is such a wonderful tribute. Thank you for nudging me along when it all felt too overwhelming to bear. Ned would be so happy about the results!

Ned, you are truly loved and missed.

Elizabeth Stuckey-French
May 2021

Grateful acknowledgment is made to the following magazines and anthologies in which some of the work first appeared, sometimes in different versions or under alternate titles:

New South: "Nightmares"
The Pinch: "South Side"
Guernica: "Backyards"
The Missouri Review: "Termites"
Cedars: "Meeting Bobby Kennedy"
Walking Magazine: "Walking the Tracks"
Why We're Here: New York Essayists on Living Upstate, edited by Robert Cowser Jr.: "The Edsel Farm," copyright 2010, Colgate University Press. Reprinted with permission from the publisher.
The Normal School: "'Don't Be Cruel': An Argument for Elvis"
middlebrow magazine: "Thank You, Jon Gnagy"
Bending Genre: Essays on Creative Nonfiction, edited by Margot Singer and Nicole Walker: "Essays and Encyclopedias," copyright 2013, Bloomsbury Press. Reprinted with permission from the publisher.
Curiosity's Cats: Essays on Research; or, A Funny Thing Happened on the Way to the Story: "An Essayist's Guide to Research and Family Life," copyright 2014, Minnesota Historical Society Press. Reprinted with permission from the publisher.

Assay: A Journal of Nonfiction Studies: "Our Queer Little Hybrid Thing: Toward a Definition of the Essay"
Brevity: "'Dear John, I'm Afraid It's Over...'"
TriQuarterly Online: "'My Name Is Ned and I'm an Addict': Facebook and the Personal Essay"

Crux, the Georgia Series in Literary Nonfiction

DEBRA MONROE, *My Unsentimental Education*
SONJA LIVINGSTON, *Ladies Night at the Dreamland*
JERICHO PARMS, *Lost Wax: Essays*
PRISCILLA LONG, *Fire and Stone: Where Do We Come From? What Are We? Where Are We Going?*
SARAH GORHAM, *Alpine Apprentice*
TRACY DAUGHERTY, *Let Us Build Us a City*
BRIAN DOYLE, *Hoop: A Basketball Life in Ninety-Five Essays*
MICHAEL MARTONE, *Brooding: Arias, Choruses, Lullabies, Follies, Dirges, and a Duet*
ANDREW MENARD, *Learning from Thoreau*
DUSTIN PARSONS, *Exploded View: Essays on Fatherhood, with Diagrams*
CLINTON CROCKETT PETERS, *Pandora's Garden: Kudzu, Cockroaches, and Other Misfits of Ecology*
ANDRÉ JOSEPH GALLANT, *A High Low Tide: The Revival of a Southern Oyster*
JUSTIN GARDINER, *Beneath the Shadow: Legacy and Longing in the Antarctic*
EMILY ARNASON CASEY, *Made Holy: Essays*
SEJAL SHAH, *This Is One Way to Dance: Essays*
LEE GUTKIND, *My Last Eight Thousand Days: An American Male in His Seventies*
CECILE PINEDA, *Entry without Inspection: A Writer's Life in El Norte*
ANJALI ENJETI, *Southbound: Essays on Identity, Inheritance, and Social Change*
CLINTON CROCKETT PETERS, *Mountain Madness: Found and Lost in the Peaks of America and Japan*
STEVE MAJORS, *High Yella: A Modern Family Memoir*
JULIA RIDLEY SMITH, *The Sum of Trifles*
SIÂN GRIFFITHS, *The Sum of Her Parts*
NED STUCKEY-FRENCH, *One by One, the Stars: Essays*